The Japanese and Europe
Images and Perceptions

The Japanese and Europe
Images and Perceptions

Edited by
BERT EDSTRÖM
Stockholm University

JAPAN
LIBRARY

THE JAPANESE AND EUROPE
IMAGES AND PERCEPTIONS

First Published 2000 by
JAPAN LIBRARY

© Japan Library (Curzon Press Ltd) 2000

Japan Library is an imprint of Curzon Press Ltd
15 The Quadrant, Richmond Surrey TW9 1BP

British Library Cataloguing in Publication Data
A CIP catalogue entry for this book is available from the British Library

ISBN 1-873410-86-7

Typeset in Bembo 12 on 12pt by Bookman, Hayes, Middlesex
Printed and bound in England by Bookcraft, Midsomer Norton, Avon

Contents

SECTION 2: Japan and Eastern Europe

SECTION 3: Japan, Europe and Cold War Issues

About the Contributors

Noriko Berlinguez-Kono graduated from the Faculty of Law, Kyoto University, and has taught in the University of Lille III and the Institut National des Langues et Civilizations Orientale (France). Her doctoral dissertation on historical and political sociology was entitled *Evolution of the perception of the foreigner and social change in Japan* (Ecole des Hautes Etudes en Science Sociales).

Sebastian Conrad is a research fellow at the Free University of Berlin. He is specializing in studies of West German and Japanese historiography in a comparative perspective.

John Crump is Wywy Professor of Japanese Studies and director of the Scottish Centre for Japanese Studies at the University of Stirling. He is the author of various books on socialist and anarchist thought in Japan and elsewhere and is currently working on a study of Japanese employers' organizations.

Selçuk Esenbel is professor of modern Japanese history at the Department of History, Bogazici University, Istanbul. Her research interests are peasant uprisings, Western culture, Asianism, and Japanese-Turkish relations. Her publications include *Even the Gods Rebel: The Peasants of Takino and the 1871 Nakano Uprising*, AAS Monograph 57, 1998; 'A fin de siecle Japanese Romantic in Istanbul', BSOAS, 59, 1996, and other articles on modern Japanese history.

Glenn D. Hook is professor of Japanese studies and director of the Graduate School of East Asian Studies at the University of Sheffield. His recent publications include *Militarization and Demilitarization in Contemporary Japan* (Routledge, 1996), *Japanese Business Management: Restructuring for Low Growth and Globalization* (co-editor, Routledge, 1998), *Subregionalism and World Order* (co-editor, Macmillan, 1999).

Kazuki Iwanaga is senior lecturer in political science at the University College of Halmstad, Sweden. He is author of *Images, Decisions and Consequences of Japan's Foreign Policy* (1993) and articles on Japanese politics and foreign policy. His current research deals with the role of women in Asian politics.

Joel Joos is research assistant of the Section of Japanese Studies at the Catholic University of Leuven, Belgium. He obtained an M.A. in political science in

Japan, and is preparing a doctoral thesis on the thought of Maruyama Masao, especially his analysis of modernity.

Rotem Kowner is senior lecturer in the Japanese Studies Cluster at the University of Haifa, Israel. He has written on the modern racial image of Japan and is currently engaged in a long-term study of the Japanese reaction to Western images during the Meiji era.

Peter Lowe is a fellow of the Royal Historical Society and reader in history at the University of Manchester. He is the author of *The Origins of the Korean War*, 2nd ed. (Longman, 1997) and *Containing the Cold War in East Asia* (Manchester University Press, 1997) and has edited *The Vietnam War* (Macmillan, 1998).

Karine Marandjian is at the Institute of Oriental Studies, St Petersburg.

Yulia Mikhailova is a professor in the Faculty of International Relations at Hiroshima City University. She is the author of several books in Russian on the intellectual history of Tokugawa and Meiji Japan. Her present research is on psychological aspects of Russian-Japanese relations.

Maria Sevela specializes in the history of Russian-Japanese relations at the Ecole des Hautes Etudes en Science Sociales in Paris. She is the author of a number of articles on the roles of history and memory in war, with oral history occupying a particularly important place in her work. The current paper is drawn from her Ph.D. thesis.

Dick Stegewerns is lecturer in modern Japanese history at the Centre for Japanese and Korean Studies, Leiden University. He is the author of *Japanese Perceptions of the Outside World during the Period of Multilateral Treaties, 1919-1933* (forthcoming) and the editor of *Japan in the World: The Dilemma of Nationalism and Internationalism in Prewar Modern Japan* (forthcoming).

Tanaka Takahiko is a professor of international history at Hitotsubashi University, Tokyo. He is the author of *Nisso kokkō kaifuku no shiteki kenkyū* [A history of Soviet-Japanese normalization, 1945-56] (Tokyo, 1993) for which he was awarded the Yoshida Shigeru Prize in 1994 and the Ōhira Masayoshi Memorial Award in 1995.

Preface

E very three years the European Association for Japanese Studies organizes an international conference which has come to be recognized as a key meeting-place for specialists in Japanese studies, with an ever-increasing number of participants. The eighth conference was held in Budapest, Hungary, in August 1997. Each of the conference sections had adopted a theme or themes to provide coherence to its sessions. For the section on History, Politics and International Relations two themes had been announced. A special session was organized on 'The Iwakura Mission in Europe', a theme which seemed appropriate since it was 125 years since the important visit to Europe of the high-powered Japanese delegation led by Prince Iwakura Tomomi visited the United States and Europe in the period 1871-73. A book edited by Professor Ian Nish based on papers presented at the conference has already been published as *The Iwakura Mission in America & Europe: A New Assessment* (Japan Library, 1998, 228 pp).

This volume contains the majority of the papers presented under the main theme of the section: 'The Japanese and Europe: historical and contemporary perceptions'. It is organized into three broad themes focusing on (1) The Japanese and Europe: Historical and Contemporary Perceptions; (2) Japan and Eastern Europe; and (3) Japan, Europe and Cold War Issues. It is our hope that these diverse but significant contributions will offer new insights into the relations between Japan and Europe and between the Japanese and the Europeans, shedding light on important events and personages, as well as giving new impetus to continued in-depth studies of a relationship of great importance, not only for Japan and Europe but for the world.

As convenor of the section, together with Professor Nish, I was truly impressed with the breadth, variety and scholarly value of the papers presented. Quite naturally, the idea to publish a scholarly volume based on a selection of the papers came up during the proceedings. This idea was enthusiastically embraced by Mr Paul Norbury of the Japan Library and Professor Nish. Their support has been a constant encouragement for me as editor of this volume and for which I must express my deepest gratitude. My thanks go also to the contributors who so painstakingly endeavoured to supply their edited contributions by the deadline. Finally, I want to reiterate my deep-felt thanks to all those who took part in the work of the section as well as to those who made the conference feasible: the Budapest College of Foreign Trade and the office-bearers of the European Association for Japanese Studies.

BERT EDSTRÖM
Autumn 1999

Editor's note
Japanese names have been rendered with the surname or family name preceding the personal name in accordance with normal Japanese practice.

The Japanese and Europe: Historical and Contemporary Perceptions

1

Unseen Paradise: The Image of Holland in the Writings of Andō Shōeki

KARINE MARANDJIAN

A ndō Shōeki (1703-62) is nowadays known as an original thinker whose ideas broke loose from the mainstream of Japanese thought of mid-Tokugawa. He rejected both Confucian and Buddhist traditions whose spread in Japan he described as resulting in the degradation of a society of ancient times once harmonious and pristine. In spite of his humble social position and life in a distant province Shōeki boldly challenged the acknowledged authorities and ways of thinking. Dissatisfied with the political and social situation of contemporary Japan he strove for what he perceived as a 'better reality'. He dreamt of travelling abroad and despite the fact that his attempts to leave the country never materialized, he used every opportunity to learn more about foreign countries.

A summary of what Shōeki knew about the outside world can be found in his treatises *Tōdō shinden* [The true explanation of the All-pervading Way] (1752) and *Shizen shin'eidō* [The true laws of nature] (1755). The 'Bankoku kikōron maki' ['Reflections on the cultural conditions of different countries'] (7 chapters) of the *Shizen shin'eidō* has been lost. 'Bankoku maki' ['On the countries of the world'] of the *Tōdō shinden* has a separate chapter entitled 'Bankoku no sambutsu, hitogara, gengo no ron' ['Reflections on products, peoples and languages of different countries'] which contains information about eleven countries.[1] Two sections deal with European countries, *Oranda* [Holland] and *Namban* [The Southern Barbarians]. In the section on the Southern Barbarians Shōeki specifies the geographical position and the abundance and productivity of land and gives the name of only four countries belonging to the Southern Barbarians (according to him there were altogether 45 countries); two countries can be recognized as Portugal and Spain. In Shōeki's words, all knowledge on the Southern Barbarians was acquired from the Dutch. Information is scarce and fragmentary.

The section on Holland is much longer and more informative. It begins with a description of exact geographical co-ordinates for Holland. In Shōeki's words, Holland and Japan are situated opposite each other: Japan lies '16 degrees north', Holland '16 degrees south'. (It seems like a mirror reflection but the geographical terms used by Shōeki are rather obscure and contradictory, so it is difficult to reconstruct his geographical conception.)

Apart from the spatial location, Holland's place within the frame of the traditional five-elements scheme is specified: in Shōeki's opinion Holland correlates with 'metal' (=west/autumn/white colour/purity/tranquillity/ etc.). Inserted in the five-element scheme Holland achieves the status of an integral part of the world. In other words, it becomes included in the 'outer world view' that traditionally embraced only China, India, Japan, Korea and countries dependent upon them.

Any reader of Shōeki's account on Oranda will be struck by the 'accuracy' of his narration. Many facts are presented some of which, as we know them now, are valid. When he writes, for example, that Oranda consists of seven provinces (although the provinces enlisted by Shōeki are not correctly named by him), it is true that the sixteenth century saw the establishment of a republic of united provinces that incorporated seven provinces. He gives a truthful description of how the Dutch appeared, depicts accurately their clothes and accessories and writes about their food and drinking preferences. He reports on several concrete technical devices such as binoculars. The factual content of the section on Oranda seems 'objective' – there is no place for obvious fantasy or fiction. Even dealing with the 'wonderful skills' [kijutsu] that the Dutch were renowned for, Shōeki tries to offer a 'rational' explanation. Some of his comments seem bizarre. One such case is when he claims that the black sailors – living on the island near Holland according to him – are black because in frames of the five-element scheme they are connected with the element 'water' that correlates with the colour black. Most of his other explanations are quite reasonable and acceptable.

2

Shōeki got the major part of his information on Holland indirectly from the Dutch. He writes in the *Tōdō shinden* that one of his students was a subordinate of the marine official in Nagasaki and acquired information about foreign lands talking with the Dutch through the interpreters (Andō, 1752 [1966]: 674). It seems that besides Shōeki's personal 'curiosity' his desire to learn more about foreign countries was quite natural in an epoch when 'interest in things Dutch was also very much present': Arai Hakuseki (1657-1725), Aoki Kon'yō (1698-1769) and Noro Genjō (1693-1761), acknowledged forerunners of *rangaku* [Dutch studies], were contemporaries of Shōeki. They were the first to seriously study Dutch science and wrote treatises on various subjects related to Holland. Several years later in the Tanuma era (1767-86) taste for luxurious exotica brought about the emergence of a number of 'Hollandophiles' [*rampeki*] (Numata, 1992, 50-5).

Certainly, due to his low social position, Shōeki did not have access to official sources of information, but there is a 'strong possibility' that he had read some works on Oranda: according to E. H. Norman, he might have known, for example, *Nagasaki yawa so* [Twilight tales of Nagasaki] (1720) by Nishikawa Joken (1648-1724) (Norman, 1949: 287).

The rapid spread of *rangaku* and appearance of numerous translations and original treatises on Holland promoted the implanting of the idea of the reality of Holland's existence in the minds of the Japanese (at least those belonging to the upper classes of society) for whom this country became no less real than China, India or Japan. Shōeki's account on Holland is an illustrious manifestation of this process.

What is more significant – Shōeki compared Holland with the traditional 'centres of the world' – China/Japan (in Confucianism) and India (in Buddhism) – and such a comparison was not in favour of the latter. He makes the remarks that 'Holland is truly a finest country that surpasses all countries in the world' (Andō, 1752 [1966]: 676) and that practical knowledge of the Dutch is 'higher than the wisdom of the Sages and Buddha' (Andō, 1752 [1966]: 677). What makes Holland superior to the other countries? Shōeki presents a number of points in evidence:

- Holland is a peaceful country. From ancient times it has not experienced war or internal strife. It never attacked any country.

3

- The country consists of seven parts (provinces?), but there is no division to the upper or lower, to the kings and lords.
- The Dutch have numerous 'wonderful skills': they construct the best ships in the world, grow various cereals, cultivate their land, and have travelled all over the world.
- The Dutch are fair by nature. One tenth of the profit they get from trade is handed over to the king. They are not greedy and thus never fight with each other.
- The Dutch are endowed by nature with sense of shame and duty.
- The Dutch are morally perfect. They practise monogamy and never deceive their wives. In case they commit adultery they are sentenced to death.

In Shōeki's words, the Dutch ridicule China, India and Japan since they are permanently engaged in internal conflicts and struggle. Those at the top are fighting with those at the bottom, which he finds a behaviour resembling a childish foolish game. Living in Japan makes Shōeki feel ashamed because of the Dutch (Andō, 1752 [1966]: 677-8).

In his brilliant work on Shōeki Norman portrays him as an 'bigoted chauvinist' but one who 'yet had such pride in his country that it was not easy for him to condemn its products whether material or intellectual' (Norman, 1949: 162).

The philosopher often criticized Japan saying that due to the selfish interests of the Sages and Buddha 'the Way of Nature was stolen' and 'disorder and lawlessness prevailed' (like in China and India). But to critizize one's country is not the same as feeling ashamed of it, especially when Japan was compared with Holland which many of Shōeki's contemporaries considered a 'barbarian country'. To openly admit admiration for Holland took real courage.

What was behind Shōeki's attitude? What made him recognize Holland as a model of justice, peacefulness and moral perfection that Japan must follow? As mentioned above concrete information on Dutch customs and institutions available to Shōeki was rather limited — his main informant evidently had no profound knowledge since his position as a petty official of the marine magistrate could not have given him free access to the Dutch. Thus Shōeki had to use various sources of information which explains the appearance of some commonplaces in his account — for example, the widespread beliefs that the Dutch were short-lived[2] and practised monogamy. Besides information obtained from his pupil, from various works on the subject and from rumours, Shōeki resorted to his imagination, combining his scarce factual data with imaginary evaluations. He did not 'invent' facts but added interpretations of 'how it should be' which resulted in the creation of an image of Holland as an 'ideal' society. Shōeki rejected the political realities of his time and was striving for an Utopian society where the people in freedom and equal simplicity cultivated their land and lived in conformity with the true Way of Nature.[3] For Shōeki antiquity (the age of gods in Japan, ancient Korea or uncivilized Ezo) was an embodiment of the true Way of Nature. This kind of Utopia can be characterized as 'retrospective', which typologically corresponds to the concept of a 'golden age'. From the beginning of its history utopian thought has embodied two visions of a better reality: 'the golden age' and 'the distant lands'. Both concepts were inherent in Chinese culture: the former was an integral part of the Confucian tradition, the latter (although present in Confucian texts) was more accentuated in Taoist thought.

Norman claims that Shōeki's critique of the Chinese Golden Age indicates that he was 'repudiating traditional Oriental Utopia and creating one conforming to his own analysis of society which was without classes and where agriculture was the chief occupation' (Norman, 1949: 225). It is difficult to agree with this assertion – rejecting the Confucian model of the Golden Age (the Utopia of 'ideal governing' where the prosperity of society was directly connected with the activity of the Confucian scholar or later the perfection of the sacral monarch) Shōeki did not reject the general pattern of the 'retrospective' Utopia as such: his 'ideal society' resembled the primitive society of the past.

At the same time Shōeki's vision of Utopia is in many respects close to the Taoist tradition with its egalitarianess and distinct 'nature-culture' antinomy – suffice it to recall his negative attitude to the learning and letters 'invented by Confucius and Buddha for selfish motives'. Shōeki's view of Holland as an 'ideal society' corresponds to the pattern of 'distant land' Utopia.

Shōeki's attempts to provide a rational interpretation of Dutch customs and institutions and his emphasis that Holland was an integral part of the world were aimed at creating a 'plausible' image of the country. He wanted to convince his readers that the ideal world existed 'here and now'. This pattern of Utopia can be designated as a synchronous Utopia of the 'escape' type.[5]

Shōeki combined two patterns of Utopia: retrospective/ golden age and synchronous/distant lands. The main modus of his philosophy is purely Utopian since its main pathos was not so much his critique of the feudal society of his time as his search for a 'better reality'. The inner laws of the Utopian mode of thinking predetermined the operation by which the image of Holland came into being. Utopian fantasy with exact geographical address was not a novelty in the history of Utopian thought. Shōeki can be seen as a traditional Eastern Utopian thinker whose philosophy developed within the context of Chinese (and Japanese) culture which included Utopianism as one of its immanent elements. Not belonging to any particular school of thinking he elaborated an original Utopian teaching shaped under the influence of the great traditions of Confucianism and Taoism.

BIBLIOGRAPHY

Andō Shōeki. 1752 (1966). *Tōdō shinden* [The true explanation of the All-pervading Way]. In *Kinsei shisōka bunshū* edited by Bitō Masahide. Nihon koten bungaku taikei, 97. Tokyo: lwanami shoten, 567-666.

———. 1752 (1966-67). *Tōdō shinden* [The true explanation of the All-pervading Way], edited by Naramoto Tatsuya. 2 vols. Tokyo: Iwanami shoten.

Martynov, A. S. 1987. 'Konfutsianskaya utopiya v drevnosti i v srednevekovje' [Ancient and medieval Confucian utopia]. In 'Kitajskie sotsialnye utopii' [Chinese social utopia], ed. Delyusin L.P., Borokh L.N., Moscow: Nauka.

Mumford, Lewis. 1962. *The Story of Utopias*. New York: Viking Press.

Norman, E. Herbert. 1949. 'Andō Shōeki and the Anatomy of Japanese Feudalism'. *Transactions of the Asiatic Society of Japan*. 3rd series, 2. Tokyo.

Numata Jirō. 1992. *Western learning. A short history of the study of Western science in Early Modern Japan*. Tokyo: The Japan-Netherlands Institute.

NOTES

1.   I have used two editions of the text: the abridged text of *Tōdō shinden* edited by Bitō Masahide in Nihon koten bungaku taikei, 97, Tokyo: Iwanami shoten, 1966, 567-666 (Andō, 1752 [1966]); and the complete text of *Todo shinden* in two vols, edited by Naramoto Tatsuya, Tokyo: lwanami shoten, 1966-67 (Andō, 1752 [1966-67]).

2.   The same assertion can be seen in Arai Hakuseki's writings (see Norman, 1949: 285).

3.   For a detailed analysis of Shōeki's Utopian thought, see Norman, 1949: 219-48.

4.   On the classicication of Confucian Utopia, see Martynov, 1987.

5.   On escape-type Utopia, see Mumford, 1962; and Martynov, 1987. A vivid example of this type is the famous 'Peach spring' by Tao Yuanming. For 'Peach spring' as a Confucian-Taoist synthesis, see Martynov, 1987: 36-9.

Debates on Naichi Zakkyo in Japan (1879-99): The Influence of Spencerian Social Evolutionism on the Japanese Perception of the West

NORIKO BERLINGUEZ-KONO

It is not yet known when the term *naichi zakkyo* was used for the first time but it appears in a memorandum written by Iwakura Tomomi in September 1871 (Inō, 1992: 4), perceived by the conservative forces as synonymous with the imminent foreign pressure.[1] On the other hand, the commoners do not seem to have reacted in the same way as the leaders did: the masses gave the expression a meaning with a positive connotation, that is, something civilized, Western, refined, certainly synonyms of *bummei*, 'civilization', and *kaika*, 'enlightenment'. For instance, a Western restaurant in a busy area of Asakusa was called *Zakkyoya*.

The expression *naichi zakkyo* can be defined as cohabitation of Japanese and foreigners on Japanese territory, by abolishing foreign settlements and extraterritoriality enjoyed by foreigners. Some Japanese could not tolerate foreigners travelling freely outside the limits of the settlements (Imai, 1975: 1-22). Shortly before and after the Meiji Restoration (1868), a certain xenophobic climate gave rise to various incidents resulting in the death of some foreigners. Nevertheless, we will not study this aspect of *naichi zakkyo*, that is, common Japanese reactions to foreigners travelling in Japan. Instead, focus will be on the controversy over the acceptance of foreigners, which will help us understand the Japanese perception of Westerners.

As Inō Tentarō has put it remarkably well, the debate on *naichi zakkyo* involved antithetical pairs such as 'approval/disapproval', 'hope/anxiety', 'interest/loss', 'likes/dislikes', in the discussion of the coexistence of Japanese and foreigners in Japan, a coexistence which in reality meant the ultimate end of the foreign settlements (Inō, 1992: 3). In order to revise the unequal treaties concluded with Western countries, the Meiji government had to deal with the controversial issue of *naichi zakkyo* and to convince the Japanese to use 'cohabitation' with foreigners to their advantage. Strangely enough, public opinion was much more attracted by the discussion of this issue than the question of equal treatment of Japan by Western powers, such as the right to determine Japanese tariffs independently and the abolition of the system of extraterritoriality. With more than four hundred articles or books published on this topic, it can easily be imagined that the idea of cohabitation with foreigners caused a great stir among Japanese whatever their origin; the new situation of *naichi zakkyo* was a preoccupation for all concerned.

This paper focuses on the way the Japanese described Westerners as a group and thus how they perceived themselves: the mirror-effect whereby the vision of the self can be seen through the vision of the other. If we are to broach the subject, we can hardly neglect the influence on Japanese intellectuals of the social evolutionism of Herbert Spencer (1820-1903). During the period in question, his ideas prevailed over the whole of Japan's intellectual society in the name of 'science', and everyone, whether democrat, conservative, socialist, or Buddhist, made frequent use of them. The ensuing discourses can be categorized into three groups, according to the characteristics of the perceptions of the Western world. It appears that both those who were for and those who were against *naichi zakkyo* were prisoners of the evolutionist idea; that is, the superiority of the white race. Let us examine each discourse in detail.

GENERAL OPTIMISM: THE WESTERNIZATION OF THE JAPANESE PHYSIQUE

In the first two decades of the Meiji period, the leitmotiv of Japanese society was *bummei kaika* – 'civilization and enlightenment'. Things Occidental were massively introduced without having been subjected to much in the way of critical judgement.[2] In such a climate of Western supremacy, it was natural that the proponents of *naichi zakkyo* should dominate the debate.The culmination of Westernization was symbolized by the balls held at the Rokumeikan ('Deer Cry Pavilion') from

1883 onwards on the initiative of Foreign Minister Inoue Kaoru (1835-1915). In response to the government's schedule for the revision of the unequal treaties, a favourable atmosphere among civilians was created for the revision as well as for *naichi zakkyo*.

Hayashi Fusatarō wrote in May 1884 in his *Naichi zakkyo hyōron* ['Comment on *naichi zakkyo*'] that he would welcome Western people and Western investments. As for Chinese people he said, 'If procreation with Japanese people is avoided, the situation is not alarming' (Inō, 1992: 7). It is noteworthy that evolutionism was an important frame of reference for him also. The leader of liberal opinion, Fukuzawa Yukichi (1835-1901), clarified his position in his book *Tsūzoku gaikōron* [Foreign policy in a popular style] published in the same year. The pseudonym Endō Aizō, for his part, pointed out in his essay 'Naichi zakkyo no rigai' [Gain and loss of *naichi zakkyo*] the overall advantage in the enforcement of *naichi zakkyo*, especially in terms of domestic economic development (Inō, 1992: 7-8). This argument based on economic reason was reiterated by the advocates of *naichi zakkyo* afterwards. In May 1886 *Mainichi shimbun* organized a prize-bearing essay contest about *naichi zakkyo*. Out of 127 essays received, 112 agreed to the idea of future *naichi zakkyo*, whereas only 15 disagreed with it. This result reflects the general state of mind of the time.

This optimism about *naichi zakkyo* generated a craze for various how-to books and science fiction novels set in the *naichi zakkyo* society. They taught the rudiments of the English language, the rules of European etiquette, ballroom dancing, European clothing and music, and so on. Tsubouchi Shōyō (1859-1935), the famous translator of Shakespeare, made a mediocre attempt to create a piece of fiction.[3]

What is more interesting to note is the diffusion at different levels of society of the idea of the superiority of the white race. The liberal economist Taguchi Ukichi (1855-1905) laid the foundations for the success of this idea, by stressing that everyone must learn the universal values residing in Western civilization. His point of view will be considered below. For the time being, let us turn to the thesis of 'racial reform' [*jinshu kairyō*] which had a favourable echo among Japanese intellectuals. The main idea consisted in improving the feeble Japanese constitution and mind by encouraging mixed marriages, promoting a meat diet, and studying English.

As for mixed marriages, the practice probably preceded the

construction of the theory, although the first Japanese to officially marry a European, Minami Teisuke, declared that he had been a long-standing 'reformist', longing for the progeny of an Anglo-Japanese breed (Koyama, 1995: 17). In fact, such a declaration seems to be typical of those who opted for mixed marriages. One who fervently supported the discourse of racial reform was Takahashi Yoshio, a journalist working for the *Jiji shimpō*. In 1884 he published a book called *Nihon jinshu kairyō ron* [Amelioration of the Japanese race] prefaced by Fukuzawa Yukichi; in January 1886 he wrote an article promoting mixed marriages in the *Jiji shimpō*, in an answer to Katō Hiroyuki (1836-1916) who had argued against this practice. Takahashi's article aroused an echo among the readers of the newspaper. One of them, Egi Yasuo, on business in Hamburg, helping administratively a certain Nishii Tomitarō's marriage to a German woman, mentioned in 1886 that if this marriage was to be accepted by the Japanese government, not only Egi himself but also the *Jiji shimpō* must be delighted at the news.[4] Thus, some explicitly advocated mixed marriages through which 'the objective of racial reform would be achieved'. Nevertheless, it must be remembered that the promotion of mixed marriages was thought to be beneficial to the Japanese only if it involved Westerners. Most of the speakers considered the marriages with other Asians as harmful.

Racial reform was not solely limited to mixed marriages. For some 'reformists', eating meat was another efficient way to bring radical changes to the Japanese body. An article in the October 1886 issue of the *Jiji shimpō*, 'Improve physical constitution before the application of *naichi zakkyo*', reported that an association named *Kōyōsha* at Kanda jimbochō in Tokyo aimed at improving the physical strength of the Japanese to that of the Westerners by encouraging a meat diet. Similarly, in order to approach Western civilization, the use of English as the official language was also discussed. For example, an article in the *Kōchi nippō* in 1887 showed the great need to resort to the English language as another official language, since it was used in a number of Asian countries (Katō, 1995: 151).

Consequently, the first two decades of the Meiji period was clearly marked by optimism regarding Westernization. Most Japanese accepted the superiority of the Western world, and with scientific guarantee of evolutionism, many internalized the hierarchy of races. The principle of *wakon yōsai*, 'Japanese spirit and Western technology', had not yet been convincing to the majority of the Japanese public.

FEAR OF MIGHTY 'COLONIZERS': HOMOGENEITY OF THE NATION

This optimistic mood was swept away, however, by a series of incidents which took place around 1886. The first incident occurred in 1886 when an English ship sank and the English captain and foreign crew left all the Japanese passengers to drown. Yet, a consular court in Kobe exonerated the captain and the crew of charges of criminal negligence. The court's decision naturally provoked public indignation and the force of pro-*naichi zakkyo* ideas weakened to a large extent. What is more, Inoue Kaoru's proposal for employing foreign jurists at every court was criticized virulently in and out of the government. The treaty-revision negotiations were extremely delicate to deal with, and turned into polemic which involved every level of society. The eloquent civil proponents of *naichi zakkyo* suddenly became taciturn.

Thus, a group of young intellectual conservatives such as Kuga Katsunan (1857-1907) came to the fore, and the wholesale delivery of Westernization was questioned. Needless to say, the promulgation of the constitution in 1889 and the convening of the first session of the Diet in 1890 galvanized public opinion into envisaging realistically the treaty revision as well as the *naichi zakkyo*. It is worth noting that this time, the spokesmen for new conservatism and, to a certain extent, those of traditional nationalism, set forth their opposition to the hasty application of *naichi zakkyo*.

Here, we will study mainly the ideas of two young intellectuals, Inoue Tetsujirō (1855-1944) and Katō Hiroyuki (1836-1916). What can be observed first is that most of the arguments against the hasty *naichi zakkyo* shared a fear of colonization by the overwhelming Western powers. In other words, these opponents of the *naichi zakkyo* were conscious of Western superiority, and thus it can hardly be said that their attitude was closely related to the xenophobic *jōi* movement – founded on a certain arrogance on the part of the Japanese – that emerged at the very end of the Edo era. Inoue emphasized the difference between his argument and the *jōi* movement, stating that the proponents of *jōi* were ignorant of overseas issues and considered the Westerners as a base and vulgar race, whereas he admired and felt friendship for the Westerners whom he considered as a superior race (Inoue, 1889 [1968]: 483-4). As for Katō, he drew a line between the unreasonable xenophobia and his, as it were, scientific position.

As mentioned above, even the opponents of 'mixed residence' were intimidated by the Western powers. Unlike the commoners who could not reformulate their opinion and theorize about it, intellectuals like Inoue and Katō made the most of the up-to-date scientific theories of European countries, in order to consolidate their arguments based on the hierarchy of races. Ironically, the recourse to science seemed to have plunged the intellectuals into a greater despair than the ordinary innocent people, over the circumstances in which a 'weak' Japan found itself. Inoue was firmly persuaded that the Japanese could not match the Westerners in every respect, that is, physically, morally, intellectually (weight, height, head size, physical strength, faculty of thinking, analytical and synthetical faculty, resistance, capital ...) (Inoue, 1889 [1968]: 475-6). In short, he affirmed that all the other races were inferior to the Westerners (Inoue, 1889 [1968]: 483). Katō shared this opinion.

This idea of hierarchy brought the Darwinian scholars to the question of inter-racial struggle and that of natural selection: they asserted that there would be no possibility of Japanese success, at least in the very near future. The major reason why they fiercely opposed the enforcement of the naichi zakkyo was to avoid a face-to-face confrontation with Westerners.

Let us have a close look at the contents of their texts. Inoue's logic was similar to that of Spencer or Darwin. His writing, abundant in technical and academic terms, was beyond the reach of the uninitiated. Inoue pedantically quoted in his article the works of renowned European scholars, accompanied by exact page references.[5] He cited especially Spencer's works such as First Principles, The Principles of Biology, The Study of Sociology as well as Darwin's The Descent of Man, The Variation of Animals and Plants under Domestication, and Journey of a Naturalist on Board the Beagle.

Inoue's considerations were as follows. First, the inferior race's contact with the superior race brings about a diminution of the population of the former. In order to prove that the 'mixed residence' would lead to a genital dysfunction for Japanese people, Inoue invoked Spencer's thesis[6] and Darwin's thesis.[7] Secondly, according to Darwin, the extinction of a race is caused chiefly by struggles between tribes and between races. Pointing to the case-study of the Pacific Islands accomplished by Darwin, Inoue alerted his readers to the danger of the extinction of the Japanese (Inoue, 1889 [1968]: 479-80). Affirming that, according to Spencer, Japanese political institutions had considerably weakened because of the tremendous social change brought from abroad, Inoue categorically rejected the 'cohabitation' with Westerners on the grounds that they would defeat and conquer Japanese people in this inter-racial struggle (Inoue 1889 [1968]: 475-6). He quoted Spencer's *The Study of Sociology* with a view to clarifying reasons for the extinction of the Japanese race (Inoue 1889 [1968]: 480).[8]

As regards another Darwinian, Katō, unlike Inoue, did not explicitly refer to the evolutionist scholars in an article in which he objected to a premature introduction of the *naichi zakkyo*. Nonetheless, his adherence to evolutionism was clear: compared to the Westerners, he regarded the Japanese race as immature and inexperienced in bitter business competition, and he was convinced that, as a result of the *naichi zakkyo*, the law of the 'survival of the fittest' would determine the winner (Westerners) and the loser (Japanese). This article was written in response to Taguchi's article which advocated the immediate abolition of foreign settlements.

Taguchi's main arguments against the *naichi zakkyo* were as follows. His prime concern was a possible Japanese defeat in the economic struggle. He claimed that the Western immigrants might predominate over the Japanese economy since they were incomparably enterprising, patient and experienced (Katō, 1893: 9, 11-3, 20-1, 25). He feared that a number of Westerners might emigrate to Japan where the climate was temperate, compared to that of India or Australia (Katō, 1893: 4-8). Clearly, Katō, known as ultra-conservative, yet firmly believed that Westerners were superior to the Japanese in that the former, as opposed to the latter, were well versed in undertaking a business, possessed large capital, showed remarkable perseverance and were highly competent (Katō, 1893: 12-3). In the field of commercial activities, he seemed to dread the Chinese for their diligence more than anyone else (Katō, 1893: 25-39).

Hence, these two leading scholars believed strongly that the 'mixed residence' was extremely harmful to an inferior race such as the Japanese, because they were under the influence of evolutionism whose adage was 'the stronger prey upon the weaker'.

Another reason for objecting to the *naichi zakkyo* was that such a radical change in a society would destroy at one sweep centuries of Japanese culture, tradition, customs, literature, religion, politics ... Some speakers, especially Buddhist and Shintō priests were of course against the Christianization of Japan. Inoue, a proponent of gradualism dear to evolutionists, was mostly concerned with the dissolution of the Japanese nation-state (Inoue, 1889 [1968]: 493-4). In his opinion, the rapid and profound transformation of society would run counter to natural evolution.

Following the example of Inoue, Katō appealed to his readers for patriotism by emphasizing a superficial and vain aspect of Westernization (Katō, 1893: 40-5). He criticized ardently the majority of the upper- and middle-class who adulated things Western without question, wished to copy all of them, as well as the lower-class people who were eager to adopt the habit of the upper-class, namely Westernization in the name of progress. Katō feared that, with the enforcement of the *naichi zakkyo*, not only Japanese culture, tradition and mentality, but also patriotism and loyalty to Japan might disappear (Katō, 1893: 45).

As mentioned above, Katō argued with Takahashi Yoshio, an advocate for 'racial' reform, over the question of mixed marriage. Katō peremptorily disapproved of the idea of making the Japanese a superior race like the white race through mixed marriages. Instead, he insisted that the Japanese were in honour bound to improve themselves on their own (Katō, 1893: 46-9). His rejection was categorical: he even suggested that the Japanese should stay a backward race if they were unable to become a superior race like Westerners on their own account (Katō, 1983: 48). It cannot be ruled out that he was an ultra-nationalist who was committed to maintaining Japanese blood pure. His position against mixed marriages was that of a nationalist, not so much that of an evolutionist. However, it is obvious to everybody that he reasoned in terms of evolutionary theory: superior race and inferior race. We must take into account the academic trends of the time that considered racialism as a deep-rooted European, and therefore thought to be authentic science. He was also one of the heirs to evolutionism.

Under the strong influence of evolutionism, it was no coincidence that Kaneko Kentarō (1853-1942), an important political figure close to the government, directly asked Spencer about the idea of the *naichi zakkyo*. Indeed, Spencer was considered by the patriarchs of the Meiji state as the most prominent intellectual of the time. Mori Arinori (1847-89), Japan's minister to the United States at that time, went to see Spencer around 1873 to ask his opinion about the re-organization of Japanese institutions (Duncan, 1908 [1996]: 161). Also, Spencer wrote to a Dr Youmans in April 1883 that the Japanese minister had informed him of the Japanese publication of his *Data of Ethics* (Duncan, 1908 [1996]: 231). Many Japanese statesmen, each time they visited London, did not fail to consult Spencer on various changes Japan was passing through (Duncan, 1908 [1996]: 318). Even Itō Hirobumi was anxious to know Spencer's opinion on the Japanese constitution (Duncan, 1908 [1996]: 320-1). Moreover, Spencer's, reputation was looming so large among Japanese intellectuals that in 1896 some of them organized an invitation trip to Japan for Spencer. We can thus tell from this Japanese attitude to Spencer that not only the intellectuals such as Inoue and Katō, close to the state's doctrine, but also a large educated population were disciples of Spencer.

Let us go back to the exchange between Kaneko and Spencer. Kaneko had consulted Spencer two years earlier. The philosopher answered in a letter that the 'cohabitation' was not a favourable solution because theoretically the superior people would dominate the less civilized. His advice consisted of the following: 1) not to authorize foreign landownership or leasehold and to permit foreigners only as annual tenants; 2) to ban foreigners from running publicly-owned and privately-owned mines; 3) to ban them from working for foreign trade; and 4) to prohibit inter-racial marriages which cause unfavourable results in the long run. According to him, the *naichi zakkyo* would be served by Western powers as a pretext for imperial expansionism (Duncan, 1908 [1996]: 321-2).

Clearly, Spencer saw the *naichi zakkyo* as a struggle between a superior race (Westerners) and an inferior race (Japanese), resulting in a Japanese defeat, that is, colonization of the Japanese by the Western powers. For Spencer, Japan was destined to be colonized sooner or later, and that is why he strongly disapproved of the enforcement of *naichi zakkyo* which would accelerate the unavoidable colonization:

> ... the Japanese policy should, I think, be that of *keeping Americans and Europeans as much as possible at arm's length* ... Apparently you are proposing by revision of the treaty powers with Europe and America 'to open the whole Empire to foreigners and foreign capital.' I regard this as a fatal policy. If you wish to see what is likely to happen, study

the history of India ... forces will be sent from America or Europe, as the case may be; a portion of territory will be seized and required to be made over as a foreign settlement; and from this there will grow eventually subjugation of the entire Japanese Empire. I believe that you will have great difficulty in avoiding this fate in any case, but you will make the process easy if you allow any privileges to foreigners beyond those which I have indicated (Duncan, 1908 [19961: 320).

In this passage we can observe Spencer's, rather sincere, compassion for what he thought of the 'uncivilized people' as well as certain anti-colonial attitude which, he feared, might 'rouse the animosity of my fellow-countrymen' (Duncan, 1908 [1996]: 323).[9] Apparently, his position was not that of an arrogant coloniser, but rather of one who sympathized with the weak nation. Simultaneously, his idea of social evolutionism was characterized by its gradualism, which implied that Japan would not be able to become at once a constitution-abiding nation (Duncan, 1908 [1996]: 319-20), and he was not in favour of rash changes harmful to Japanese society.

As for inter-marriage between foreigners and Japanese, Spencer recommended that it should be forbidden for biological reasons. He asserted that as for the inter-breeding of animals and the inter-marriages of human races alike, when they mixed, 'they must form a bad hybrid' and a 'chaotic constitution' (Duncan, 1908 [1996]: 322-3). In favour of regulations to restrict the Chinese immigration in America, Spencer regarded the immigration as a major cause of 'social disorganization' (Duncan, 1908 [1996]: 323).

Few will dispute the claim that the same arguments can be seen in those developed by Inoue or Katō. It is undeniably true that Spencerian sociology exerted a great influence on the intellectuals of the time.

POSITIVE THINKING BASED ON ECONOMIC LIBERALISM: THE DIVERSITY OF THE NATION

As opposed to the conservatives, the advocates of 'mixed residence' appeared to be much less overwhelmed by the supremacy of the white race. It is certainly possible that they saw between the Japanese and the Westerners a gap small enough to be easily bridged: the former could soon match the latter. Taguchi, a supporter of 'laissez-faire', made it clear that even though he believed in evolutionism, he refused to think the Japanese inferior (Taguchi, 1891: 707-9). In addition, the Liberal

Party, headed by Itagaki Taisuke (1837-1919), defined the Japanese as a civilized people who had the potential to defeat even Westerners (Jiyūtō tōhō gōgai, 1893 [1992]: 6). Shimada Saburō (1852-1923), a politician close to Ōkuma Shigenobu (1838-1922), shared the same point of view (Shimada, 1889 [1968]: 372).

For Taguchi, Westerners had to be an ideal model and must not be a threat to Japan (Taguchi, 1893 [1992]: 21). Indeed, he was only too aware of the threat of colonization. That is why it was imperative that the government should enforce the *naichi zakkyo* which put an end to the existence of foreign settlements. The argument for the abolition of foreign settlements seemed to be inherited from that of Hermann Roesler, a German adviser to the foreign ministry (Roesler, 1879 [1992]). Taguchi thought that the foreigners living in the settlements were capable of becoming the vanguard of any advance on Japan by the Western powers, and if it happened, Japan would be colonized just like India (Taguchi, 1893 [1992]: 25-6). As we pointed out, on the contrary, his opponents feared that the 'cohabitation' might lead to a territorial invasion by the law of 'racial struggle'. It is important to note that the intellectuals, both proponents and opponents of the *naichi zakkyo*, shared, implicitly or explicitly, the same feeling that the Westerners are a menace to Japanese society, for 'the Japanese people are inferior to the Westerners'.

What is most interesting in Taguchi's thesis is that he believed Japan to be a land of welcome, capable of assimilating foreigners. His model country was obviously the United States, proud of the diversity of the nation, whose citizens nevertheless remained highly patriotic (Taguchi, 1893 [1992]: 40-1). Stressing the Japanese history of integration by naturalization – incidentally, Inoue was a surname of foreign origin – giving various examples of successful integration all over the world, he asserted that once foreigners were naturalized, they would become devoted patriots. His vision of naturalization offers a great contrast to that of Katō. Similarly, he laid a special emphasis upon the Japanization of children of mixed Japanese-foreign parentage. The acquisition of the Japanese language and culture by the child was considered as extremely beneficial to Japan (Taguchi, 1893 [1992]: 48).

Moreover, he was of the opinion that the Japanese compatriots ought to take the initiative to go overseas for settlement, so that the number of descendants outside Japan would multiply. Quoting the case of Great Britain whose emigration policy made her a great nation with a large population, he urged the Japanese to run the risk of going abroad to settle down for the sake of the Japanese nation (Taguchi, 1893 [1992]: 49-50). Somehow he happened to find that the Japanese and the Hungarians shared the same root, and applauded the exploits of these 'Asians' who survived despite the 'Aryan' aggression. The Darwinian concept of 'racial struggle' was present in Taguchi's reasoning as well.

On the other hand, Inoue's conviction lay in a theory that a country's strength originated from the homogeneity of its nation (Inoue 1889: 476). Thus, the diversity of cultures made the state difficult to govern, damaging the unity of the nation. Also, he thought that the foreigners who had decided to settle in Japan would remain foreigners because of their cultural background. In view of the situation in America or India, the Europeans, in particular, would refuse to learn the Japanese language, culture, religion and customs, showing great attachment to their own way of life (Inoue, 1889 [1968]: 496-7). As for the Japanese, he judged them incapable of emigrating, due to their feeble character (Inoue, 1889 [1968]: 475).

To sum up, in order to maintain Japanese independence, Taguchi and Inoue stood for two distinct visions of the nation. Taguchi proposed a plan that the Japanese, inside Japan, should try to assimilate foreigners and, outside Japan, settle in a foreign country with a view to spreading Japanese culture, while Inoue's project was to prioritize the homogeneity of the nation, hence no immigration, no emigration.

Before moving on to a conclusion, we must refer to the general reaction on the eve of the enforcement of the *naichi zakkyo* in July 1899. Yokoyama Gen'nosuke (1870-1915), a journalist concerned with the lot of the destitute, published in May 1899 a book called *Naichi zakkyogo no Nihon* [Japan after the enforcement of the *naichi zakkyo*]. It conveys very well the excitement at all levels of society:

> Schools of English language sprang up like mushrooms, the number of students of language increased rapidly, printing offices of European writing were thriving, educationists researched on new pedagogy adapted to the situation of *naichi zakkyo*, ambitious men of letters familiarized themselves with world literature ... in the business world, merchants dream of the *naichi zakkyo* day and night, industrialists accumulate capital to strengthen their position, nowadays every Tom, Dick, and Harry speaks of the *naichi zakkyo* looking beyond July, asks

himself about his future, in the public bath at the corner of the barber, all the town talk of the *naichi zakkyo* even in the depths of the country far from the railway . . . (Yokoyama, 1899 [1954]: 14).

Yokoyama himself qualified the *naichi zakkyo* as a time of war against the West which was much more difficult to win than the Sino-Japanese War. It is clear that this strong pessimism came from his sympathy for the labouring class. His description of society, however, tells us that the overall reaction was positive, if anxious, about the new situation of 'mixed residence'. From the books and articles of the time, the pragmatic mind of people who wished to adapt themselves quickly to social change can be observed. Surprisingly enough, there were picture books or toys (snakes and ladders, for example) on the *naichi zakkyo* specially designed for children (Inō, 1992: 21).

As for the entrepreneurs and bankers, they were unanimously optimistic about this extensive reform (Boa, 1899: 180-207). They also understood that the new world required them to be highly competitive. It is interesting to note that most of them considered the Westerners as dynamic, positive, active and independent. By contrast, the image of the Japanese was, of course, at an opposite extreme. Nevertheless, it seems that these economic leaders did not totally adhere to this negative image of the Japanese population which was a prisoner of erring ways. By comparing the Japanese with the Westerners, the Japanese leaders were particularly hopeful that they would have some success in exhorting the population to modernize its state of mind.

CONCLUSION

What conclusions can be drawn from all this? First of all, the whole of Japan without exception received the message that one had entered into the era of permanent competition. The internalization of the eternal struggle in each mind was possible mainly because of the intellectuals' efforts to interpret precisely the modern world and the attitude necessary to accomplish the modernization of the country. Undoubtedly, the large diffusion of evolutionism played a key role. Yet, we can hardly overlook the fact that ordinary people revealed a capacity for adaptation, a competitive mind, an idea of progress, an optimistic attitude, in short, a 'predisposition' to become the dynamic actors in the process of modernization.

Furthermore, the hierarchy between races which forms a

central part of social evolutionism, no longer was fervently emphasized in public by Japanese intellectuals, probably because they preferred not to stress the determinism of the biological differences between races. Even the argument for the improvement of the Japanese race strongly recommended by Takahashi Yoshio was later dismissed by Takahashi himself since 'the idea was preposterous' (Takahashi, 1933: 113-4). Instead of recalling that the Japanese race was inferior to the whites, the intellectuals preferred to create a founder myth of the Japanese nation and to believe in the Japanese capacity to step up in the hierarchy of interational society. However, that does not mean that the intellectuals were finally liberated from an inferiority complex regarding the Westerners. The problem of identity crisis seemed to be all the more serious, since Taguchi claimed in 1904 in his article (Taguchi, 1904 [1985]: 722) and in his book (Taguchi, 1904 [1927]: 485-6, 499, 500) that the Japanese were essentially different from the 'yellow race': '. . . it is indisputable that the Japanese belong to the Aryen (linguistic) group' (Taguchi, 1904 [1927]: 499), '. . . we can reject the ill repute that the Japanese are yellow' (Taguchi, 1904 [1927]: 500). It is true that Taguchi did not completely deny a certain relation between the Japanese and the yellow race, but at the same time he vigorously asserted that the Japanese were not related to the yellow race: 'I know that some of the Japanese also share a trace of blood of the so-called yellow race; however, those who maintain superiority and excellence in Japanese society are by no means of the yellow race' (Taguchi, 1904 [1927]: 485-6).

Another important observation is that since the enforcement of the *naichi zakkyo*, the thesis of diversity had officially become a main current of nationalism to the detriment of that of homogeneity.[10] This choice meant that the Japanese no longer defined themselves as belonging to an inferior race condemned to limit themselves to the archipelago, but as a 'future' superior race fully capable of prospering all over the world. Westerners no longer monopolized the position of the only civilized race described by Inoue Tetsujirō, but became merely one of them – at least many Japanese leaders wished to adopt such a positive thinking while striving to dissimulate an inferiority complex towards Westerners.

Finally, it is hard to underestimate the consequence of this choice from these two perceptions. It is probable that the two seemingly opposite discourses directly or indirectly paved the way for later expansionism for Greater Japan: on the one hand, the discourse for diversity, offering a self-image of a powerful, enterprising and brotherly nation to the Japanese people, proposing that the future of Japan should lie in a policy of expansion, especially after the victory over the Sino-Japanese War; on the other hand, the discourse regarding homogeneity was used to foster notions of ultra-nationalism which later crystallized into a fanatical form of patriotism characterized by piety for the emperor and the 'family state'. Both camps, even the conservatives, chose not to reject social evolutionism which nevertheless brought 'dishonour' on the Japanese nation by classifying the Japanese as uncivilized. Instead, they fully accepted the theory as a scientific truth, and interpreted it freely; in a positive or negative manner. The application of the *naichi zakkyo* marked a temporary victory for those who endorsed the principle of 'cohabitation', which signified that many shared the idea of Spencerian social evolutionism, but Spencer's pessimism towards Japanese society was shared only by the intellectuals close to the imperial regime.

BIBLIOGRAPHY

Boa Sanshi. 1899. *Zakkyo no keishō* [Warning against cohabitation]. Tokyo: Jimmin shimbunsha.
Duncan, David. 1908 (1996). *The Life and Letters of Herbert Spencer*. London: Routledge/Thoemmes Press.
Imai Shōji. 1975. 'Meiji nijūnendai ni okeru naichi zakkyoteki keikō ni tsuite' [Trends toward *naichi zakkyo* in the second decade of the Meiji period]. *Kokushigaku*, 104:1-22.
Inō Tentarō, ed. 1992. *Naichi zakkyoron shiryō shūsei* [Compiled materials for the discourses on *naichi zakkyo*], 1. Tokyo: Hara shobō.
Inoue Teorsed the principle of 'cohabitaakkyoron' [On *naichi zakkyo*]. In *Meiji bunka zenshū: Gaikōhen* [Complete works on Meiji culture: Foreign policy]. Tokyo: Nihon hyōronsha, 471-520.
Jiyūtō tōhō gōgai [Liberal Party: extra of the party organ]. 1893 (1992). 'Naichi zakkyoron' [On *naichi zakkyo*]. In *Naichi zakkyoron shiryō shūsei* [Compiled materials for the discourses on *naichi zakkyo*], 3, edited by Inō Tentarō. Tokyo: Hara shobō, 1-12.
Katō Hidetoshi. 1995. 'Gendai ijin kō' [Contemporary reflections on the foreigner]. *Chūō kōron*, February, 144-64.
Katō Hiroyuki. 1893. *Zakkyo shōsō* [Premature cohabitation]. Tokyo: Tetsugaku shoin.
Koyama Noboru. 1995. *Kokusai kekkon daiichigō* [The first case of mixed marriage]. Tokyo: Kōdansha.
Roesler, Hermann. 1879 (1992). 'Naichi zakkyoron' [On *naichi zakkyo*]. In *Naichi zakkyoron shiryō shūsei* [Compiled materials for the discourses on *naichi zakkyo*], 1,

edited by Inō Tentarō. Tokyo: Hara shobō, 49-60.

Shimada Saburō. 1889 (1968). 'Jōyaku kaiseiron' [The revision of the unequal treaties]. In *Meiji bunka zenshū: Gaikōhen* [Complete works on Meiji culture: Foreign policy]. Tokyo: Nihon hyōronsha, 365-408.

Taguchi Ukichi. 1891. 'Inoue Tetsujirō shi ni tadasu' [Questions to Mr Inoue Tetsujirō]. *Tōkyō keizai zasshi*, 573: 707-9.

——. 1893 (1992). 'Iryūchi seido to naichi zakkyo' [Foreign settlements and *naichi zakkyo*]. In *Naichi zakkyoron shiryō shūsei* [Compiled materials for the discourses on *naichi zakkyo*], 3, edited by Inō Tentarō. Tokyo: Hara shobō, 15-55.

——. 1904 (1927). 'Hakōka ron: Nihon jinshu no shinsō' [Against the theory of the yellow peril: The truth of the Japanese race]. (Tokyo: Keizai zasshisha). In *Teiken Taguchi Ukichi zenshū* [Complete works of Taguchi Ukichi], 2. Tokyo: Teiker. Taguchi Ukichi zenshū kankōkai, 483-500.

——. 1964 (1985). 'Nihonjin wa ōshoku jinshu ni arazo' [The Japanese do not belong to the yellow race]. *Tōkyō keizai zashi*, 1231: 722-5.

Takahashi Yoshio. 1933. *Hōki no ato* [After sweeping]. Tokyo: Shūhōen.

Yokoyama Gen'nosuke. 1899 (1954). *Naichi zakkyogo no Nihon* [Japan after the enforcement of the *naichi zakkyo*] Tokyo: Iwanami shoten.

NOTES

1   Iwakura's memorandum 'Meiji yonen Yokohama shutchō shisetsu no gi naidan no koto' [An envoy to the Yokohama settlement discussed in private in the fourth year of the Meiji period (i.e., 1871)].

2   The resistance against the Enlightenment movement existed, but it is only from 1880 that these kinds of voices were heard.

3   Under the pseudonym 'Haru no yaoboro sensei', he published in 1886 the fiction-story *Naichi zakkyo mirai no yume* [Dream about the future of *naichi zakkyo*].

4   'Naigai jimmin kekkon zakken' [Miscellaneous cases of international marriages], in the archives of the Japanese Ministry of Foreign Affairs.

5   Apart from Spencer and Darwin, Inoue cited Baelz, Machiavelli, Savigny, Montesquieu, Rousseau, Dühring, Schopenhauer, Hegel, Hobbes, Guizot, Comte, and so on.

6   According to Inoue, Spencer developed in *The Principles of Biology* a thesis that the more human beings use their brains the less they procreate, for the energy in a body concentrates in the brain, not in the genital function.

7   Inoue invoked Darwin's *The Descent of Man* and *The Variation of Animals and Plants under Domestication* in order to stress the idea that the social transformation would inevitably result in a genital function, and very often, dysfunction.

8   Inoue argued that the 'mixture' would give rise to phenomena such as propagation of new diseases, alcoholism and moral depravation.

9   For this reason, Spencer asked Kaneko not to publicize this 'confidence' during his lifetime, but implied that it should be published after his death. Thus, it was published in *The Times* (18 January 1904).

10   The victory of the advocates for 'diversity' were by no means suggesting that the advocates of 'homogeneity' would lose influence on the political leaders in power. These advocates had instituted, through education, the idea of homogeneity of each Japanese subject *vis-á-vis* the emperor. After metamorphosis by the enforcement of the *naichi zakkyo* they succeeded in achieving a metamorphosis by integrating imperialism to a certain extent into their philosophy.

3

Two Japanese on Modernity: Fukuzawa Yukichi and Japanese Images of Europe and the World as Interpreted by Maruyama Masao

JOEL JOOS

When doing research on the life and works of a scholar, especially an influential intellectual such as Maruyama Masao, perhaps a first step is to gain a general overview of the works and philosophy of that person. In Maruyama's case this is not an easy task, since there are only few comprehensive studies on the author.[1] There may be many reasons for this. First of all, he passed away only recently. Other factors may be the vast array of topics he tackled and his enormous influence, the continuously 'acute' and problematic nature of some of the subjects he dealt with, and not in the least the reaction against his 'modernistic' views propelled by recent developments in sociology and philosophy.[2] We will have to make our own way here and try to develop some encompassing interpretation ourselves.

Maruyama is often called the foremost 'intellectual leader' of the postwar era in Japan. The range of his works is very wide and goes from comments on the *Kojiki* (712 AD) to an incisive analysis and rejection of the militarist system of the pre-war period. His activity was most conspicuous in the 1950s, when he was known as the intellectual, descending from his ivory tower to discuss publicly the policy of the government, in this case that of Prime Minister Kishi Nobusuke and the renewal of the peace treaty with the US. But a career that spans almost half a century gave Maruyama many opportunities to invest energy elsewhere, and left us a heritage full of contrasts and continuities, straight lines and complex fractures.

Major contrasts can be discerned in Maruyama's works, differences precariously united in one person. We can point at the distinction between the early Maruyama trying to safeguard modernity from the attacks of proponents of nationalism and the later Maruyama trying to uncover a Japanese individuality, or that what is characteristic of Japan's intellectual history. Equally striking is the distinction between the scholar penetrating old Japanese sources, and the intellectual responding to current developments, writing articles on miscellaneous topics and prone to lend his ear to numerous Western theories. There seems to be some gap between the professor at Tokyo University, the zenith of the Japanese academic world, and the commentator fulminating against the policy of the government or establishment in general. He is known as the progressive scholar venting bitter comments on the imperial system, but in the mean time not sparing criticism on the Communist Party, otherwise often depicted as the main victim of pre-war repression. Finally, while being accused of 'Euro-centrism', he never devoted any great effort to producing essays and works that focused directly on Europe or the US, etc.

On the other hand, I think it is possible to discern in Maruyama's works some recurrent themes; or better: some patterns of thought that have not changed basically over more than forty years. In one of his last interviews he categorized his own thought as one of permanent, continuous revolution [*eikyū kakumei-ron*]. He relentlessly stresses the importance of more Japanese efforts to self-understanding and self-consciousness [*jikaku*], the making of a Japanese tradition of individual dignity and liberty. And as far as the topic of the present paper is concerned, we can consider Maruyama's positive stance towards modernity and the location he sees as its 'home base', Europe and America [*ōbei*] as another of those continuing elements.

Contrary to a lot of too easy criticism, Maruyama certainly is not blind to the weak or ugly spots of the Western world and its traditions. Still, he wholeheartedly commits to its ideals, and its academia [*gakumon*] in general; he relies on it hoping to inspire his fellow-countrymen to a spiritual revolution at least as far-reaching as the one the West went through in the last centuries. This commitment, however, cannot leave Maruyama's understanding of the world unattained; his works and especially – surprisingly or not – the ones in which he presents a profound analysis of Japanese tradition bear the clearly visible stamp of

Western methods, world views and presuppositions. Our starting point will be the following: Maruyama tackles some problems in Japanese intellectual tradition by means of Western methods, and, unwillingly or voluntarily, these impinge upon the result of his analysis, the outcome of his search, the gaps he finds to be filled. This pattern does not change over the years; although Maruyama encounters numerous new theories, his main aim remains unaltered. In the immediate pre-war period he showed appreciation for some very distinct characters in Japanese history. This appreciation which to a considerable degree seemed to be inspired by the context of anti-fascist feelings and the need to redefine Japanese history *in toto*, did not loose any of its essential meaning to Maruyama, nor its relevance. He just did not feel like changing models or paradigms because of the general optimism concerning Japan's modernization and democratic character, or because of the growing critique on modernism itself. Nonetheless, one should not overemphasize the point of this paper: we do try to go to the core of Maruyama's thought, but we do not pretend to cover exhaustively his works, the essence of which indeed is not the view on Europe or the outside world. It is no exaggeration to state that Maruyama is a 'universalist', discerning the same possibilities for Japan as for Europe, and that any attempt to understand the true sense of his endeavours should primarily concern itself with these topics.

That Maruyama did not seem to change the above-mentioned model is not a fatal error in itself, in fact it is not an error at all. It is one way of coping with the enormous challenge the modern world poses even today to the traditional Japanese frame of mind. It is the interpretation and the appeal of a great mind that wants to reach a helping hand to those who share the same anguish (the resurgence of ultra-nationalism). Certainly, Maruyama was not the only one to do such a thing, nor did he ever occupy a truly and explicitly dominant position on the polarized stage of Japan's recent intellectual history. To right-wing authors he was an 'outsider' who did not add valuable insight in the spirit of Japanese uniqueness, leaning too heavily on universal values – he was considered a 'Euro-centrist' and his definition of modern themes as 'nationalism' was and is labelled unpatriotic and evasive (Satō, 1996). To the Marxist camp that was very influential in the immediate post-war period, he represented the model of the liberal bourgeois too preoccupied with matters of 'mind' and unorthodox descriptions of Japanese historical and intellectual evolution. From their particular point of view, these criticisms are not meaningless. Yet it is Maruyama's 'detached' attitude, namely to transcend this kind of bipolarity to face up to far greater and deeper problems, that elevates him above the level of the average scholar. It is as if he stood between Japan and the West in much the same way as many stood and were forced to choose between left or right within Japan, and the West for that matter.

An early work of Maruyama, in fact the work that made him famous, is *Nihon seiji shisōshi kenkyū* [Studies in the Intellectual History of Tokugawa Japan] (translated by Mikiso Hane). This *magnum opus* on the history of political ideas in feudal Japan begins with a quotation from Hegel, in which he depicts China, or the East in general as an area where no development ever took place or could be imagined (Dauer).[3] Maruyama expresses doubts as far as the term 'East' is concerned, because he wants to distinguish clearly between China and Japan (cf. Maruyama, 1974: 7). He writes:

> Because he [Hegel] describes the development of the world spirit in terms of the rise and fall of the peoples who have served as its bearers, historical stages come to coincide with a certain geographical classification. A positivist historian would see this scheme as somewhat arbitrary. ... But what is significant is the fact that in China these characteristics did not constitute only one phase; they are constantly reproduced. ... With characteristic acumen, Hegel's interpretation strikes to the root of the matter: Chinese history remained 'unhistorical' despite frequent dynastic changes, not because of internal dissension but precisely because it lacked such dissension. (Maruyama, 1974: 3-5)

Confucianism then is said to be in a very close relationship with the perpetuation of such a condition, teaching the 'necessity of maintaining the distinctions between father and son, ruler and servant rigidly' (Maruyama, 1974: 4), from the earliest stages of the Han dynasty. The next step Maruyama undertakes is to elucidate two distinct developments. First of all, he holds that specific historical circumstances in Japan enhanced the appeal of Confucianism for the Japanese leaders of the day. And secondly, he attempts to show that within this officially incorporated Confucianism an evolution took place that was a first leap out of and beyond the traditional paradigm identifying nature and society, and thus politics. I will not penetrate this any further here, but at least concerning this point the contrast with the Chinese situation – or better: Maruyama's description of it – is striking. In order to rid ourselves of any doubt about it: this is *not* a result of any deeply felt contempt for China on the part of Maruyama. It is the consequence of a method that in essence relies on the revealing of contrasts between large entities, in combination with his single-minded preoccupation with the problems of his day [*mondai ishiki*], i.e. the attack on modernity by the ultra-nationalists and the urge to react against it.

The main purpose of his book is to show that there has been an evolution within Confucianism in Japan, a shift of thought structure that prepared the relatively swift adaptation to Western modernity, in a material sense at least. By doing so he wants to prove that the so-called Western distinction between morality and politics had its own early version in Japan, more specifically in the thought of Ogyū Sorai (1666-1728). On China, however, the author remains silent and by doing so, he ends up accepting Hegel's description of the East, and China as its major part, as an immobile region.[4] This point may become even clearer through another quotation of a scholar commenting on Hegel's historical views:

> Rather than allowing his metaphysics to emerge from his analysis of the subject matter, he classifies and examines his subject matter according to his metaphysics. The dialectic proceeds from China to India ... because the idea of an organism means that a moment of diversity should follow that of unity. The division of history into the Oriental, Classical and Germanic worlds according to the principle of one, some, or all being free derives from Hegel's treatment of the forms of judgement in his Logic. In general, Hegel does not hesitate to pass harsh judgements upon foreign cultures according to the standpoint of Western individualism, falling to prey to the very ethnocentrism from which historicism should liberate us (Beiser, 1993: 287).

As we know now, Maruyama's method is above all dialectic and is inspired to a great extent by German idealist thought, of which Hegel certainly is representative. This implies the creating of large spiritual entities and the search for a continuous dynamics between thesis, antithesis and synthesis. Undoubtedly, the East (without Japan in this case) is seen as an antithesis to the West, modern thought as an antithesis to pre-modern thought. And in the same way as Hegel initially worked on his model and then tried to fit reality in, Maruyama applies a very similar framework to the early intellectual developments in Tokugawa Japan. But as we said before, the circumstances of the immediate post-war era should be taken into consideration. Maruyama's writings should be understood as an addition to previous scholarship, and cannot be expected to answer questions that pop up now out of totally different conditions. And exactly at this point we are faced with what we could call an 'unusual' tenacity. Most of us, however, would agree that the situation in the 1980s is quite different. One may expect that, although it is in the autumn of Maruyama's career, his treatment in this period of the works of Fukuzawa Yukichi and their relevance should be able to offer more.

FUKUZAWA YUKICHI'S AN OUTLINE OF A THEORY OF CIVILIZATION

Fukuzawa Yukichi (1834-1901) is an important figure in the intellectual history of early Meiji Japan, and he is recognized as such: it is no coincidence that his effigy can be found on the 10,000-yen note. He introduced contemporary Western ideas in Japan and translated several Western, or better English, works that were to become of primary importance in the foundation of Japan's intellectual and educational modernization. Fukuzawa enjoys even today attention and appreciation, but he certainly is not uncontroversial. His career can be divided in two periods. The earlier period has left us with an heritage of numerous translations and introductions, in which he aims to educate the Japanese people and realizing in each individual an independent spirit. Only this will enable the Japanese to stand up against the colonial threat of the great powers and maintain Japan's political independence [isshin dokuritsu shite, ikkoku dokuritsu su]. The second period is characterized by Fukuzawa's contributions to the journal Jiji shimpō, commenting on the events of the day, propagating the war effort against China, and emphasizing the importance of the state power [kokken] rather than that of the people [minken].

These two periods are often seen as separate faces of Fukuzawa and Japanese scholars have discussed whether Fukuzawa should be appreciated because of his earlier efforts or condemned for his later activities. Some say the earlier period constitutes the real face of Fukuzawa, others say the later does. Some do not see a distinction at all and wholly condemn Fukuzawa's contribution. Many of those who state there is a fissure in his thought, consider the mid-1870s as pivotal years. One of Fukuzawa's most famous products of this period was the *Bummeiron no gairyaku* [An outline of a theory of civilization] (1875), a somewhat ambivalent work in which both above-mentioned elements in his thought are present to a certain degree. The main theme still is the education of the Japanese and an urgent demand for their political 'coming-of-age' by learning from the West (cf. the didactic connotation of the term *gairyaku* in the title of the book). At the same time a new perception surfaces: conflict will be unavoidable and Japan needs to preserve its independence, to the detriment of the feudal heritage, even that of the Asian mainland. The opening paragraph of the *Outline* may serve as an appropriate example:

> The characters for *light* and *heavy*, *long* and *short*, *good* and *bad*, *right* and *wrong* are born out of a relative way of thinking. This means, if there is no such thing as *light*, there can not be *heavy* and if there is no such a thing as *good*, there can not be *bad* either. Hence, *light* is lighter than *heavy*, and *good* is better than *bad*. So if we do not relate this thing here and that one there, we cannot talk about *light* and *heavy*, *good* and *bad*. We call this kind of relating, and fixing of what is heavy and what is good, the 'standard' of the discussion. There is a saying: one cannot change the belly into the back; one also says: one sometimes has to kill a small bug to save a big bug. . . . When handling animals, one considers a crane greater and more valuable then a loach [*dojō*]; so one can say that there is no objection using the loach to feed the crane. (Fukuzawa, 1875a)

Endless discussions have been held in Japan on the true meaning of this statement. For us it is nor the time nor the place to elaborate on it: for the time being it is worth mentioning that it reflects the 'imperialistic' intention some ascribe to Fukuzawa. And this in its turn relates to Fukuzawa's vision of the world, of Japan's independence in this world, if necessary at the expense of, for example, the backward Korean kingdom.

As the above quotation indicates, the first chapter of the book is devoted to the fixing of a standard of discussion, limits within which the arguments used should be understood, in casu the safeguarding of Japan's national integrity [*kokutai*]. The other chapters basically explain that the only way to obtain this, is getting rid of the erroneous and suffocating Confucian feudal bonds, moral views and understanding of nature, a loathsome heritage Fukuzawa contemptuously calls *wakudeki*, 'uncritical faith'.[5] Civilization is the goal to be reached, nothing else, and in this respect, independence is a condition *sine qua non*. The West is not the ideal in an absolute sense. It is considered most successful among the world's nations in turning the newly discovered knowledge on nature's ruling principles into its own advantage, in subdueing less developed regions, laying hands on the world's riches.

The reason Asia has fallen into arrears with the powerful nations of the West is its lack of a multifaceted tradition. The fortuitous West enjoys an intellectual tradition that combines several centres of power. The Church (religion), nobility (politics), merchants (economy), the German, Roman and Christian lineage intertwined in the course of time, a phenomenon that obliged each opponent to the mutual admittance of liberties, leaving protracted strife, struggle and war as the only alternative. In Japan, on the contrary, since time immemorial religion and trade have been subjected to political power. This inclination to always yield to the holder of power is repeated in a limitless way over time and in space. This means that on every social level in Japan a similar phenomenon takes place: the position of the superior is uncontested in any matter and thus almost absolute. The way to change this and to approach the ideal of a civilized society cannot be achieved through the effort of some individuals. It is paramount to change the whole nature of social behaviour in Japan, to study carefully Western sciences, to engage in public debate with other citizens and the government itself, all in order to preserve Japan as a independent state.

MARUYAMA INTERPRETS FUKUZAWA

Maruyama's reader on Fukuzawa's *Outline* is not the first comment he wrote on Fukuzawa's thought (actually it was one of the last). In fact, Maruyama's fondness of Fukuzawa, probably due to the common trait of strong commitment to the cause of modernity, has often been called 'in love with Fukuzawa' [*Fukuzawa-bore*]. Similarly, the way Maruyama interprets Fukuzawa has not changed all that much over the years: he evaluates Fukuzawa in a very positive way.

It is curious to notice that Maruyama falls back on the old method of 'annotation' in a somewhat similar vein to a Confucian scholar's work that follows in the footsteps of his old teacher. It is a mixture of extensive quotation and explanation, even on a word level. This method can be expected to have some unavoidable weaknesses: the final result could be too 'close' to the original, failing to create some necessary distance. There is a considerable chance that themes that are not handled explicitly in the base text lack in the annotation as well. In Maruyama's case, the decision to stick to this one work of the author hinders the positioning of the work in a larger context of history and career. One could even conclude that the parallel between Meiji and Maruyama's own period is laid with too great an ease and Fukuzawa's short-comings end up being equal to those of Maruyama and vice versa. The problematic character of Fukuzawa's later works is seldom mentioned and Maruyama's overall appreciation seems almost too optimistic.[6] Nevertheless, Maruyama seems prepared to put up with these limitations. From his point of view, the advantages offered by this approach enabling him to elaborate on the main purpose of the project, clearly outweigh the possible risks.

Generally speaking, Fukuzawa's intent is to achieve moder-nization in Japan. He is not interested primarily in preserving some unique Japanese identity, but rather in maintaining Japan's national defence. A first essential step to be taken in this process is the 'independence' of each Japanese individual, the creation of new moral ties, based on rational rules and discussion of important topics. Still, the immediate goal ahead is Japan's self-rule. Maruyama never stops emphasizing the importance of this critical situation: the onslaught of the Western colonial powers is nigh, and Japan is not prepared. It is this sense of crisis that inspires Fukuzawa. But what is inspiring Maruyama to be so 'close' to Fukuzawa? Why can Maruyama in the opulent 1980s keep on 'falling in love' with a thinker that lived more than one hundred years ago? Might not the answer be that, on a basic level, the conviction that the difficult task Fukuzawa imposed on the Japanese intellectuals has not been brought to a favourable conclusion yet? Maruyama laments the failure of modernization in Meiji, and even points out the growing distance between pre-war Japanese reality and Fukuzawa's initial ideals.[7] Fukuzawa's shortcomings could be pardoned to a certain degree by the international threat he is witnessing. Maruyama's espousing of the same visions is not the result of intellectual laziness. Rather it is due to the intention to save Fukuzawa from his critics, and to show how the possibilities of the early Meiji period have been aborted. By doing so, however, he does not seem to manage to overcome Fukuzawa's limited (due to the character of the goal itself) schemes.

One of these 'flaws' is Maruyama's silent approval (how else can we interpret his 900-page long silence?) of Fukuzawa's representation of Asia, Europe and the gap between them. We are not talking about outright indifference and error: Fukuzawa has been to Europe several times and has devoted numerous works to the introduction of not only European thought but also everyday life, economy, geography and so forth.[8] Moreover, Fukuzawa uses some European works as a foundation for his *Outline*, namely those of François Guizot and Henry Thomas Buckle,[9] and to a lesser extent John Stuart Mill[10] and William and Robert Chambers' educational books. The problem lies deeper: the purpose of the work is to picture the (common) foundations of power of the Western countries, not to give a detailed account of their possible differences. And indeed this is what happens: differences between countries are minimized in order to make visible the general heritage, the common traits that constitute the success of the European system. In fact, Fukuzawa points at those deeper tendencies in the history of the West that are lacking in Japan – one might ask if the gap between the worlds can ever be overcome, since the differences seem to be so fundamental? On this point both Maruyama and Fukuzawa are carefully optimistic: it can be done, it is our only hope, it will take great effort. At the same time the process of learning is very much a one-way street. Again the argument can be used: this was about the only possibility. But is this equally valid for Maruyama? He still is convinced, about ten years ago that is, that more can be learned from the West than the other way round.

VIEWS ON THE WEST

This is not the place to engage in a discussion on whether this is true or not. Instead, let us go back to the work of Fukuzawa: as we said, he uses a lot of English materials to compose it. Now, the England of his time was indeed very powerful and by almost all standards a very developed nation, and it should not surprise us that it served as an example for an intellectual, wanting to make his country great and strong and independent. He relies on the general theory of Buckle concerning civilization in the world, the evolution of which is depicted in three steps: *mikai* [not yet developed], *hankai* [half developed] and *bummei* [civilized]. The last step in the eyes of Fukuzawa is an ideal even the West has not reached yet, but it is closest to achieving it and, in view of the unilinear movement that is presupposed, in this world it can be taken as the example:

> When we take a look at the situation in the different countries of the West [seiyōshokoku], we see that their knowledge grows from day to day and the courage to undertake great feats increases; it is as if there is nothing between heaven and earth, natural things nor man-made facts, that can obstruct the thought of man; they freely investigate into the reason of things, and they install laws with which men freely comply. They already know the true nature of natural things and their workings and following it they have found the rules to subdue it in numerous cases (Fukuzawa, 1875a: 166–7).

It should be clear that this description of development is in some way reminiscent of the one Hegel presented to us. This is not all that strange when we realize that German idealism had quite some influence in late nineteenth-century England. It is easy to discover how Buckle puts Asia and the whole non-Western world in a lower category, and even goes as far as to attribute some of the differences to climate.[11] This kind of division into three steps tells us more about the world view of the people using it, than it sheds light on the true nature of development, at least to our generation. Maruyama finds it sufficient to point out that Buckle had a vision that already spanned the whole world and not just Europe. Maruyama admits that Buckle had a 'typically Victorian' sense of superiority towards all that was not English, but does not elaborate on it. He does not point out that Fukuzawa implements the same vision of Asia and Europe in his theory, not even once actually.

Fukuzawa's faith in the theory of the Westerner Buckle is not absolute. In some striking remarks Fukuzawa tries to put into perspective the Western success or to differentiate between nations. He points out that Ireland actually is a poor and occupied region (Fukuzawa, 1875a: 55), where people survive by eating nothing but potatoes [imo], how difficult it is for people in India to become a member of the administration that rules the country because of discrimination by the British, how even in the West religion is not the single determinant of civilization because Catholic France is far greater than Protestant Sweden, etc. He clearly is aware of differences and weak points, but he still considers the West as the place where things happen. This kind of perspective does not stop Fukuzawa from the frequent usage of terms such as seiyō, 'the West', seiyōshokoku, 'the countries of the West' or Yōroppa/Ōshū, 'Europe'.

Maruyama sometimes calls Fukuzawa's method 'dialectic'. The question exits if this is an apt qualification: to some it may seem that by using the term 'dialectic' Maruyama blesses or sanctifies Fukuzawa. It illustrates beautifully the use of the East-West paradigm in both authors' work, and how it leads to a contrast, to a gap the bridging of which requires drastic measurements. Fukuzawa praises the English people for their gradual and evolutionary attainment of a considerable degree of civilization (contrary to the French Revolution for example) and obviously would like to see the same happening, be it much faster, in Japan. Although there may be discussion on what Maruyama thinks of the feasibility of such an 'evolution', clearly this is also Maruyama's view: a sudden leap (as was provided by the defeat in 1945) could be necessary. If Europe is put at one extreme of the civilization scale, Asia is at the other extreme and the good points of Europe are the bad ones for Asia.[12] Fukuzawa does not make this distinction at an individual moral level, but he does so at a public-intellectual one. Asia is a region mired in old and useless beliefs, rituals, systems and its only chance to face up to the colonial powers is to get rid of these. The interesting and controversial point is that Fukuzawa sees a difference between Japan and the rest of Asia: certainly they have a common background, this he admits even in his infamous essay *Datsua ron* [Dissociation from Asia] (Fukuzawa, 1875b: [1989]). Japan, however, has the advantage of the 'opposition' within its own society between emperor on the one hand, and warriors with their relatively distinct habits and attitude of opposition and struggle at the other. The tension between these has proven strong enough to reappear after several centuries of institutionalized warrior rule and has put Japan on the road to change. In China and Korea no such distinction existed and Fukuzawa insists that, if they do not change quickly, they will become colonies of the stronger nations. Their passive stance towards a foreign threat inspired him to this famous conclusion in another work:

> Thus, to fulfill our plans in this day, our country does not have the time to wait for the enlightenment of our neighbouring countries and to resuscitate Asia together. Rather, we should leave this company and share our course of action with the civilized countries of the West. The way to attend to China and Korea ought not be special just because they are neighbouring countries: we should dispose of them just in the same manner as Westerners attend to them. People that are close with

bad friends cannot avoid sharing their bad reputation. In our hearts, we have to severe our bonds with those bad friends of East Asia (16 March 1885) (Fukuzawa, 1875b [1989]: 224).

And again, this kind of thought is never mentioned by Maruyama, not because Maruyama 'hates' China, but rather because he is too preoccupied with the challenge Western thought poses to Japan to encompass the niceties of Asian brotherhood.

CONCLUSION

Fukuzawa is a great thinker indeed. He not only introduced a lot of modern Western thought into Japan but also assimilated great parts of it and made it accessible to a large Japanese audience in an era where information was scarce and the demand huge. His thought is clear and 'rational', it transcends the narrow Japanese condition and tackles universal themes. He never went into government service in spite of numerous offers, and always kept a critical attitude towards the new Meiji administration that achieved a lot but still turned to old-fashioned methods. Fukuzawa was democratic as far as contemporary standards were concerned, not in a direct political way – he did not agree of the aims of the Freedom and People's Rights Movement [Jiyū minken undō] – but as far as the relationship between the individual and the nation is concerned. He is probably not, however, the champion of modern values and ideas to the extent Maruyama wants us to believe. Fukuzawa's whole project cannot escape the limits of its immediate goal: the safeguarding of Japan against foreign threat. His motto is 'if you cannot beat them, join them', and not in a vague, eclectic sense.

This undoubtedly reflects on Maruyama: for him, the difference in age and circumstance was not sufficient to justify a drastic shift of paradigm. He takes a more attenuated stance on some topics that are all too obvious, for example Japanese integrity, but in general he adopts rather than adapts Fukuzawa's model.

It is clear that the evaluation of China and Asia is not an isolated fact, that it is based on specific presuppositions. In the first place, it presupposes a line of development from pre-modern to modern. This line is expressed in geographical terms [datsua nyūō]. Europe and America are seen as the stronghold of civilization and modernity. Seiyō and other terms are rarely differentiated, and the traditions of the West are reduced to some very fundamental, and even idealistic principles. Theory is stronger than reality and its meaning is transferred to us by means of contrast, of extremes. Even within a universalistic view on the world and history, a vague idea of superiority is adopted: the example to be emulated is the West, Japan manages to follow and Asia lags far behind. A distinction may be made between Asian and European experiences respectively (England is not France is not Germany; India/China), but the moving principle and the ultimate goal remains unchanged.

Maruyama's annotation and interpretation of the *Outline* shows why he is one of the most appealing intellectuals of his time: his commitment is unshakeable and inviting; it also shows us that he is one of the leading modernists of his age. This is not a condemnation: Maruyama is not an Euro-centrist in the explicit sense of the word – he almost never wrote on anything else but Japan. He adopts a universal theory that has been developed in Europe and unavoidably bares this stamp. He fails to see, or pretends not to see, the traps it includes and does not make remarks on a scholar that did the same one hundred years ago. This is not a proof of intellectual inadequacy, it is the sign of committed determinacy, the fate of all academic endeavour.

BIBLIOGRAPHY

Beiser, Frederick B. 1993. 'Hegel's Historicism'. In *The Cambridge Companion to Hegel*, edited by Frederick B. Beiser. New York: Cambridge University Press, 270-300.

Blacker, Carmen. 1964. *The Japanese Enlightenment. A study of the writings of Fukuzawa Yukichi*. Cambridge: Cambridge University Press.

Distelrath, Günther. 1996. *Die japanische Produktionsweise*. München: Iudicium Verlag.

Fukuzawa Yukichi. 1869 (1989). *Sekai kunizukushi* [Everything about the countries of the world]. In *Fukuzawa Yukichi senshū* [Selected works of Fukuzawa Yukichi], 2. Tokyo: Iwanami Shoten, 103-86.

——. 1875a. *Bummeiron no gairyaku* [An outline of a theory of civilization]. Tokyo.

——. 1875b (1989). 'Datsua ron' [Dissociation from Asia]. In *Fukuzawa Yukichi senshū* [Selected works of Fukuzawa Yukichi], 7. Tokyo: Iwanami Shoten, 221-4.

Gendai shisō. 1996. 'Maruyama Masao tokushū' [Special issue on Maruyama Masao], 22(1): 55-250.

Hegel, G.W.F. 1930. *Die Vernunft in der Geschichte*. Leipzig.

Imai Juichirō and Kawaguchi Shigeo. 1987. *Maruyama Masao chosaku nōto* [A note of Maruyama Masao's writings]. Tokyo: Gendai no rironsha.

Maruyama, Masao. 1974. *Studies in the Intellectual History of Tokugawa Japan*. Translated by Mikiso Hane. Tokyo: University of Tokyo Press.

——. 1986. '*Bummeiron no gairyaku*' o yomu [Reading Fukuzawa's An outline of a theory of civilization]. 3 vols. Tokyo: Iwanami shoten.

Mill, John Stuart. 1859 (1974). *On Liberty*. Harmondsworth: Penguin.

Sasakura Hideo. 1988. *Maruyama Masao ron nōto* [Notes on a theory of Maruyama Masao]. Tokyo: Misuzu shobō.

Satō Seizaburō. 1996. 'Maruyama Masao ron: Sono kindai Nihon kan' [On Maruyama Masao: His view on modern Japan]. *Chūō kōron*, December, 190-208.

Tsuzuki Tsutomu. 1995. *Sengo Nihon no chishikijin* [Intellectuals of postwar Japan]. Tokyo: Seori shobō.

NOTES

1. There are of course many books and articles by Maruyama, see the comprehensive presentation by Imai and Kawaguchi (1987). Although there are hundreds of articles on Maruyama, not many books on him have appeared and few of them transcend the scope of one aspect of his works. Two examples of the former are Tsuzuki (1995) and Sasakura (1988). More limited studies of Maruyama's thought have been presented by, for example, Takimura Ryūichi, basically critiques on the influence of Max Weber and Harold Lasswell on Maruyama's works.

2. For some articles, see *Gendai shisō*, 1996: 55-250.

3. In Hegel (1930). The same idea is reflected by Max Weber in his treatment of Chinese Confucianism (cf. Distelrath, 1996).

4. In the 'Author's Introduction to English Edition', Maruyama comments on his own prejudice and also refers to the Korean influence (Maruyama, 1974: xv-xxxvii). However, to the extent that it accepts the fundamental pattern laid out in the book, that is, a development towards the ultimate goal of modern understanding, it does not constitute a fundamental shift.

5. Carmen Blacker, who has published a study on Fukuzawa, admittedly had trouble in translating *wakudeki* into English (Blacker, 1964; cf. Maruyama, 1986, 1: 108).

6. An example can be given. In a comment Maruyama deals with Fukuzawa's call to intellectuals to educate the people, to alter the whole 'atmosphere' [*kifū*] of society (Maruyama, 1986, 2: 81). Maruyama interprets this as Fukuzawa's version of a 'long revolution', much in the vein of Maruyama's own stance which he once described as an 'eternal revolution' [*eikyū kakumei*]. In the light of events that took place later in Fukuzawa's career, this is an optimistic evaluation, indeed. Of course, such ideas may be ascribed to Fukuzawa, but they are certainly not the only ones he had; as a typification they are rather insufficient.

7. Examples of this position are numerous and can be found in all three volumes; see Maruyama, 1986, 1: 154-5, 210-13; 2: 74; 3: 132-9.

8. One well-known example is Fukuzawa's *Sekai kunizukushi* [Everything about the countries in the world], in which he writes, for instance, of my home country: 'Belgium is a country split off from Holland, and its population is active in agriculture: there is no piece of land that is not productive. It obtains iron and coal from its soil and makes many things. It is a small country, but it looks much like England'; and also: 'The neighbouring country in the west is Belgium, formerly a part of Holland, and its manners and customs are much like it; its riches are based on the character [of its people] that spares no effort in the fields of agriculture, manufacturing and trade' (Fukuzawa, 1869 [1989]).

9. François Guizot, *Histoire de la civilisation en France depuis la chûte de l'Empire romain jusqu'à la Révolution française*. Paris, 1828 (Fukuzawa used the English translation); Henry Thomas Buckle, *The History of Civilization in England*, 2 vols. London, 1858-61.

10. Especially Mill's *On Liberty* and *On Representative Government*. Fukuzawa seems to have assimilated many of Mill's ideas, sometimes too eagerly: in Fukuzawa's *Outline* we find a passage on the evils of 'the tyranny of the majority'. Maruyama is aware of the fact that this was hardly an urgent topic in early Meiji Japan. However, it seems as if he – intentionally or not – fails to notice that to some extent the same was true of England in 1859. The omission of any reference to nineteenth-century European political practice suggests that he interprets 'tyranny of the majority' as 'tyranny of any political majority', even a majority of a very limited political scope – which is rather improbable. And as we can infer from some remarks in *On Liberty*, Mill was not void of the typical view on Asia of his time: he even states that his theory on the liberty of the individual as resisting the demands of an ardent majority is non-valid for underdeveloped races:

> Those who are still in a state to require being taken care of by others must be protected against their own actions as well as against external injury. For the same reason we may leave out of consideration those backward states of society in which the race itself may be considered as in its nonage. . . . Despotism is a legitimate mode of government in dealing with barbarians, provided the end be their improvementa nd the means justified by actually effecting that end (Mill, 1859 [1974]: 69, 153).

11. Fukuzawa refutes this argument, since it is deterministic and deprives the Japanese of all hope; it is baffling to notice that scholars as Watsuji Tetsurō decided to use the same model again in the twentieth century.

12. Fukuzawa does not neglect to point out that the ideal civilized society is far superior to the present Western one. This ideal society involves, among others, the absence of government – an ideal so far ahead and away from the nineteenth century present that it remains no more than that, an ideal and definitely not a valid alternative.

4

The Break with Europe: Japanese Views of the Old World after the First World War

DICK STEGEWERNS

U p to the First World War Europe was the model civilization
on which Japan was trying to pattern itself. The period
following the opening-up of Japan springs to mind, with the
short-lived Rokumeikan as the most conspicuous example of
Europeanization. Nationalist reactions against the excessive
Westernization of Japanese society ensued but, even in the first
decade of the twentieth century, Europe remained the guiding
light for the Japanese intelligentsia in ideological, philosophical,
cultural, scientific, military, political and economic matters.

In the case of the Japanese intellectuals, Europe was the cradle
of their modern professions and their frame of reference; it was
the destination of their travels and the place of sojourn for their
research. However, the term 'Europe' must be specified, since
after a brief period of popularity of France immediately following
the Meiji Restoration, Europe in the eyes of the Japanese élite
consisted mainly of the great power England and its upcoming
economic rival Germany.

To many, England was the political, economic and naval ideal
and, of course, the country which reinforced Japan's international position by means of the Anglo-Japanese Alliance.
Germany, on the other hand, was the philosophical, scientific
and military model. Most students going abroad for study and
those sent abroad by the government or army for training went
to one of these countries, and the scholarly élite could be
roughly divided into an English-speaking and a German-
speaking part, depending on their subject of study. And while
other Japanese went to the United States, usually to study at

universities connected to the Protestant mission in Japan, there were not many who looked up to the country as an ideal in a particular field. Moreover, except for a political realist like Hara Takashi, there were not many who conceived the US as the strong, great power-to-be.

As a result of the First World War and the ensuing reshuffle of international power relations, Japanese views of the outside world changed considerably, and the share which Europe – that is England and Germany – occupied in the outside world as perceived by the Japanese was to diminish rapidly. By means of two case studies of contemporary opinion leaders in the area of international relations, namely Horie Kiichi and Mizuno Hironori, we will examine more exactly when, how and why Japanese views of Europe changed.

Horie Kiichi and Europe

THE LIFE AND CAREER OF HORIE KIICHI

Horie Kiichi was a prominent commentator on economic matters in the first quarter of this century. His total publications run to some sixty volumes, including standard works on banking and currency that went through many reprints.[1] He also contributed regularly from 1897 onwards to the newspapers *Jiji Shimpō* and *Tōkyō Nichi Nichi Shimbun* and to various magazines, ranging from scholarly journals to more popular periodicals like *Taiyō*, *Chūō Kōron*, *Kaizō* and *Ekonomi-suto*.[2] While up to his second visit to the West in 1910 his articles were concerned mainly with monetary and economic topics, afterwards his interests were more and more oriented towards social policy, the labour movement and international relations.

Horie was born in Tokyo in 1876 into a family of hereditary retainers of Tokushima *han*.[3] His father served as a career officer in the navy, but committed suicide before his son's birth, taking responsibility for the *Ōsaka-maru* accident of December 1875 (Horie Otoo, 1977: 18). At the age of 12 Horie enrolled in the junior course of Keiō University and, with a few brief interruptions, he would remain associated with this institution for the rest of his life. From early on he had an interest in economics and he is said to have surprised his fellow students by reading the entire *An Inquiry into the Nature and Causes of the Wealth of Nations* by Adam Smith when only sixteen years of age (Takahashi, 1970: 390-1). Smith's theory of free trade was to remain a primary influence on Horie's thought. After his graduation from Keiō's economic department in 1896, he joined Fukuzawa Yukichi's *Jiji Shimpō* and three years later he became a lecturer at Keiō himself, eventually rising to the post of Chairman of the Economy Department in 1908 and subsequently to Dean of the newly established Faculty of Economics in 1920. Horie visited the West twice for research. During his first stay from 1899 to 1902 he spent most of his time in England. Horie was much impressed by the democratic advances and the policy of free trade (Horie, 1928-29, 10, 663-771; Tamaki, 1990: 48-52). Back in Japan, he became a prominent member of the Social Policy Society [*Shakai Seisaku Gakkai*] and accordingly his second visit to Europe in 1910 was devoted mainly to studying British social policy and the system of poor relief (Horie, 1928-29, 10: 815-29). Horie also had strong sympathy for the working class and the aims of the trade union movement. He was a councillor of the Yūaikai from the very start in 1912 and today he is best known for the drafting, together with Yoshino Sakuzō and Abe Isoo, of the founding proclamation of the non-Communist proletarian party, the *Shakai minshūtō*, in 1926 (Large, 1972: 16; 1981: 105-7). At the end of the following year he suffered a stroke and died at the age of 51.

HORIE AND ENGLAND: THE SOCIAL AND POLITICAL EXAMPLE

Horie abhorred the 'Great European War' – the way the First World War was known amongst the Japanese at the time, despite the fact that their country was one of the participants – since it was precisely the phenomenon of war that resulted in the greatest restriction of free trade. The process of increasing international economic interdependence and prosperity would come to a halt, the total volume of world trade would dwindle, and Japan, a member of the world economy, was sure to suffer the unfavourable effects of these developments. (Horie, 1915: 30-1) Although Horie soon had to retract this last pessimistic prediction as the Japanese economy was reaping the profits of the war, he did not stop warning that the boom conditions were not of a structural economic nature and that postwar Japan would face a correspondingly severe crisis (Horie, 1916a: 51-6; 1916b: 57-9). Horie did not openly side with either party of 'practitioners of uneconomic activities', although he principally blamed the German nationalist policy of economic autarky for the outbreak of the war. (Horie, 1919a: 22-3; 1928-29, 8: 703-7) It was also clear that his sympathies lay with the British, whom he considered cosmopolitan and relatively free-tradist. However, he did not refrain from taking them to task over the Allied Economic Conference in Paris in 1916, which Horie character-ized as immoral, because the postwar policy decided on – the economic isolation of Germany – was at loggerheads with the same principle of free trade (Horie, 1916d: 60-2; 1928-29, 8: 691-702). Nor was Horie very pleased with the Peace Treaty of Versailles and the newly created, overwhelmingly European, League of Nations. The boycott of Communist Russia and the harsh treatment of defeated Germany implied a major setback to the recovery of the European economy and, by extension, the world economy (Horie, 1921e: 55-9; 1922c: 153-5). Moreover, he despaired of the League which in his eyes was too weak (Horie, 1920a: 168). And indeed, it failed to bring about the desired disarmament, which Horie considered the principal means of reactivating the economic spiral of free trade, international division of labour and economic interdependency, resulting in lasting peace (Horie, 1921b: 64-6; 1921c: 94). He thus occasionally aimed his criticism at England and, for example, demanded that it abandon its monopolistic policy towards its colonies and put an end to its unfair competition in China (Horie, 1919a: 25-26). However, at the same time Horie's thought was showing its first socialist tendencies and, in addition to a drive towards democracy, he now also acknowl-edged an international trend away from capitalism (Horie 1919b: 32-3; 1920a: 170; 1928-29, 10: 874). It was on this point that Horie was extremely critical of his own country. He thought that Japan, at the Peace Conference and the associated International Labour Conference, had publicly shown that it was lagging far behind in the field of social and labour policy. (Horie, 1919b: 35-6; 1920a: 170). Again it was England he looked up to as the symbol of parliamentary democracy and a strong trade union movement (Horie, 1921d: 57). Thus Horie seemed to be capable of making a distinction between the English nation and the British Colonial Empire.[4]

HORIE AND THE US: THE THREAT OF THE NEW ECONOMIC SUPERPOWER

Horie recognized that the US was the new economic superpower which, by means of investments, had to assume the role of driving force of the world economy (Horie, 1916c: 83; 1919c:

27). However, Horie did not seem to know what to think of the sudden exit of Wilsonism from the international scene and retained a rather neutral attitude towards the US. But this was to change radically at the time of the Washington Conference of 1921. The Washington Treaties signalled a turning point in history according to Horie. He now spoke of 'the new age of Taishō', which was characterized by the rejection of militarism and economic imperialism. In the form of the Five Power Treaty, which prescribed substantial naval disarmament, the US had succeeded whereas the European League of Nations had accomplished nothing. Horie was convinced that the Treaty would be the impetus that could put the world economy back on track again (Horie, 1921f: 209-10; 1922a: 25-9). Moreover, he was full of praise for the Nine Power Treaty, which in his eyes had banned economic imperialism from China and would cause an international open economy to arise in the Far East with China at its centre (Horie, 1922b: 79; 1922d: 62).

In contrast, Horie had become very critical of Japan's policy towards its colonies and China. He thought his country's record, as a militarist and economic imperialist power, was far worse than those of the US and England. According to Horie, the Koreans were looking with envy to their Indian and Filipino fellow-sufferers and the Chinese people were looking for support to· the West and not to Japan (Horie, 1923b: 82). Yet now the Washington Treaty had forced Japan to change, and thus had saved its China policy, which had been at deadlock. On the basis of the Nine Power Treaty co-existence would become possible and China, he predicted, would also reap the profits from this new situation (Horie 1922b: 74-6).

It would not have been surprising if Horie, who greatly admired the Washington Treaties, had then turned to the US as his guiding light. However, matters were slightly more complicated. Apart from his support for free trade and economic internationalization, Horie had always stressed that there was one vital condition, namely the safety of trade routes (Horie, 1919a: 23-4; 1921c: 95). In the case of Japan, the problem was that its main trade routes stretched all over the Pacific Ocean and could not be protected by the Japanese navy on its own. In addition, Japan was to such a large extent dependent on the US for its exports that not only the eruption of a war involving one of Japan's major trade partners but merely a boycott of Japanese silk stockings by American women could wield the Japanese economy a deadly blow (Horie, 1918e: 67-8; 1929, 8: 716). This awareness of Japan's economic vulnerability had become even more acute with the Washington Conference, which was not just the start of a new era of disarmament and international cooperation but at the same time implied the supremacy of the US on the East Asian scene. In this situation Horie did not consider it wise to put all one's trust in an American signature on a sheet of paper. The passing of an anti-Japanese immigration law, the Japanese Exclusion Act, in the American Congress in May 1924 only strengthened this feeling (Horie, 1924a: 48, 58).

HORIE'S SEARCH FOR A STRATEGIC ALLY

Despite his country's difficult situation, Horie did not despair and came up with various solutions, some of which made him turn towards Europe again. In his opinion the most fundamental solution would be to industrialize Japan thoroughly in such a way that it would export only essential goods of prime quality which were not liable to become the object of a boycott (Horie, 1925a: 76-7; 1926b: 111). Another solution was the formation of an interregional economic unit close to home, which would include Japan, Korea, Taiwan, Manchuria and parts of China, in order to shorten trade routes and to diminish Japan's dependency on the US and the British colonies. In view of the Japanese need to procure natural resources within its sphere of influence Horie especially urged for closer economic relations with China (Horie, 1923c: 42; 1924c: 54-6). However, these solutions were both long-term policies and could not bring immediate relief. It was in this context that Horie turned his attention to the 'European' League of Nations, which he had hitherto ignored, in the hope that it could become a counterbalance to the US. His hopes were bolstered by the fact that in 1924 England had a Labour and France a socialist cabinet, which were both more lenient towards Germany and Russia and were even trying to have them join the League of Nations. Such a reinforced League, Horie hoped, might support the weak Japan when confronted by 'immoral highhandedness on the part of the US' (Horie, 1924c: 47-8).

By this time socialism had become a strong influence on Horie's thought, and he had made the link between the plight of the working class and the suffering of the colonized coloured people as both being the result of the same capitalist oppression (Horie, 1922e: 72; 1923d: 210). So why did Horie have no hesitation in pinning his hopes on the two largest colonial empires in the world? He must have been aware that his was a weak bid, yet he could not find an alternative. There was no force as yet which could lead the anti-capitalist and anti-colonialist movement. China was still tormented by internal strife and did not show any signs of recovery. As for Japan, Horie of course wanted his own country to become an international harbinger, in national affairs, by surpassing the English Fabian Society through the socialization and democratization of industry, as well as in international affairs, by exceeding the framework of the Nine Power Treaty on China and adopting an autonomous policy to improve the position of the Chinese (Horie, 1925b: 53; 1926b: 128). However, he had to admit that during the 1920s there was no change in the situation that Japan lagged far behind the Western nations and was not even able to attain the absolute international minimum in terms of its social, labour, and China policy (Horie, 1923a: 42-5; 1924b: 110). In sharp contrast, England was still the example of political democracy, with a government led by a proletariat party, an ideal shared by most of the Japanese intelligentsia who had lost confidence in the established political parties.[5] Moreover, although it was the largest colonial empire, England remained the only non-protectionist country in Horie's opinion (Horie, 1924d: 13). And it also remained the example of the economic goal he had in mind, since England had succeeded in establishing economic superiority within its own economic block from a disadvantageous geographical and geological position comparable to Japan (Horie, 1921a: 82-9).

But as the Labour cabinet only lasted for 10 months and was followed again by another conservative administration, Horie finally lost all hope and turned his back on the old empire, and thus on Europe (Horie, 1925a: 68). It was only at the beginning of 1927 that he, this time primarily driven by socialist ideas, found an alternative in China, when he foresaw that it would be unified under a nationalist – and, in his eyes, an anti-capitalist and anti-imperialist – government (Horie, 1927a: 24-5). Although Horie unfortunately did not live to see the unification of China, he fully expected that it would succeed in expelling all imperialist forces from its territory, Manchuria included. Moreover, as a supporter of this anti-imperialist aim he strongly opposed the policy of armed intervention of the Tanaka Cabinet, which he feared to be mainly inspired by the impossible aim of countering Chinese nationalism or, even worse, the disastrous aim of annexating Manchuria (Horie, 1927b: 42-3, 47). Thus Horie was one of the few who even seemed to sanction the sacrifice of Japan's established position in the north-eastern part of China, in the hope that his country could help China to take the lead in the struggle against capitalism and make the world safe for democracy, socialism, and free trade.[6]

Mizuno Hironori and Europe

THE LIFE AND CAREER OF MIZUNO HIRONORI

Mizuno Hironori was a maverick in the circles of *bummei hihyōka*, the intellectual élite of so-called 'civilization critics' who dominated the pages of the popular magazines in the 1910 and 1920s. As he came from a background of poverty and had not been to university, his style of writing was considerably different from the others. He hardly ever mentioned Western influences and the theoretical foundation of his arguments was definitely not his forte; instead his writing made a direct appeal to common sense and his style betrayed the strong influence of the traditional Confucianist education Mizuno had received.[7] Nevertheless, he was accepted by his colleagues and warmly welcomed by the general magazines in 1921, when he made the extraordinary step from the navy to the media. On the eve of the Washington Conference Mizuno, a former captain in the navy, had precisely the specialist knowledge that the other opinion leaders lacked. Moreover, as a 'defector' from the navy who now openly sided with the movement for naval disarmament, he had the novelty value and the right amount of 'political correctness' to launch his new career successfully. During the 1920s he continued to advance the cause of disarmament in his articles on military matters and international relations, until he was silenced after the Manchurian Incident.[8]

Mizuno Hironori was born in 1875 in Ehime prefecture as the son of a former low-ranking samurai of the Matsuyama *han*.[9] Unable to finish his middle school due to poverty, he eventually managed in 1895 to get into the naval academy, where one was exempted from tuition fees. After his graduation he climbed step by step up the navy ladder, serving as a torpedo boat commander during the Russo-Japanese War. In 1906 he was suddenly summoned to Tokyo to compile a history of the naval battles during this war, an assignment which took him five years to complete. In 1911 he published *Kono Issen* [The decisive battle], a popular adaptation of the official war history which became an instant bestseller and made Mizuno into a prosperous man. However, while doing his desk work in Tokyo, he had become estranged from life on board and became the odd man out in the navy. He clashed with his superiors and was sidetracked to a leisurely post ashore, again in Tokyo. This enabled him to indulge in more writing which, however, was only to cause him further problems with the naval establishment and, after his second disciplinary punishment in 1921, he finally decided to shed his uniform and trade his sabre for the pen.

MIZUNO AND GERMANY: THE MILITARIST MODEL

Mizuno was over 40 years old when in 1916, at the height of the fighting, he visited Europe for the first time. Although still in the navy he went, rather exceptionally, at his own expense to observe modern warfare. He did indeed experience the first air raids on London, where he inevitably spent most of his time, although he would have much rather headed for Berlin (Mizuno, 1978: 313-41). At the time Mizuno still shared the unofficial world view of the army, in the sense that he believed that the world was ruled by the law of the jungle and the international struggle for survival dictated a militarist policy (Mizuno, 1919: 111-4). According to Mizuno, militarism did not necessarily result in expansionist aggression; it was nothing but an administrative policy to strengthen the nation, which was prescribed by the needs of his time, was based on the presence of an army, and was aimed at national defence (Mizuno, 1919: 110-3, 123-4).

Although it was the enemy of the country he served, he did not even try to hide his admiration for Germany as the strongest militarist nation. England and France were also considered strong powers [*kyōkoku*], since they, unlike the US, Russia and Japan itself, did live up to the two conditions of a rich nation [*fukoku*] and a strong army [*kyōhei*], although not to the same degree as Germany. Thus the latter, Mizuno emphasized, was the example his country should follow (Mizuno, 1915: 34-5; 1919: 113). Even a second visit to Europe immediately after the war, which this time included the battlefields of France and hunger-stricken Berlin, could not make him change his opinion (Mizuno, 1978: 373-405). He supported the thesis that Germany had won the battle, but lost the war; in the end the German army had been betrayed by its own nation and its political leaders, as a result of the unlawful economic blockade and the devious propaganda by the British (Mizuno, 1919: 123; 1920: 21-3, 40-4).

It will be clear that Mizuno's ideas were in sharp contrast to the general opinion amongst the Japanese intellectuals in the immediate post-war years.[10] He did not subscribe to the viewpoint that the war had brought about the victory of justice, humanity, and democracy; it had been just another struggle between militarist rivals, so the inevitable outcome was the victory of militarism, which continued to rule the world as before (Mizuno, 1919: 111, 123). Neither did Mizuno have any sympathy for the newly established League of Nations (Mizuno, 1919: 111). In his eyes it was not a peace-keeping organ, but a white, European, and Allied-biased institution to implement the Peace Treaty of Versailles, which he considered the most severe and revengeful peace treaty ever known. The German people, he remarked, had been deceived by Wilson's hollow words and would have been better off if they had continued the war (Mizuno, 1920: 27, 46-8; 1921b: 37).

Although Mizuno, unlike many of his contemporaries, was not of the opinion that the war had changed the nature of international relations significantly, he did admit that Germany's defeat called for a few adjustments to Japan's militarist model. First, it should try to attain complete autarky, since international law, which forbade the blockade of non-strategic goods, was not being obeyed. Therefore Japan should not aim to be an industrialized state instead of an agricultural state; it should try to be a combination (Mizuno, 1920: 32). Secondly, the European War had been a war on a formerly unknown scale and of a character completely different from the Russo-Japanese War. Mizuno discerned that the world had arrived at a new stage of warfare which involved mobilization of the whole nation. Defensive power was no longer a monopoly of the armed forces, but had become a multi-layered structure in which the economic, financial and popular elements played an equally vital role. He emphasized the need for one cooperated effort from all levels of society towards the aim of national defence and accordingly advocated the rapprochement of state and society, in particular, of the army and people. The people had to be imbued with national pride and society should be militarized (Mizuno, 1919: 113, 124; 1921a: 46-7).

MIZUNO AND THE US; THE BANKRUPTCY OF MILITARISM

However, the Japan Mizuno came home to in 1920 was no longer the country he used to know. The anti-militarist post-war climate had been anything but favourable to the army and the unpopularity of the unsuccessful Siberian Intervention only aggravated matters. For the first time in their history the armed forces were being looked down upon and applications for the army as well as the navy declined sharply (Matsuo, 1970: 220-44; Humphries, 1995: 43-9). Mizuno realized that in this situation the militarization of society was no longer a realistic proposition. It had to be the other way round: the army had to socialize, which at that time meant to democratize, in order to cast off its unpopularity. Although he was aware that this 'democratic militarism' might have some negative effects on the power of the army, Mizuno considered this only a minor loss compared to the harm which would be caused by further isolation from society (Mizuno, 1921b: 38, 42-5).

Yet it was the changed international situation after the war which made him more and more aware of the fallacies in his design to protect his country by means of militarism. He had previously emphasized autarky and complete independence and had not put much trust in bilateral treaties such as the Anglo-Japanese Alliance (Mizuno, 1914: 9-10; 1920: 27). However, the fact that even the strongest militarist power had been defeated and the threatening realization that, unlike the prewar situation, a new and hostile superpower had its military outposts in the vicinity of Japanese territory, gradually brought home the message that there was no such thing as absolute security anymore. Just like the German supreme command, Mizuno had underestimated the US during the war, but in the post-war world he had to admit US dominance (Mizuno, 1921a: 48-50; 1921c: 98). He now regarded economic strength and the presence of an infrastructure of civilization as the major factors determining national strength. A country had to be an economic power [fukoku] and a civilized power [bummeikoku] to be able to rise to the position of a strong power [kyōkoku]; military power [kyōhei] seemed to have become a matter of minor importance. He concluded that the world was in a process of transition, from an era of military nation-building to an era of economic nation-building (Mizuno, 1922a: 131-7). However, the problem was that this transition was clearly not advantageous to Japan, whose economy was still weak and extremely vulnerable.

Mizuno called on his country to wake up to the changing tide and regauge its position in the world. Japan, he stated, had become the common enemy of the US and China, the latter being openly hostile. Accordingly, it had a navy to oppose the US and an army to oppress the Chinese. Yet he deemed Japan's power insufficient to sustain this stance, especially when it was obvious that England, Japan's ally, would be more likely to support the US than Japan in case of war (Mizuno, 1922a: 50-3). And even when one assumed that a clash between Japan and its naval enemy would occur within in a vacuum and one left other third countries out of one's consideration, Mizuno was convinced that his country on its own would never be able to win a war of attrition against the US. There was no way by which Japan could oppose the US any longer. Therefore Mizuno did not consider it realistic to take part in the search for an ally to bolster Japan against the US, like Horie did (Mizuno, 1922a: 48). He merely concluded that his country had better try to avoid war at all costs and, therefore, it was most urgent that it relinquish all dreams of territorial expansion; it had to switch 'from militarism based on armed opposition to economism based on international cooperation' (Mizuno, 1921c: 99; 1922c: 132).

Just around this time Japan received an invitation from the US for a conference on naval disarmament and the adjustment of interests in the Pacific region. Mizuno seized the chance and openly declared himself 'a proponent of comparative, treaty-based arms reductions' (Mizuno, 1921c: 95-6). He welcomed the Washington Conference as a heaven-sent opportunity for the Japanese navy and economy. In contrast to those who interpreted the conference as a national crisis, Mizuno lauded the economic realism of the participants and subscribed to what he referred to as 'the spirit of the Washington Treaties' – partial sacrifice of sovereignty by the economically weaker, generosity by the economically stronger. He considered this conciliatory spirit the solution to the dilemma of Japan's national safety, in the sense that a non-militarist US would also enable Japan to abandon militarism (Mizuno, 1921c: 102-4;1922a: 42, 56).

As a result of Mizuno's total revocation of militarism Germany was no longer mentioned, and with it Europe faded away from his view as well.[11] He now turned to the US as the strongest representative of the new economic and democratic age. Moreover, in his eyes the US, instead of the squabbling European League of Nations, had become the champion of disarmament by showing the magnanimity to sacrifice part of its power and had thus brought about a degree of arms reduction far more drastic than anybody had foreseen (Mizuno, 1922b: 88-90; 1922c: 134-7).

MIZUNO'S SEARCH FOR AN ANTI-CAPITALIST ALTERNATIVE

However, in the years following the conference Mizuno gradually converted to socialism and by 1923 he had already reached the stage that he proclaimed capitalism the root of all evil (Mizuno, 1923a: 103; 1923b: 19). While he continued to support disarmament, he no longer considered it a fundamental solution, which could bring about a substantial reform to the unequal capitalist world order (Mizuno, 1925c: 21 ; 1925d: 58). Neither could he any longer champion the US, the general headquarters of capitalism, as the international example to be followed, although he did not become too harsh on the country and still valued the Washington Treaties as 'the greatest accomplishment by man in the first quarter of the twentieth century' (Mizuno, 1922b.10: 243; 1925b: 139).

As an extension of his support for the embryonic Japanese proletariat parties, Mizuno placed his hopes on a supra-national league of labourers which would bring about world peace (Mizuno, 1924a: 78). It was in this context, which was very different from Horie's motives, that in 1924 he suddenly redirected his attention to Europe, where an English Labour and a French socialist cabinet had come to power. Apart from his ideological support, he was also particularly charmed by Ramsay MacDonald's suspension of plans to build a naval base in Singapore (Mizuno, 1924b: 98-100; 1925a: 23-4). Nevertheless, Mizuno's focus on Europe was to be as short-lived as the afore-mentioned cabinets and, much earlier and more radically than Horie, he shifted his attention from the European colonialist empires to their victim, the rising nationalist China, where it was to remain the rest of the interbellum.

While Mizuno had at first pardoned the colonialist powers, saying that their colonial possessions were a legitimate historical legacy, he now advocated the liberation of the international proletariat, that is, the coloured races (Mizuno, 1925a: 34-5; 1926: 188, 195). As a first step he wanted Japan to side with their foremost representative, China, and he admonished his country not to exploit China any longer under the pretense of international cooperation with the Western powers. International socialist justice had now become Mizuno's criterion, and within this context he considered it his country's most important task to assist China, aware of the fact that this would imply opposing Europe and the US (Mizuno, 1925e: 175-8; 1928: 326).

CONCLUSION

Whereas in prewar days Europe was associated with progressivism and most Japanese intellectuals were predominantly focussed on European developments, during and after 'The Great European War' was exposed as being conservative and imperialist by US Wilsonism, Soviet communism, and the carnage it had brought upon itself. A vacuum ensued, during which many opinion leaders gave free rein to their idealistic fantasies, which had at least one common aspect in the fact that these either ignored or rejected the newly established and Europe-dominated League of Nations. Yet there was no way to ignore the US when in 1921 the superpower of the new economic era took the main stage in the East Asian theatre by means of the Washington Conference. In fact, most Japanese commentators even reacted favourably to the Washington Treaties, although one should not forget that their support was directed mainly at the Five Power Treaty on naval disarmament. From this moment onwards, Europe's share in the world view of the Japanese intellectual dwindled. He was almost completely preoccupied by 'the Japan-US question' [*Nichi-Bei mondai*] and 'the Japan-China question' [*Nisshi mondai*], and in this context Europe, or more precisely England, was often no longer regarded as a force to consider in East Asia, neither as a potential enemy nor as a useful ally.

However, the US did not become the exemplary symbol of civilization pre-war Europe had been to the Japanese intelligentsia; to some it became the symbol of capitalism, to others it merely remained Japan's only serious potential enemy. This last aspect was aptly demonstrated by anti-Japanese legislation approved by US Congress in 1924. Indignation, a feeling of international isolation, and socialist influence resulted in a tendency of renewed interest in Europe and Russia.[12] However, the first British and French social-democratic cabinets did not last long, and the Italian fascist experiment was generally slighted as an act of irrationality by a second-rate nation.[13] In contrast, there was a considerable amount of sympathy amongst the *Taishō bummei hihyōka* for the 'rational and idealistic' Communist model of the Soviet Union, but eventually it was probably considered too heterogeneous to receive continuous attention as a potential ally to Japan.

Thus, out of the few countries that constituted the Japanese outside world there remained only one, namely China. Although calls for a Sino-Japanese alliance were not new, up till then China had not been treated as a serious partner and was merely seen as Japan's main field of operation.[14] Yet as China was growing stronger and chances of national unification were rising, many of the Taishō civilization critics distanced themselves more and more from such a Japan-centred form of 'Asianism'. In the meantime, the gradually growing influence on the Japanese intelligentsia of socialism, which they from the mid-1920s onwards applied to international relations as well, for the first time enabled some of them to view China not merely as a potentially strong neighbour but also as an equal partner. These developments made opinion leaders like Horie and Mizuno direct themselves to China and added the finishing touch to their process of breaking with Europe.

BIBLIOGRAPHY

Horie Kiichi. 1915. 'Ōshū sensō to hompō keizai shakai no shōrai'. *Chūō kōron*, 30(5): 18-31.
——. 1916a. 'Keiki kaifuku to ippan keizaikai'. *Chūō kōron*, 31(2): 48-57.
——. 1916b. 'Ōshū sensō no eizoku to waga kuni keizai shakai no rigai'. *Chūō kōron*, 31(5): 57-67.
——. 1916c. 'Ōshū sengo ni okeru keizai shakai no hendō'. *Taiyō*, 22(8): 76-83.
——. 1916d. 'Kokusai keizai to dōtoku'. *Taiyō*, 22(10): 57-64.
——. 1918. 'Takahashi zōsho no zaisei iken wo shissei su'. *Chūō kōron*, 33(12): 65-9.
——. 1919a. 'Sekai saikensetsu to kokusai keizai'. *Taiyō*, 25(1): 21-8.
——. 1919b. 'Masa ni kitaran to suru keizai seikatsujō no kakushin'. *Chūō kōron*, 34(5): 29-36.
——. 1919c. 'Tai-Shi shakkandan mondai to Nisshi keizai kankei'. *Chūō kōron*, 34(7): 24-31.
——. 1920a. 'Ōshū sensō to keizai shichō no dōyō'. *Chūō kōron*, 35(1): 164-70.
——. 1920b. 'Shina ni okeru Nichi-Ei-Bei sankoku no kankei'. *Chūō kōron*, 35(2): 53-6.
——. 1921a. 'Nihon no keizai seikatsu wo kaizō suru michi'. *Kaizō*, 3(1): 78-90.
——. 1921b. 'Kokuminkeizai to [miritarizumu]'. *Kaizō*, 3(3): 64-75.
——. 1921c. 'Shōgyōchūshinshugi yori kōgyōchūshinshugi ni'. *Chūō kōron*, 36(4): 81-99.
——. 1921d. 'Keizaigan de mita Nihon genji no seiji'. *Kaizō*, 3(5): 57-65.
——. 1921e. 'Doitsu no shōkin shiharai o chūshin to shite kokusai keizaijō ni shōzuru hendō'. *Chūō kōron*, 36.6: 51-9.

——. 1921f. 'Kafu kaigi no dai-issei ni sesshite'. *Kaizō*, 3(13): 205-10.

——. 1922a. 'Buryokuteki kyōsō kara kokusai keizaiteki kyōsō e'. *Chūō kōron*, 37(2): 20-30.

——. 1922b. 'Shikoku kyōshō narabi ni Kyokutō kyōyaku no seiritsu to tai-Shi keizai seisaku'. *Chūō kōron*, 37(3): 69-79.

——. 1922c. 'Sekai keizaijō yori mitaru Zenoa kaigi'. *Chūō kōron*, 37(4): 149-59.

——. 1922d. 'Keizai seisaku o sasshin sezareba kokuun wa kizutsuku'. *Chūō kōron*, 37(7): 57-70.

——. 1922e. 'Shihonshugiteki keizaikan o aratamezareba sekai heiwa narabi ni jinruiai no jitsugen muzukashi'. *Chūō kōron*, 37(8): 60-72.

——. 1923a. 'Tai-Shi bunka jigyō no keizaiteki kansatsu'. *Chūō kōron*, 38(5): 38-49.

——. 1923b. 'Chōsen keizai shikan'. *Chūō kōron*, 38(6): 67-85.

——. 1923c. 'Kokusai taishaku riron to waga kuni keizaikai no kiki', *Kaizō*, 5(7): 32-54.

——. 1923d. 'Tai-Shi keizai seisaku no komponteki kaizō'. *Kaizō*, 5(8): 206-18.

——. 1924a. 'Beikoku no hai-Nichi rippō to waga kuni no keizaiteki fuan'. *Chūō kōron*, 39(7): 47-66.

——. 1924b. 'Gumbi shukushō ni taisuru keizaikan'. *Kaizō*, 6(10): 110-14.

——. 1924c. 'Keizaiteki yūsei no jōken o ronzu'. *Kaizō*, 6(12): 37-56.

——. 1924d. 'Tai-Shi keizai seisaku to Nihon'. *Ekonomisuto*, 2(23): 12-4.

——. 1925a. 'Sakoku keizai no kiken waga kuni ni semaru'. *Kaizō*, 7(2): 58-86.

——. 1925b. 'Shina no kanzei jishu shuken to Nihon no tai-Shi keizai kankei'. *Kaizō*, 7(12): 44-61.

——. 1926a. 'Keizai jiji mondai'. *Kaizō*, 8(6): 99-112.

——. 1926b. 'Shinkeizai seisaku no kichō ikaga'. *Kaizō*, 8(11): 120-8.

——. 1927a. 'Shina wa hatashite sekika suru ka'. *Ekonomisuto*, 5(7): 24-6.

——. 1927b. 'Nihon no Mammō keizai seisaku'. *Kaizō*, 9(11): 38-48.

——. 1928-9. *Horie Kiichi zenshū*, 10 vols. Tokyo: Kaizōsha.

Horie Otoo. 1977. 'Miyake, Takiyama, Fukuzawa to chichi Horie Kiichi.' *Fukuzawa techō*, 13: 17-22.

Humphries, Leonard A. 1995. *The Way of the Heavenly Sword: The Japanese Army in the 1920s*. Stanford: Stanford University Press.

Iida Taizō. 1983. 'Taishōki bummei hihyōka chosaku ichiran'. *Hōgaku shirin*, 80(3/4): 179-211.

Itō Yukio. 1987. *Taishō demokurashii to seitō seiji*. Tokyo: Yamakawa shuppansha.

Large, Stephen S. 1972. *The Rise of Labor in Japan - The Yūaikai, 1912-19*. Tokyo: Sophia University.

——. 1981. *Organized Workers and Socialist Politics in Interwar Japan*. Cambridge: Cambridge University Press.

Matsuo Takayoshi. 1970. *Mimponshugi no chōryū*. Tokyo: Eibundō.

Matsushita Yoshio. 1950. *Mizuno Hironori*. Matsuyama: Shishūsha. Reissued as Maesaka Toshiyuki, ed. 1993. *Kaigun taisa no hansen – Mizuno Hironori*. Tokyo: Yūzankaku.

Miyamoto Moritarō. 1993. 'Mizuno Hironori ni okeru shisō no tenkai'. In *Kindai Nihon seiji shisōshi hakkutsu: heiwa, kirisutokyō, kokka*, edited by Miyamoto Moritarō et al. Tokyo: Fūkōsha, 3-20.

Mizuno Hironori. 1914. 'Sensō gakan'. In *Mizuno Hironori chosakushū* (below Chosakushū), 2: 8-21.

——. 1915. 'Ōshū-taisenkan – kenkō jūkei'. In *Chosakushū*, 2: 26-33.

——. 1919. 'Waga gunkokushugiron'. *Chūō kōron*, 34(1): 104-24.

——. 1920. 'Doitsu no haiin'. *Kaizō*, 2(7): 20-48.

——. 1921a. 'Busō heiwa no kyōi: Kokusai Remmei kaizō no kyūmu'. In *Chosakushū*, 4: 46-58.

——. 1921b. 'Gunjin shinri'. In *Chosakushū*, 4: 37-45.

——. 1921c. 'Washinton kaigi to gumbi shukugen'. *Chūō kōron*, 36(10): 94-111.

——. 1922a. 'Gumbi shukushō to kokumin shisō'. *Chūō kōron*, 37(1): 42-56.

——. 1922b. 'Gunjijō yori mitaru kaigun kyōtei'. *Chūō kōron*, 37(2): 88-98.

——. 1922c. 'Iaku jōsō to tōsuiken'. In *Chosakushū*, 4: 131-43.

——. 1922d. 'Doku-Ro o dō suru?'. In *Chosakushū*, 4: 233-44.

——. 1923a. 'Ichiji no handō genshō ni kommei suru nakare'. *Chūō kōron*, 38(1): 94-106.

——. 1923b. 'Kokusai Remmei o kaizō subeshi'. In *Chosakushū*, 5: 15-21.

——. 1924a. 'Sensō ikkagen'. *Chūō kōron*, 39(7): 67-78.

——. 1924b. 'Gunkan bakuchin to shidan genshō: kokusai heiwa to gumbi shukushō'. In *Chosakushū*, 5: 84-106.

——. 1925a. 'Beikoku kaigun no Taiheiyō daienshū o chūshin ni shite'. *Chūō kōron*, 40(2): 22-40.

——. 1925b. 'Beikoku kaigun to Nihon'. *Chūō kōron*, 40(4): 135-45.

——. 1925c. 'Sekai heiwa to gumbi shukushō kaigi'. *Kokusai Chishiki*, 5(4): 14-24.

——. 1925d. '1921-2 no Kafu kaigi to kitarubeki gunshuku kaigi ni tsuite: shitsumon to tōgi'. *Kokusai chishiki*, 5(5): 51-9.

——. 1925e. 'Nisshi shinzen to taitō jōyaku'. In *Chosakushū*, 5: 170-8.

——. 1926. 'Kaikyū mondai to minzoku mondai'. In *Chosakushū*, 5: 188-96.

——. 1928. 'Ei-Futsu kyōtei no muenryo-hyō'. In *Chosakushū*, 5: 318-26.

——. 1978. *Hankotsu no gunjin: Mizuno Hironori*. Tokyo: Keizai ōraisha. Reissued as volume 7 of Mizuno Hironori. 1995. *Mizuno Hironori chosakushū*.

——. 1995. *Mizuno Hironori chosakushū*, 8 vols. Tokyo: Yūzankaku.

Nishikawa Shunsaku. 1985. *Fukuzawa Yukichi to sannin no kōshintachi*. Tokyo: Nihon hyōronsha.

Oka Yoshitake et al., eds. 1973. *Ogawa Heikichi kankei monjo, 2*. Tokyo: Misuzu shobō.

Ozeki Motoaki. 1997. 'Mimponshugiron no shūen to ni-daiseitōseiron no kaizō'. *Shirin*, 80(1): 109-46.

Peattie, Mark R. 1990. 'Forecasting a Pacific War, 1912-1933: The Idea of a Conditional Japanese Victory'. In *The Ambivalence of Nationalism: Modern Japan between East and West*, edited by James W. White and Michio Umegaki. Lanham: University Press of America, 115-29.

Saeki Shōichi. 1975. 'Images of the United States as a Hypothetical Enemy'. In *Mutual Images*, edited by Akira Iriye. Cambridge: Harvard University Press, 100-14.

Stegewerns, Dick. (forthcoming). *Japanese Perceptions of the Outside World during the Period of Multilateral treaties, 1919-33*. Leiden: CNWS Publications.

Takahashi Seiichirō. 1970. 'Ko Horie Kiichi hakase o shinobu'. In Takahashi Seiichirō, *Zuihitsu: Keiō gijuku*. Tokyo: Mita bungaku raiburarii, 381-409.

Tamaki Norio. 1988. 'The American Professors' Regime: Political Economy at Keiō University, 1890-1912'. In *Enlightenment and Beyond: Political Economy comes to Japan*, edited by Sugiyama Chūhei and Mizuta Hiroshi. Tokyo: University of Tokyo Press, 75-95.

——. 1990. 'Horie Kiichi no Rondon'. In *Kindai Nihon Kenkyū, 7*. Tokyo: Keiō gijuku Fukuzawa kenkyū sentā, 45-61.

Uji Jun'ichirō. 1962. 'Keizaigakubu'. In *Keiō gijuku hyakunenshi: bekkan (daigaku hen)*. Tokyo: Keiō gijuku, 1-203.

NOTES

1.   There are no postwar reprints of any of Horie's books. The ten-volume series *Horie Kiichi zenshū* [The complete works of Horie Kiichi] (Horie, 1928-9) was published soon after his death, but in spite of its title it can hardly be called complete. It is a compilation of a fair part of his books but not all of them, and, furthermore, it completely omits the many articles Horie had been writing since 1897 for scholarly journals, newspapers and general magazines. His diaries for the years 1899-1927 and a few letters are included.

2.   There is a list, although not complete and impeccable, of the articles Horie wrote for scholarly journals and popular magazines in his *Complete works* (Horie, 1928-9, 10: 962-77). After having been led in the wrong direction for several years, recently I was able to trace Horie's private belongings which had been donated to Keiō University by Horie's son. Gathering dust in the basement of the Fukuzawa Research Centre were a dozen cardboard boxes which contained amongst others his diaries, the manuscripts of most of his books, a part of his correspondence and scrapbooks of all the articles Horie had written for the *Ōsaka mainichi shimbun* and the *Tōkyō nichi nichi shimbun* in the period 1913-27. I have not been able to take these materials into account in this article but will do so in my forthcoming book on Mizuno, Horie, Yoshino Sakuzō and Sugimori Kōjirō.

3.   Biographical information on Horie is most easily found in Nishikawa, 1985: 127-57; and Uji, 1962: 55-61. In English there is only Tamaki, 1988: 85-95, which gives a brief account of Horie's education received at Keiō University.

4.   This is also evident from the fact that Horie occasionally characterizes the English living in China as despicable and cunning while he not once uses such qualifications when dealing with the non-colonial English living in the British Isles (see Horie, 1920b: 55; Horie, 1921d: 57-9).

5.   Since the introduction of male suffrage in 1925 many Japanese opinion leaders cried out loudly in public for the overthrow of the corrupt established political parties and the establishment of proletariat party rule. Nevertheless, it is hard to deny that many were predominantly inspired by an intense hatred of the Seiyūkai and were actually putting their hopes on a Kenseikai-proletariat party coalition in the near future. Yoshino Sakuzō, the most eminent representative of the Taishō opinion leaders, clearly stands out for such an attitude (Ozeki, 1997), but Horie, who openly proclaimed Takahashi Korekiyo to be his greatest ideological enemy and who actively supported the election campaign of Keiseikai candidates, also nicely fits the case.

6.   It is hard not to get the impression that Yoshino Sakuzō, who was hardly trained in economic theory, was considerably influenced by Horie. Most of Yoshino's rare economic arguments, such as his rejection of emigration as a solution for solving Japan's overpopulation problem, his stress on the relative importance of industrializa-tion, his economic comparison of Japan and England, and his priority to China proper over Manchuria, seem to have had their precedent in articles by Horie. When one considers the influence Horie had as one of the most prominent economists of his day, whose articles on a regular basis adorned the pages of the three major general magazines of the 1910s and 1920s, this impression seems to be even more plausible.

7.   The fact that Iida (1983: 180-2) omitted Mizuno from his extensive list of *Taishō bummei hyōka* is a clear sign of Mizuno's somewhat controversial status.

8.   The bulk of Mizuno's oeuvre, including his books, his autobiography, his diaries and his correspondence, has recently been reissued through the good offices of a television station in Mizuno's native Matsuyama as *Mizuno Hironori chosakushū* [Collected works of Mizuno Hironori] (Mizuno, 1995).

9. Biographical information on Mizuno can be found in either his autobiography *Hankotsu no gunjin* [A recalcitrant soldier]' which regrettably only covers the period up to his resignation from the navy, or the detailed biography by Matsushita Yoshio, a pupil of Mizuno who was later best known as an authority on the military history of pre-war modern Japan (Mizuno, 1978; Matsushita, 1950). In sharp contrast to the war period, when a critical pre-war article by Mizuno was used by the US army in order to incite the Japanese people against their military leaders, there has hardly been any interest in Mizuno outside Japan in the postwar period. As far as I have been able to ascertain, in the English literature Mizuno has only been dealt with briefly in two articles on 'war scare literature' in pre-war modern Japan (Saeki, 1975: 103-4; Peattie, 1990: 119-20).

10, Mizuno's January 1919 article in *Chūō kōron* was a reaction to articles in magazines and newspapers by such heavyweights as Anezaki Masaharu and Yoshino Sakuzō and was stridently called 'My argument in support of militarism'. Thus he collided head on with the general trend of the immediate post World War I period, in which militarism indeed was a topic profusely dealt with but strictly in a negative context. Mizuno's lonely protest could not change the fact that the term 'militarism' ever afterwards would not be spoken of in a positive sense.

11. This assessment of Mizuno's revocation of militarism goes against previous interpretations, which usually place this revocation in 1919, when Mizuno was in Europe for the second time and saw the ruins of modern warfare with his own eyes (Miyamoto, 1993: 9-11). However, these interpretations seem to be merely based on an uncritical reading of Yoshino's autobiography, which has a chapter on his 'Great conversion of thought' on the battlefields of France. They leave one wondering why Mizuno after his return from Europe first wrote an article on the causes of German defeat in which he advocated the creation of a garrison state and why it took him until the autumn of 1921 before he publicly renounced militarism.

12. Yoshino Sakuzō, who is usually treated as uniquely representative of the *Taishō bummei hyōka*, actually often took an exceptional stand when it came to international affairs. In sharp contrast to the general trend he expressed great faith in the League of Nations, he hardly had any attention for the substantial and detailed Five Power Treaty and rather concentrated on the generally slighted formalistic Five Power Treaty, and his interest in Europe was only reawakened after the first 'socialist' cabinets had collapsed and most opinion leaders had already turned their eyes away again (Stegewerns, forthcoming).

13. This contempt of Italy in general and fascism in particular is evident in all case studies of *Taishō bummei hyōka* I have done up to now (Stegewerns, forthcoming). Itō Yukio has also done some research on the reactions in Japan to the establishment of the fascist regime in Italy, as seen in the major newspapers of the day (Itō, 1987: 141-56).

14. A well-known example is Finance Minister Takahashi Korekiyo's plan for a Sino-Japanese economic alliance of May 1921, which was the object of severe attacks by Horie (Oka, et. al., 1973: 144-9).

5

Perceptions of 'Europe' in Japanese Historiography, 1945-65

SEBASTIAN CONRAD

E ver since the Meiji period, 'Europe' played a major role in the development of Japanese historiography. This influence was sometimes overt and willingly recognized, while at times one needed to read between the lines of historical scholarship in order to detect its 'European' thematic. Three complementary aspects of this influence can be differentiated: First, Europe constituted an important object of study for Japanese academic historians. In fact, when a faculty of history was set up at Tokyo University in 1887, at first it was solely concerned with the European past. Academic historiography in Japan, in other words, began as the study of European history. Not least, this was due to the strong influence of the European model on the establishment of history as an academic subject in Japan. Especially the impact of German historicism was very marked; the Japanese government had commissioned Ludwig Riess, a young historian at Berlin University, to serve as first professor of history at Tokyo University. Riess, who was a specialist of English constitutional history, lectured on European history and on universal history in the fashion of German historicism (most notably Leopold von Ranke). Most of his students, consequently, were trained to use European source materials and had studied the European past.

Moreover, and this brings us to our second point, the interest in things European had a methodological background as well. With the establishment of history as a discipline, Japanese historiography had adapted to the European methodology of research and history writing. Shigeno Yasutsugu, one of the foremost historians at the time, expressed the appeal this new methodology had for Japanese historians: 'Unlike Japanese and Chinese histories, which confine themselves to factual statement, Western histories inquire into causes and consider effects, provide detailed accounts of their subjects and vivid pictures of conditions of the time with which they are concerned. There can be no doubt that their form and method embody many points of value to us' (quoted from Numata, 1961: 277). The institutionalization of history as a discipline thus entailed the appropriation of European standards of historiography. One of the methodological imperatives that came with German historicism was the dogma of the primacy of foreign policy. This concept served to reinforce an interest in the foreign relations of early modern Japan, most notably with the European powers (see Blussé, 1979).

There was, however, a third aspect to the preoccupation with European history in Japanese historiography, and it is with this aspect we will primarily be concerned here. For Japanese historians, European history continuously served as a yardstick for an evaluation of the Japanese past. The historiography of the so-called enlightenment historians like Fukuzawa Yukichi, but also of the Min'yūsha historians in the late nineteenth century – all looking to European history in order to extract the universal laws of development – are the best known examples of this approach (see Iwai, 1963; Duus, 1974). But also in the twentieth century, and more specifically in the wake of World War II, Europe figured prominently in the discussions on Japan's history and the appropriate steps towards a democratic future. Europe here appeared not so much as a remote object of disinterested study, but rather implied the possibility of drawing conclusions about oneself. 'Europe' did not primarily designate a geographical location, but rather served to locate Japan. In this sense, also the scientific investigation into European history was the means to a larger end; studying the European past represented an approach towards a historiographical knowledge of Japan and its future.

As a result of the complicated process of institutionalization, the faculties of history at Japanese universities were subdivided along geographical lines: the field of History was differentiated into Western [seiyōshi], Japanese [kokushi] and Oriental [tōyōshi] history (the latter dealt with Asia, but not Japan) (see Conrad, in press). Seiyōshi in this set-up comprised the history of the 'West', which in historiographical practice was epitomized by Europe.

Europe, however, was itself narrowly defined and limited to a small number of national pasts. Most faculties followed the example of Tokyo University and installed courses in German, French, and English history. Eastern or southern Europe, on the other hand, were almost entirely excluded and confined to the margins. At the same time, American history was only rarely considered a subject matter of *seiyōshi*. Before 1945, Western Europe [*seiō*] and the 'West' [*seiyō*] were taken to be virtually identical.[1]

Accordingly, the practice of *seiyōshi* was part of a discursive construction of the 'West'. Through a selective reading of the European past, an image of 'Europe' (as the 'West') was constantly reproduced. Europe was depicted as the progressive and modern model society that could serve as the norm for Japanese development. Drawing on Edward Said's discussion of European encounters with the non-European Other, the constant reference to Europe in Japanese historiography could be read as an example of a 'Self-Orientalization'. Edward Said had described 'Orientalism' as a practice by which Europe discursively defined a backward 'Orient' that was then juxtaposed to a progressive West. Part and parcel of European imperialism in the nineteenth century, this discourse tended to turn the Orient into the passive object of European domination and represented it as the prehistory of the modern West (Said, 1991). By a characteristic and inverse move, Japanese historians of Europe contributed to this 'imaginative geography'. The Japanese representation of European history produced an idealized version of the West that served as yardstick for the evaluation of the Japanese past. The European road to modernity was presented as the natural and sound development that all other nations would eventually follow. By implication, this European success was contrasted to a Japanese failure; the fullness of European modernity corresponded to a Japanese lack. Japanese identity, in other words, was discursively constituted as the negative image of the 'West' (see also Dirlik, 1996).

This mechanism had permeated Japanese historiography and was especially conspicuous in the period under consideration here. After 1945, military defeat and the subsequent occupation had palpably demonstrated the superiority of the 'West'. Consequently, the asymmetrical comparison that measured the difference between this 'West' and Japanese society became the dominant mode of historical argument. While during the war the heated debates among Japanese intellectuals had also displayed feelings of animosity with respect to the allegedly overbearing Western influence, after 1945 the priority of the 'West' as model was reinstated and hardly ever questioned. Japanese historians who dealt with European history, therefore, presented their analyses of the European past as operating manuals for the future course of Japanese society.

Within the academic discipline of Western History, or *seiyōshi*, the interpretive strategies associated with the school of Ōtsuka Hisao (1907-96) soon emerged as the leading paradigm of a Japanese historiography of Europe. Otsuka taught at the Faculty of Economics at Tokyo University, and his analyses of the transition from feudal to modern societies relied to a large extent on the study of economic history. Nevertheless, in a postwar setting that saw Japanese historiography heavily dominated by Marxist historians, Ōtsuka and his colleagues at Tokyo University introduced the methodology of Max Weber to compensate for what they perceived as shortcomings of the Marxist orthodoxy. Soon this fusion of Marx and Weber championed by the Ōtsuka school established itself as the leading paradigm in the historiography of Europe. Ōtsuka's studies of English capitalism, Takahashi Kōhachirō's analyses of the French Revolution, and Matsuda Tomoo's investigations into the peculiarities of Prussian modernization both defined the problematic of European history and limited the range of valid patterns of argument.[2] In the function of 'Europe' in the studies of the Ōtsuka school we can detect the mechanism of a 'Self-Orientalization' along the lines described above.

The dominant field of research for the historians of the Ōtsuka school was the pre-modern era. This extensive research into eighteenth-century Europe was by no means a self-sufficient enterprise, however; rather, the course of the European past seemed to bear direct implications for an understanding of Japanese history. Since the transition to modern capitalism and civil society was understood as a universal task that Western Europe had already successfully mastered, studying Europe promised to reveal what History still held in store for Japan's future. Thus, when analyzing the French Revolution or early English capitalism, the historians of the Ōtsuka school implicitly made statements about Japanese history as well. Japan figured as the unsaid Other of European history. Takahashi Kōhachirō, a professor of French history at Tokyo University, explained this relationship in the preface of a volume on European economic history he edited in 1947. It was the aim of this collection of essays to analyze 'the emergence of the structure of the modern world in Western Europe', since these structures 'embodied the stages of development of world history (universal history) in their "pure and classical" form.' The focus of attention was not so much on Europe, but on the universal laws governing all histories; by extension, Japanese modernity was the hidden agenda of the Ōtsuka school's studies of Europe. 'Even if we deal with this problem only in a hypothetical way, it is possible to claim that from the perspective of the classical European stages of development we can deduct a new point of view for the analysis of Japanese society as well' (Takahashi, 1947: 1, 16f).[3] In short, Ōtsuka and Takahashi stressed the instrumental character of Japanese studies of European history.

The central theme of the scientific oeuvre produced by historians associated with the Ōtsuka school was the transition from feudalism to modern capitalism in Western Europe. The emergence of a modern civil society that seemed to have failed in Japan thus became the principal concern of *seiyōshi* historiography. Ōtsuka himself dealt with the formation of early capitalism in his extensive studies of sixteenth-century England. Drawing on a Weberian interpretation of categories introduced by Marx, Ōtsuka analyzed what to him seemed two competing roads leading to industrial capitalism. One of these alternatives was the so-called 'merchant' path by which he understood the accumulation of capital through commerce. In his analysis, however, Ōtsuka denied any revolutionary significance to this historical alternative. All ages had witnessed some form of commerce, and the pure accumulation of wealth could be motivated by greed or other decidedly pre-modern considerations. For Ōtsuka, the early merchant class in their pursuit of profit still relied entirely on pre-modern motivational structures. Therefore, only pursuit of the 'producer' path promised to lead to industrial capitalism and modern society. As Ōtsuka found in his studies of sixteenth-century England, it was the accumulation of capital in the hands of the early capitalist middle-classes that brought about the Industrial Revolution. In his extensive research on early modernity in England, Ōtsuka identified the independent yeomanry as the driving force behind this development. These producers from the rural middle-classes were attributed the role of the subject on the only sound and revolutionary path towards modernity. Only after overcoming resistance by a stratum of rich merchants, freedom of trade and the capitalist differentiation into entrepreneurs and paid labourers was possible (Ōtsuka, 1944, 1952).

Japan's modernization, by contrast, had to be measured against this developmental matrix as observed in the history of Western Europe. By these standards, Japanese development appeared as backward and incomplete. Compared with the independent yeomen and the rural middle-classes in sixteenth-century England who advanced, due to 'their modern, in other words democratic character ... to the role of subject and agent of modern society', the Japanese peasants had completely failed to fulfil their historical task. There was a marked 'difference between the agrarian productive forces in England and in our country – and in more general terms: between West and East.' Ōtsuka attributed these differences not to fate, geography, or climate – as earlier theories of spheres of culture had frequently done – but his Weberian background lead him to postulate a certain kind of ethos responsible for the emergence of a capitalist spirit. And unlike the Marxist majority in postwar Japanese historiography, Ōtsuka did not rely on purely economic factors to explain the persistence of feudal and pre-modem structures in Japanese society. In opposition to the Marxist determination of superstructure by economic base, for Ōtsuka the essence of modernity could be found in the realm of culture (Ōtsuka, 1969d: 248, 255).

This insight led to a description of Japanese society as characterized by feudal and pre-modern social structures that had seriously impeded the emergence of a capitalist spirit. In Japan, according to Ōtsuka, paternalistic social relations prevailed through a paternalistic ethos [oyagokoro]: 'Those above us in a leadership capacity are supposed to have the authority of parents. The people, or those "below", must be obedient to this authority. The leaders who have this authority as parents show "love and mercy" toward those below, who obey them. In any case, according to this pattern the people are treated as immature. Indeed ... to be immature is considered a virtue ... [Therefore] it can be said that the people of our country have no inner originality [jihatsusei]' (Ōtsuka, b: 177).[4]

The introduction of Europe as a standard of history served a political purpose as well. The scholarship of the Ōtsuka school aimed at bringing about a truly liberal, democratic society – a political programme that rested on the conviction that Japan's modernity so far had utterly failed. This point of view and the problem consciousness [*mondai ishiki*] it entailed held wide sway over Japanese historians after the war. This is not to say, however, that all historians agreed with Ōtsuka's analysis of European and Japanese history. Let us digress for a moment and take a comparative look on attempts to define the relation between Japanese and European history differently.

Within the field of *seiyōshi*, the group associated with Ōchi Takeomi, for example, depicted English modernization in a manner that sharply differed from the interpretation of the Ōtsuka school. For Ōchi, but also other historians like Tsunoyama Sakae in Kyoto, not the rural middle-classes (as Ōtsuka had insisted) but the gentry and merchant capital were the decisive factor of the development of English capitalism (Ōchi, 1954). Consequently, not some romantic version of modernization 'from below', but the 'merchant' road towards capitalism was presented as the appropriate model of development. This interpretation had its specific implications for the evaluation of Japan as well. Also Japanese modernization, by extension, had not failed – on the contrary: it had essentially followed the English example and therefore could be characterized as sound and successful (see Kondo, 1991).

Revisionism of this kind gained in importance since the mid-1950s, when economic growth began to be palpable and make the image of a structurally backward Japan seem more and more implausible. Historians had long been preoccupied with measuring the (temporal) distance between Japan and the West. But when the occupation period ended (1952), a peace treaty with the United States and other countries was signed (1951), and the buds of economic recovery could no longer be overlooked, this distance seemed gradually to decrease if not to vanish. This observation led to attempts to compare Japanese and European pasts in a more balanced way. The analyses of the Meiji Restoration by the French historian Kuwabara Takeo and the philosopher Ueyama Shumpei are other cases. Their interpretations can be read as attacks on what they considered uneven comparisons between French and Japanese history.

The Meiji Restoration was usually interpreted as an incomplete version of the French Revolution and therefore an aborted attempt to institutionalize a civil society in the bourgeois sense. In fact, the French Revolution served as the comparative cornerstone for the Marxists' and the Modernists' interpretation of Japanese history. Since the 1930s, therefore, interest in French history had continuously been high; this was also reflected in the large number of translations of European works on the French Revolution. In the early 1930s, in the context of the 'Debate on Japanese capitalism' [*Nihon shihonshugi ronsō*] among Marxist historians, Jean Jaurè's *Histoire socialists de la Révolution française* (by Muramatsu Masatoshi, 1930-32) and Kropotkin's *La Révolution française* (by Tan Tokusaburō, 1931) were rendered into Japanese. After the war, Albert Mathiez's *La Révolution française* (Nezu Masashi, Ichihara Toyota, 1958/59), Georges Lefebvre's *Quatre-vingt-neuf* (Suzuki Taihei, 1952), Lefebvre's *La Révolution et les paysans* (Shibata Michio, 1956) and Albert Soboul's *La Révolution française* (Obase Takuzō, Watanabe Jun, 1953) were all translated in an attempt to come to terms with Japan's failed modernization. The comprehensive land reform [*nōchi kaikaku*] undertaken by the occupation forces had stimulated an intensive interest among Japanese historians in the works of Georges Lefebvre and Ernest Labrousse on the agrarian politics in France on the eve of the revolution (see Takahashi, 1960). Given this background, Takahashi Kōhachirō stressed the unique importance of studies on the French Revolution for an understanding of Japanese history. 'The structure of Japanese agriculture and landownership is by far more similar to small scale agriculture and small peasant property in France than to large scale agriculture ... in England or ... in Germany' (Japanese National Committee of Historical Sciences, 1965: 361).

The argument, put forward by the Japanese Marxists of the *kōzaha* group and likewise by Takahashi and other historians of the Ōtsuka school, referred to the fact that in Japan, the bourgeoisie had not taken full control of politics and the economy. But for Ueyama, the *Meiji ishin* in this respect was not unlike but very much resembled the French Revolution. Ueyama taught philosophy at the Research Center for the Human Sciences [*Jimbun kagaku kenkyūjo*] in Kyoto, and his critique was directly aimed at the then hegemonic discourse of Marxist historiography. For Ueyama, the Meiji Restoration appeared not as the bourgeois revolution in the pure and theoretical sense, but as a transitional phase. Such a transitional phase, however, could be witnessed in any country bridging the deep gap between absolutism and modernity. As Ueyama surmised from English and French development as well, at this stage the bourgeois class does not attain to full control of state power. From this perspective, the Meiji Restoration did not differ from the French Revolution. In other words, remnants of feudal structures of domination in the wake of the social upheavals of modernization did not have to be considered a Japanese peculiarity. And also in terms of class relations and class antagonisms Japan after 1889 appeared as the equal of Napoleonic France. By thus rewriting a chapter of French history, Ueyama also came to alternative conclusions about Japan's modernity. 'The Meiji Restoration', he concluded, 'was a form of the bourgeois revolution' (Ueyama, 1956: 91).

Ueyama's colleague at the Research Centre in Kyoto was the expert on French Literature, Kuwabara Takeo. Although not a historian proper, his revisionist interpretation of the Meiji Restoration had a great impact on the re-examination of the standard historiography. On New Year's Day 1956 Kuwabara published his call for a 'renewed appreciation of the Meiji period' in the Japanese daily *Asahi shimbun* that he was to repeat in later publications. 'I believe we have to admit that Japanese modernization in the Meiji period was successful' (Kuwabara, 1956; cf. Kuwabara, et al., 1962). Kuwabara especially admired the speed of the Japanese attempt to catch up with Western industrialization, even though this concentrated effort entailed certain social costs in the form of uneven development. Kuwabara's argument rested on the findings of an interdisciplinary group of scholars that under his leadership had worked on the comparative evaluation of the French Revolution. In the light of this research, he arrived at a much more positive reading of the Meiji Restoration than, for example, the Ōtsuka school. 'I do not mean to bypass all the problems industrialization has wrought, but the point is that Japan was a backward nation in Asia, and it became a leading industrial power within the span of one hundred years. This is one of the wonders of world history' (Kuwabara, 1983a: 136). The reason for this unparalleled development was not to be found in the uncritical adaptation of Western civilization, but for Kuwabara rested in the uniqueness of Japanese culture. 'Japan, too, was economically and in other ways very undeveloped at the beginning of the Meiji era, but it had a unique and relatively well-integrated, sophisticated culture' (Kuwabara, 1983b: 39).

As a last example of the kind of revisionism that flourished in the mid-1950s and that attempted to redefine the complex relation between Japanese and European history, we will for a moment turn to the cultural anthropologist Umesao Tadao. In February 1957 he published an article in the journal *Chūō kōron* that solicited reactions from a variety of sources, not least the historians. Umesao, who was inspired by the work of Arnold Toynbee (who had visited Japan in the preceding year), was interested in defining the 'exact co-ordinates' of Japan's position in the world. His aim was to demonstrate that Japan was not part of the 'Orient', as was usually held, but rather essentially European. Although Japanese culture incorporated a number of 'Eastern aspects', for Umesao not the genealogy of cultural influences but rather the social function of culture determined the character of a nation. In this respect he found stunning parallels between European and Japanese societies, both of which could be called 'highly civilized'. To account for these similarities Umesao looked for regularities that could be aggregated to a law of world history. In this project he was inspired by the ecological theories of a succession of life-forms:

> Just as the theory of the succession of life-forms made it possible to understand the history of the natural communities of animals and plants in a lawful manner, we may be able to understand the history of the human community . . . – to a certain degree – as a lawful evolution as well (Umesao, 1957: 34f, 43).

As a result of his phenomenology of human life-forms Umesao divided the globe into an old and a new world. The 'old world' [kyūsekai] that he was interested in consisted of Europe, north Africa, and Asia. Within these regions, only few countries were associated with a successful development towards 'high civiliza-tion' [kōdo bummei] – it was precisely the countries that were located at the periphery of the Eurasian continent:

> In parts several regions have reached this stage, but on a national scale only Japan, and – on the opposite side [of the continent] – the Western European countries have developed a highly civilized state. There is still a huge difference to countries like China, southeast Asia, India, Russia, the Islamic countries or Eastern Europe (Umesao, 1957: 37).

From a perspective based on economic growth and national independence as measures of modernization, the geographical margins of Eurasia – Western Europe and Japan, that is – appeared as a coherent cultural sphere. And this coherence for Umesao was not due to the massive import of European modernity to Japan after the Meiji Restoration. Rather, the similarities of development had to be attributed to the regularities of universal history: 'The development of Japanese civilization since the Meiji period was nothing but a necessary process determined by the laws of world history and . . . was not due to cultural conversion or Europeanization' (Umesao, 1957: 41).

In his attempt to anchor these parallels of development in the history of this European periphery, Umesao took recourse to the experience of feudalism common to both regions. For him, only the social formation of feudalism made a bourgeois revolution possible, which in turn was a necessary prerequisite for the emergence of capitalism. The 'highly civilized' countries of the periphery, in other words, owed their success to feudalism. This was a condition of development that lacked in other countries which had been governed autocratically or had lived under colonial status. According to this logic, then, 'feudalism' held positive connotations. While in Marxist (and also in Ōtsuka's) discourse 'feudal' was an attribute of social backwardness, for Umesao this social formation advanced to the status of an indispensable precondition of modernity. This argumentative strategy allowed him, from his world-historical perspective, to define Japan – in a certain sense – as an integral part of Western Europe. Both regions were situated at the periphery of the 'old world' and had utilized the common experience of feudalism to a modernization that turned them into 'highly civilized' societies. Ōtsuka and most historians associated with him had stressed the need for Japanese society to catch up and to level out the immense differences – measured in world historical time – they detected between Japan and Europe. For Umesao, then, this time-lag did not exist; Europe was not so much a norm or model, but an equal companion. In Umesao's narrative, Japan was now a part of the West.

To sum up this cursory treatment of attempts to situate the Japanese past on a par with European history: Ōchi's 'gentry-thesis', the revisionist reading of the French Revolution by Ueyama or Kuwabara, and the ecological theories by Umesao underlined the fact that the critical perspective on Japan with which the Ōtsuka school treated European history did not remain unchallenged. The differences pertained to the interpretation of European history and by implication also affected the evaluation of the Japanese past. It is important to note, however, that in all these controversies the status of Japanese history was measured in terms of European development. In the process, both the Ōtsuka school and the critique by the revisionists did not transcend the bounds of the overall paradigm: the subject [*shutai*] of change was controversial, but the direction of development and the definition of its ruptures and stages remained unquestioned. And even though the assessment of the gap between Japanese and European history might differ: idealizing the European path to modernity – the dogma of the 'West-as-model' – was common currency in all interventions in this debate.

For Ōtsuka, to resume our argument, Japan's modernity was characterized by stagnation and backwardness when compared to the laws of development he had detected in European history. He believed that this difference could be overcome and that Japanese cultural heritage would be able to develop a modern spirit of its own. Ōtsuka thus reduced the problematic of progress and backwardness to a question of culture. He quoted attempts to attribute the differences between Europe and Japan to historical fate, to climate, or racial differences. In explicit opposition to these essentializing strategies of explanation, Ōtsuka located the principal deficiency in the minds of the Japanese people. Neither geography nor ethnicity, but Japanese culture to him seemed the pivotal point on which modernization hinged. According to Ōtsuka, it was due to the still despotic and pre-modern patterns of domination that an independent entrepreneurial ethos had not yet developed in Japan. His historical analysis led him to the conclusion that at some decisive moment Japan had deviated from the revolutionary path to modernity and instead followed the 'merchant' path of capital accumulation. Therefore, the Meiji Restoration did not bring about a modern society; rather, feudal remnants persisted and facilitated the emergence of the so-called 'emperor system' and, eventually, of fascism. Only some kind of cultural revolution, the adoption of what Ōtsuka termed the 'modern human type' [*kindaiteki ningen ruikei*], promised to bring Japan back on the right track of development. What was needed was 'inner autonomy, rationality, consciousness of social solidarity, and ... a realistic emphasis on economic life. ... [When] a decisive portion of the people is moulded into this modern human type, the results will be modern productivity and a potential for managerial construction, along with the endogenous formation of a democratic regime' (Ōtsuka, 1969b: 184).

By dissociating modernization from geographical conditions

and instead connecting progress to culture, Ōtsuka took recourse to a pattern of explanation that is typical for the kind of 'Self-Orientalization' described here. Differences between Japan and the 'West' were not due to constant restrictions of geography or ethnicity, but were subject to change in history. Japan thus was not eternally destined to a subaltern position in world history. The political optimism that Ōtsuka's works conveyed translated the modernization gap between Europe and Japan into a mere lag in time.

In a sense, translating differences into a temporal language implied an emancipation of non-European history. All nations could count on their own modernity, the differences being reduced to a matter of arriving 'early' or 'late'. This operation did not, however, question two basic tenets of historiography: on the one hand, the direction history took was not open to debate; the 'West' appeared as the natural *telos* of all non-Western history. This seemed sufficiently plausible in the light of the political world order after World War II, but it was also a result of the theoretical approach of the Weberian problematic (which also guided Ōtsuka's endeavours) that asked for the reasons for Europe's uniqueness – a uniqueness that was hardly ever questioned in the course of research. On the other hand, the means by which to bridge the historical gap between societies was also predetermined; in Weberian fashion, Ōtsuka looked for and found the cause of all social and economic differences in the sphere of culture – and consequently, the modernization of this culture under Western auspices appeared as the precondition of a modernization of society.

The reliance on a linear process of modernization also implied that Europe was not only prototype but also furnished the time frame with which to understand Japanese history. Events in the Japanese past that did not immediately reveal their true meaning to the innocent observer were elevated to historical importance only when compared to European history. Japanese history, in other words, seemed to make sense only when perceived through a European lens. When inquiring into the prehistory of the French Revolution, for example, Takahashi considered the 'attention to the economic and social problems under *l'ancien régime* in France as a means of analyzing the economic structure of Japanese absolute monarchy' (Japanese National Committee of Historical Sciences, 1965: 363). The study of European history, thus, was considered instrumental for any analysis of contemporary Japanese society. This aspect was reinforced by Okada Tomoyoshi: 'It should be noted that the socio-economic conditions confronting the bourgeois revolutions in seventeenth and eighteenth-century Europe were, for us Japanese, not things to be dealt with as belonging to the past or as someone else's business, but were with some differences the realities of the present' (Comité Japonais des Sciences Historiques, 1960: 429).

Only through this European subtext Japanese history was charged with meaning. Seemingly unconnected events in Japanese history made sense only through a comparative mapping of the European experience. This strategy, however, did not confine Japanese politics to the status of a blind follower of European precedents. Not only Ōtsuka stressed that the heuristic reference to European history did not 'force our country ... into a Procrustean mold' of historical development. Nevertheless, in his empirical studies he continually relied on a rhetoric of universal necessities. Thus, European developments were classified, for example, as 'an obligatory transitional stage' in the process of modernization, or as a 'general fact' of the law of world history – a law, to be sure, before which 'there is neither East nor West' (Ōtsuka, 1969c: 326).

The comparisons with European history not only served to map the Japanese past, but also contributed to a specific image of the 'West'. For Ōtsuka, examining European economic history served two different purposes: on the one hand, this representation of the 'West' was the background against which 'the Japanese peculiarities – the parallels and differences, or to be precise: the question whether Japan witnessed the development of capitalism in the Western European sense' – could be tackled. On the other hand, studying Europe 'served to understand the essence of the 'West' ['seiyō' no shin]' (Ōtsuka, 1969a: 294). Through the gradual reinterpretation of Europe's history, this essence was subject to a constant (if not always palpable) redefinition. The 'West' was not a natural and unchanging category, but a discursive space that was permanently reconstructed. Germany, for example, had long served as a model for both Japan's modernization and historiography. The university structure, but also the profession of history had relied on cultural borrowings from German institutions (for details, see Conrad, in press; Martin, 1995). After fascism, however, Germany was no longer taken as an undisputed element of the 'West'. Rather, Germany was now considered a companion on Japan's flawed, backward and incomplete road towards modernity. These changes were sometimes reflected in apparently minor but nonetheless revealing adjustments. The oldest academic journal of the historical profession, for example, the *Shigaku zasshi* in 1949 abolished its German-language résumés and instead began to publish summaries in English.

In the period under review, what was comprised by the signifier the 'West' gradually shifted. This constant reconfiguration colluded with changes in the global arena that also left Japanese historians not unaffected. The occupation of Japan and the subsequent reforms, but also the emerging cold war order with the US-Japanese security treaties in its wake transmitted powerful images of the postwar 'West'. The definition of Europe in historical scholarship was always negotiated with what appeared as the current incarnation of the 'West'. A major shift in this definition of the 'West' occurred at the end of the 1950s with the advent of modernization theory in Japan. The Hakone Conference and Edwin O. Reischauer's appointment as US ambassador to Tokyo, both in 1960, implanted a different narrative of modernity. The 'West' was still the model, but this time 'modernity' had a strong American connotation. Before 1945, American history had been virtually excluded from Japanese faculties of history. The only chair for the study of American history at the Tokyo University was the Hepburn Chair of American History and Government (held by Takagi Yasaka) that had been established in 1924 at the Faculty of Law. Now, through the detour of theory import, American modernity was established as the yardstick for the evaluation of Japanese history. And also the institutional development reflected this change in political and historiographical outlook. After 1945, the newly founded faculties of general education [kyōyō gakubu] also included seminars on American culture and history alongside the traditional courses in French, English, and German civilization. Also the topics chosen for the graduation thesis [sotsugyō rombun] reveal this growing interest in things American. At the private Waseda University, for example, more than half of the graduate theses written in modern Western history [kindai seiyōshi] dealt with US history.[5] But also at the more conservative Tokyo University and Kyoto University, interest in US history rose sharply and did not decline after the end of the occupation. The most frequent topics included the American civil war, Wilson's politics of peace, the New Deal, but also the issues of slavery and racial conflicts. The growing importance of American history, however, was not confined to the student level. In addition, a historical association was established to explicitly deal with American developments. The Japanese Association for American Studies [*Amerika gakkai*] that was founded under Takagi's leadership in 1946 soon published the five-volume *Genten Amerikashi* [A documentary history of the American people]. And also Nakaya Ken'ichi's volume on American history, *Beikokushi* (Tokyo 1948), documented the shifting emphasis in the study of 'Western history' [*seiyōshi*] (Jansen, 1965; Ide, et al., 1973-82; Homma, 1985).

The 'West', thus, had gradually moved. This geographical reconfiguration did not necessarily imply, however, that Europe lost its ontological priority; rather, Europe now seemed to encompass America as well. So, when Ōtsuka appealed to the 'West-as-model' for historical development, he defined it as 'Western Europe, above all England and the United States of America' (Ōtsuka, 1969c: 321).

I have attempted to show that the Japanese definition of 'Europe' was subject to constant reconfiguration and did not remain unchanged. Rather than constituting a neutral category of reference and orientation, it was always charged with ideology and meaning. Thus unstable and never fixed, Europe nevertheless remained the model to follow. Even after 1945, Japanese studies of *seiyōshi* continued to cast light on a historical development that was interpreted as Japan's future. At a historical moment when European hegemony was finally threatened on a global scale, 'Europe' (epitomizing the West) thus remained the sovereign subject that seemed to endow all history with meaning. The European past was always studied with this comparative perspective in mind. On a theoretical level, the European experience thus provided a historiographical yardstick that was used to measure Japan.

BIBLIOGRAPHY

Blussé, Leonard. 1979. 'Japanese Historiography and European Sources'. In *Reappraisals in Overseas History: Essays on Post-war Historiography about European Expansion*, edited by P. C. Emmer and H. L. Wesseling, Leiden University Press, 193-222.

Comité Japonais des Sciences Historiques. 1960. *Le Japon au XIe Congrès International des Sciences Historiques à Stockholm. L'etat actuel et les tendances des études historiques au Japon.* Tokyo.

Conrad, Sebastian. In press. 'World History, Japanese Style. Reading the Japanese Past Through a European Lense'. *Storia della Storiografia*, 27.

Dirlik, Arif. 1996. 'Chinese History and the Question of Orientalism'. *History and Theory*, 35(4): 96-118.

Duus, Peter. 1974. 'Whig History, Japanese Style. The Min'yūsha Historians and the Meiji Restoration'. *Journal of Asian Studies*, 33: 415-36.

Homma Nagayo. 1985. 'The Teaching of United States History in Japan'. In Lewis Hanke, ed., *Guide to the Study of United States History Outside the U.S., 1945-1980*, 3. New York, 18-33.

Ide Yoshimitsu, et al., eds. 1973-82. *Amerika kenkyū hōgo bunken mokuroku* [Bibliography of Japanese materials on American research]. 3 vols. Tokyo.

Ienaga Saburō. 1957. *Nihon no kindai shigaku* [Modern Japanese historiography]. Tokyo.

Iwai Tadakuma. 1963. 'Nihon kindai shigaku no keisei' [The establishment of modern Japanese historiography]. In *Iwanami kōza: Nihon rekishi, bekkan* [Iwanami's lectures on Japanese history, appendix], 1. Tokyo: Iwanami shōten, 59-102.

Jansen, Marius B. 1965. 'American Studies in Japan'. *American Historical Review*, 70: 413-7.

Japanese National Committee of Historical Sciences, ed. 1965. *Japan at the XIIth International Congress of Historical Sciences in Vienna*. Tokyo.

Kondo Kazuhiko. 1991. 'Ichinichi mo hayaku bummeikaika no kado ni hairashimen. Sengo shigaku to seikinha' [Let's open the door to civilization one day earlier. Postwar historiography and the *seikin* group]'. In *Eikoku o miru. Rekishi to shakai* [Looking at England. History and society], edited by Kusamitsu Toshio, et al. Tokyo, 269-98.

Koschmann, J. Victor. 1996. *Revolution and Subjectivity in Postwar Japan*. Chigaco.

——. 1995. 'Kiritsuteki kihan to shite no shihonshugi no seishin' [The capitalist spirit as disciplinary regime]. In Yamanouchi Yasushi, Victor J. Koschmann and Narita Ryūichi, eds, *Sōryokusen to gendaika* [Total mobilization during the war and modernization]. Tokyo: Kashiwashobō, 119-40.

Kuwabara Takeo, Takeuchi Yoshimi, Hani Gorō. 1962. 'Zadankai: Meiji ishin no imi' [The meaning of the Meiji Restoration. A Symposium]. *Chūō kōron*, February, 174-89.

Kuwabara Takeo. 1956. 'Meiji no saihyōka' [A reevaluation of the Meiji Restoration]. *Asahi shimbun*, 1 January.

——. 1983a. 'Japan and European Civilization'. In Kuwabara Takeo, *Japan and Western Civilization. Essays on Comparative Culture*. Tokyo, 115-54.

——. 1983b. 'Tradition versus Modernization'. In Kuwabara Takeo, *Japan and Western Civilization. Essays on Comparative Culture*. Tokyo, 39-64.

Martin, Bernd. 1995. *Japan and Germany in the Modern World*. Providence: Berghahn Books.

Matsuda Tomoo. 1948. *Kindai no shiteki kōzōron* [Studies on the historical structure of modernity]. Tokyo.

Matsumoto Akira. 1995. 'Sengo rekishigaku to "Otsuka shigaku"' [Postwar historiography and the "Ōtsuka school"]'. *Rekishi hyōron*, 542: 52-9.

Mehl, Margaret. 1998. *Historiography and the State in Nineteenth-Century Japan*. New York: St Martin's Press.

Numata Jirō. 1961. 'Shigeno Yasutsugu and the Modern Tokyo Tradition of Historical Writing'. In *Historians of China and Japan*, edited by W. G. Beasley and E. G. Pulleyblank. Oxford University Press.

Ochi Takeomi. 1954. 'Eikoku jinushisei no ichi kōsatsu' [Reflections on the system of landownership in England]. *Seiyō shigaku*, 24.

Ōkubo Toshiaki. 1988. *Nihon kindai shigaku no seiritsu* [The establishment of modern Japanese historiography]. In *Ōkubo Toshiaki rekishi chōsakushū*, [Collected works of Ōkubo Toshiaki], 7. Tokyo Yoshikawa kōbunkan.

Ōtsuka Hisao. 1944. Kindai Ōshū keizaishi josetsu [Economic history of modern Europe. An introduction]. In *Ōtsuka Hisao chōsakushū* [Collected works of Ōtsuka Hisao], 2. Tokyo: Iwanami shoten, 1-384.

——. 1947. *Kindai shihon shugi no keifu* [A genealogy of modern capitalism]. Tokyo.

——. 1952. *Shihonshugi no seiritsu* [The establishment of modern capitalism], *Shakai kagaku kōza* [Lectures in social sciences], 4. Tokyo.

——. 1960. 'Shogen. Wareware wa hōkensei kara shihonshugi e no idō katei o dono yō ni mondai to suru ka' [Preface: How to problematize the transitional phase from feudalism to capitalism?]. In Ōtsuka Hisao, Takahashi Kōhachirō, Matsuda Tomoo, eds. *Seiyō keizaishi kōza. Hōkensei kara shihonshugi e no ikō* [Lectures on the eonomic history of the West. The transition from feudalism to capitalism], 1. Tokyo, 1-44.

——. 1969a. 'Hompō ni okeru seiyō shihonshugi hattatsushi no kenkyū ni tsuite' [Japanese studies on the development of modern capitalism]. In *Ōtsuka Hisao chōsakushū* [Collected works of Ōtsuka Hisao], 4. Tokyo, 293-306.

——. 1969b. 'Jiyū to dokuritsu' [Freedom and autonomy]. In *Ōtsuka Hisao chōsakushū* [Collected works of Ōtsuka Hisao], 8. Tokyo, 176-86.

——. 1969c. 'Keizai saikenki ni okeru keizaishi no mondai' [Problems of economic history in an era of reconstruction]. In *Ōtsuka Hisao chōsakushū* [Collected works of Ōtsuka Hisao], 4. Tokyo, 321-6.

——. 1969d: 'Seisanryoku ni okeru tōyō to seiyō. Seiō hōken nōmin no tokushitsu' [Productive forces in East and West. The peculiarities of the peasantry in West-European feudalism]. In *Ōtsuka Hisao chōsakushū* [Collected works of Ōtsuka Hisao], 7. Tokyo, 246-58.

Ōtsuka Hisao, Takahashi Kōhachirō, Matsuda Tomoo, eds. 1960-62. *Seiyō keizaishi kōza. Hōkensei kara shihon shugi e no ikō* [Lecturer on the economic history of the West. The transition from feudalism to capitalism]. 5 vols. Tokyo.

Said, Edward W. 1979. *Orientalism: Western Conceptions of the Orient*. New York: Vintage.

Schwentker, Wolfgang. 1998. *Max Weber in Japan. Eine Untersuchung zur Wirkungsgeschichte 1905-1995* [Max Weber in Japan. A study on the reception of his work]. Tübingen Mohr Siebeck, 220-56.

Takahashi Kōhachirō. 1947. *Kindai shakai seiritsu shiron* [The establishment of modern society in historical perspective]. Tokyo Ochanomizu shobō.

——. 1950. *Shimin kakumei no kōzō* [The structure of the bourgeois revolution]. Tokyo Ochanomizu shobō.

——. 1960. 'Georges Lefebvre et les historians japonais' [Georges Lefebvre and the Japanese historians]. *Annales historiques de la revolution française*, January-March, 117-25.

Tōkyō daigaku hyakunenshi henshū iinkai, ed. 1987. *Tokyo daigaku hyakunenshi. Bukyokushi* [100-year history of Tokyo University: the history of its departments], 1. Tokyo.

Ueyama Shumpei. 1956. 'Meiji ishin ron no saikentō. Shisōshi kenkyū no kenchi kara' [Reappraisals of the theories on the Meiji Restoration. From the perspective of intellectual history]. *Shisō*, 390: 72-91.

Umesao Tadao. 1957. 'Bummei no seitai shikan josetsu' [Preliminary thoughts concerning a history of civilized forms of life]. *Chūō kōron* February, 32-49.

NOTES

1.   For the founding of the discipline, see Ienaga, 1957; Ōkubo, 1988; Mehl, 1998; Tōkyō daigaku hyakunenshi henshū iinkai, ed., 1987.
2.   Representative works of the Ōtsuka school include Matsuda, 1948; Takahashi, 1947, 1950; Ōtsuka, 1947, 1952; Ōtsuka, et al., 1960-62. For the history of the Ōtsuka school, see also Matsumoto, 1995; Schwentker, 1998:220-56.
3.   See also Ōtsuka Hisao, 1960: 1-44, 3-4. Okada Tomoyoshi summarized the problem-consciousness of the Ōtsuka-Takahashi group in the following way: 'They tried to clarify the classical pattern of the process of the formation of modern capitalism, or of the modernization of society, in the history of modern western Europe, in order to find out a criterion for research on the specific structure of Japanese capitalism. . . . In short, it was their main task to criticize modern Japan through the study of modern European history.' See Comité Japonais des Sciences Historiques, 1960: 428.
4.   English translation quoted from Koschmann, 1996: 160.
5.   According to figures compiled from the journal *Shirin*, 343 graduate theses were written in the field of Western history [*seiyōshi*] at Waseda University between 1952 and 1959, 144 theses were dedicated to the epoch of modern history, of which 79 dealt with American history.

6

Japanese Employers' Perceptions of European Labour Relations

JOHN CRUMP

After the Meiji Restoration of 1868, for many years Japan sought to learn from Europe and America in the field of industrial development. Japanese employers became avid students of Western know-how and practices, but their enthusiasm for industrial technology did not extend to labour relations as they developed in Europe and elsewhere. Japanese employers stressed Japan's uniqueness or peculiarity [*tokushusei*] which meant that the labour relations that were appropriate for European countries were not suited to Japan. Initially, there seem to have been two lines of thinking at work here in Japanese employers' heads. One was that Japan was different to the West in its social arrangements, culture and history, and that different labour relations were just one more aspect of this overall *distinctiveness*. The second train of thought emphasized *backwardness* more than distinctiveness since, according to this way of thinking, the Japanese approach to labour relations was a necessary compensation for Japan's technological disadvantages. Japan could not afford Western-style labour relations because, if the playing field were levelled in this way, Japanese companies would be outperformed and could not compete with their Western counterparts.

These rationalizations by Japanese employers of their rejection of Western-style labour relations during the early decades of Japan's modernization became deeply ingrained as ideology. As the decades passed, however, the line of thinking that proceeded from a consciousness of Japan's backwardness became increasingly uncomfortable for reasons that I shall explain. In order to compensate for this, the national distinctiveness argument came to be pushed ever more assiduously. To this end, even in the postwar period, Japanese employers have projected highly selective and self-serving images of Western-style labour relations in order to justify their own practices and in an attempt to convince their employees that the labour relations they experience are best suited to their national character as 'Japanese'.

This paper examines the unfolding image of European labour relations that Japanese employers have fostered over the years. It focuses on comparing *European* and Japanese labour relations, even though the main pole of comparison for most Japanese employers has been a vaguely defined notion of 'the West' [*ōbei*] which has encompassed America as much as Europe. America has been exluded from my investigation partly for reasons of time and space, but also because America has featured relatively prominently in the existing literature on the subject. Most previous studies have been by American scholars and for them, naturally, the main axis of comparison has been between the USA and Japan.[1] In order to redress the balance somewhat, I have chosen to focus on the Europe-Japan axis and I have done so by considering Japanese employers' perceptions of European labour relations in three distinct periods. These are: (i) the interwar years; (ii) the high growth era of the 1960s/1970s; and (iii) the recessionary decade of the 1990s. To represent employers' perceptions, I have taken as my principal sources documents associated with some of the major employers' federations of these periods, such as the Kanto Federation of Industrial Organizations [*Kantō sangyō dantai rengōkai*] and the Japan Federation of Employers' Organizations [*Nihon keieisha dantai renmei* or *Nikkeiren*] in the pre- and postwar eras respectively and the *Nihon kōgyō kurabu* (Japan Industrial Club) which has existed continuously since 1917. To those who might object that these federations have been dominated by major companies and that my chosen sources therefore over-represent this section of capitalist opinion, I would reply that this study is concerned with the collective ideology of the capitalist class, which is principally manufactured by precisely these major companies and their spokesmen. Having given an account of Japanese employers' perceptions of European labour relations at these various stages of Japan's capitalist development, I shall then try to draw some conclusions at the end of the paper.

When the Japan Industrial Club was formed in 1917, the spectre of European-style labour relations was invoked as a warning of what Japan had to avoid. In a speech delivered at the Club's formal launching on 10 March 1917, the Vice-President of the Privy Council, Kiyoura Keigo, asserted that:

> ... the problem on which the industrialists of Japan must concentrate their attention and research in the future is the problem of labour. There have already been clear manifestations of this problem in the various countries of Europe, and its beginnings have appeared in our country (quoted in Marshall, 1967: 80).

Although this implied that Japan was susceptible to the same contagion that was affecting Europe, Kiyoura was optimistic that the problem could be headed off by means of the 'mutual understanding' that supposedly all elements of Japanese society could achieve. Such views expressed the ideology which the Japan Industrial Club has promoted throughout its long existence. This attributes antagonistic labour relations not to universal features of capitalism, such as the fact that labour power is purchased as a commodity by the employers and used to pursue their own sectional interests, but to the cultural matrix from which societies other than Japan have emerged.

For example, in the volume which the Japan Industrial Club published in 1972 to mark its fiftieth anniversary, it was argued that:

> The European and American view of labour is that labour is human suffering and without value, so that wages are turned into compensation. Also, in Christianity, labour is punishment inflicted on man as atonement for original sin. Compared to that, the Japanese view of labour is entirely different: the human being feels labour to be what makes life worth living and labour becomes one type of happiness. In Buddhism, labour is service thankfully to repay benefit [*on*] in the light of the so-called four benefits [*on*] that humans receive. Ideas such as that it constitutes punishment do not arise (Nihon kōgyō kurabu, 1972: 641).

This alleged contrast between Western and Japanese concepts of labour was used by Japanese employers in the interwar years to justify their sustained opposition to the attempt by a section of the state bureaucracy to introduce union legislation. The employers' argument ran that union legislation was a Western device to solve labour problems that flowed from the antagonism that existed between labour and capital in Europe and North

America. Supposedly, it was inappropriate in Japan because workers and employers there, unlike the West, were partners in a common endeavour.

In 1919 the first International Labour Conference was held in Washington and the introduction of some basic protection for workers was on the agenda. The proposed reforms included the eight-hour day, unemployment prevention, a minimum working age and banning night-time employment of women and minors. The Japan Industrial Club prepared a paper on these issues and argued there that:

> ... since the industrial and labour situation in our country is different from that found in the advanced countries of Europe and America, we must give these measures sufficient thought. Since it is a unique [tokushu] country, Japan should be treated as an exception on various counts, in such a way that the foundations of our country's productive organization are not endangered (Nihon kōgyō kurabu, 1972: 140-1).

As can be seen, national distinctiveness was strongly invoked in the Japan Industrial Club's paper, but at the conference itself it was the backwardness argument that came to the fore in the context of a determined effort by the employers' and government's representatives to gain exemption for Japan from the proposed restrictions on work to eight hours per day and 48 hours per week. Both the employers' and the government's representatives portrayed Japan as being in a different league to the advanced countries and more on a par with India and China as far as the proposed restrictions on working hours were concerned. The labour representative argued the opposite, but was in the minority, so that Japan got its exemption (Nihon kōgyō kurabu, 1972: 140-1).

For reasons of backwardness as well as distinctiveness, the same contrast between Japanese and Western labour relations was frequently remarked on when the Japan Industrial Club sent a mission of prominent capitalists to the USA and Britain in 1921-2 (Morita, 1958: 73ff). This was a major commitment of both personnel and time, since 24 leading figures from important companies such as Mitsui, Mitsubishi and Sumitomo were away from their businesses for six months, conferring with their opposite numbers and discussing questions of mutual concern, among which labour problems were conspicuous. The reason why such a commitment was considered a sound investment has to lie in Japanese capital's self-perception of backwardness. If Japan had simply been 'distinctive', there would have been little point in journeying to the other side of the world in order to study how labour relations were handled differently there. Only if 'advanced' countries such as Britain and the USA offered 'backward' Japan a picture of its likely future could an extended study tour be seen as paying dividends. As we shall see, this perception of Japanese backwardness was certainly shared by the British capitalists with whom the delegation came in contact. They had no doubt, as they interacted with the Japanese, of the essentially teacher-pupil relationship that existed between the two countries.

The seriousness of the intention in 1921-2 to learn from the 'advanced' countries is also conveyed by the fact that when, a generation later, Morita Yoshio came to write his history of Japanese employers' organizations (published in 1958), the records of individual discussions were still carefully preserved. This enabled him to 'excerpt from the records the essential points of the speeches and discussions we held on the subject of labour problems so that we may hear the views of the authorities [*senkakusha*] of that time in Britain and the USA (Morita, 1958: 76). These records are valuable evidence of the patronising attitude which British capitalists took towards Japan. For example, the Japanese delegation visited the Manchester Chamber of Commerce on 9 January 1922 and was treated to a speech by Sir Edwin Stockton which was as patronising as it was complacent. Seemingly unaware that Lancashire's pre-eminence was under threat from Japan, Sir Edwin gave a highly self-satisfied account of the state of the industry he represented:

> For as long as we can remember, very good feelings have existed between labour and capital in the cotton-spinning environment of Lancashire. The deep mutual affection which manifested itself on the occasion of the recent slump in trade has, I believe, strengthened these feelings still further. We are proud of the high level of skill of the Lancashire spinning operatives. I believe that even to praise them as being the best weavers in the world is not to put it too highly. They possess a spinners' union which is the most steadfast in Britain, besides being the most cleverly led... (Morita, 1958: 85)

Turning to the Japanese side of things, Stockton lectured his audience on the theme that all classes within society deserve to be treated fairly, including the workers.

> I suppose that for Japan labour problems are comparatively new problems, but if so I believe that the Lancashire weavers' union would

be an object worthy of careful study by our distinguished guests. In Britain these days, it has become generally accepted that in industry a good union is an organ that we cannot do without. If there were a case where one class ignored [the interests of] other classes, that class could not prosper for long... (Morita, 1958: 85)

Similarly, when Minister of Labour MacNamara delivered a speech to the Japanese delegation on 24 January 1922, the Whitley Council was held up as a model for harmonising the interests of labour and capital. In the course of his presentation, the minister expressed the hope that the delegates would recommend a similar approach to labour relations when they returned to Japan (Morita, 1958: 86).

In these discussions between the representatives of Japanese and British capital, the former came across as far more authoritarian and far less accommodating than the latter. When the Japanese delegation visited Birmingham on 4 January 1922, T. Henry Wright, the secretary of the local Chamber of Commerce, gave a talk on agreements over wages, hours of work and working conditions and also on the merits and disadvantages of organs for mediating in labour disputes. Nakajima Kumakichi replied for the Japanese side and, while he conceded that the same labour problems as those outlined by Wright existed in Japan, he emphasized that the Japanese response was different. Nakajima explained that Japanese capitalists were resolutely opposed to group negotiations, the implication being that these would undermine the relationship between a particular employer and his workers. Furthermore, in the case of public utilities, they favoured compulsory arbitration (Morita, 1958: 84).

After the delegation's return to Japan, it issued a report on its principal conclusions, a large part of which was devoted to labour relations (Morita, 1958: 86-9). One section in particular, entitled 'The True Meaning of Labour-Capital Cooperation', showed the basically ambivalent reaction of these representatives of Japanese capital to the influences which had acted on them during their time abroad. On the one hand, the report echoed the platitudes which British capitalists had intoned in the passages where it averred that labour and capital must 'live together and help each other' and it even went so far as to suggest that Japanese employers should not seek to oppress labour unions. On the other hand, establishing a legal framework for unions to work within was clearly a leaf which the delegates still felt unable to take out of the British book. It was asserted that Japan should not simply mimic the laws of other countries, since the country's circumstances had to be taken fully into account (Morita, 1958: 89). This ambivalence can best be explained by the conflict that frequently existed between the twin trains of thought (one rooted in distinctiveness and one in backwardness) that co-existed within the collective consciousness of the Japanese capitalist class and, indeed, often even within the heads of individual capitalists.

What eventually resolved this conflict in favour of distinctive-ness in the pre-war period was that Japan's 'backwardness' became an argument that was increasingly used by foreign capitalist interests in the 1930s when they criticized alleged 'social dumping' practices. If Japanese capitalists had persisted in pleading for special treatment on the grounds that Japan's economy was still 'backward', as for example they had done at the 1919 International Labour Conference, they would have played into the hands of their Western critics, who attributed the low prices of Japanese goods on the world markets to corollaries of 'back-wardness', such as low wages. Hence, when the Kanto Federation of Industrial Organizations produced a paper on the 'social dumping' issue in 1934, it specifically denied that the competitive prices of Japanese goods were due to factors such as low wage levels. Rather, it attributed Japan's competitive advantage to 'conditions within our country' [*waga kuni jō*], 'the singularity [*tokuisei*] of industry and labour-capital relations,' 'the control [*tosei*] of capital and labour' and so on (Morita, 1958: 411).

Elaborating further on 'the special character [*tokushitsu*] of labour-capital relations' in Japan, the Kanto Federation of Industrial Organizations' paper argued:

> The Japanese are a nation which from ancient times has attached importance to human feelings [*giri ninjō*]. Ideas of rights and duties, which are based on individualism and have been transmitted along with modern European civilization, have not taken root to any great extent. This national character, which attaches greater importance to *giri ninjō* than to concepts of right and duty, develops into a spirit of familism and it is also a striking fact that it prevails within our industrial sector. The concept of labour as a commodity [*rōdōshōhinshugi*], which is based on the individualism found, for example, in Europe and America, is incompatible with Japan's national character (Morita, 1958: 417-8).

To this was added a note, which read in part:

> This type of national character would in the end appear as a special
> relationship of friendship and morality between labour and capital. This is
> the fundamental reason why the trade unionism associated with foreign
> countries cannot prevail in our industrial sector (Morita, 1958: 418).

This distillation of the national distinctiveness argument became
the hallmark of the period and, as time passed, it was delivered in
increasingly militarist language, as for example when in 1942 the
All-Japan Federation of Industrial Organizations [*Zenkoku sangyō
dantai remmei*] praised 'the industrial patriotic movement' and
retrospectively explained its purpose at the time of its formation
in 1931 as being to combat ideas that would 'disrupt the *kokutai*
and poison the *kokutai*' (Morita, 1958: 300, 305). These days,
statements such as those emanating from the Kanto Federation of
Industrial Organizations and the All-Japan Federation of
Industrial Organizations are commonly criticized because of
the extent to which they represented a capitulation to the
militarist state, revealed for example by the acceptance of state
control [*tosei*] of industry, by the sophistry over government
repression of labour unions, and by the invoking of the
authoritarian political system known as the *kokutai*. However,
while militarism was in the long run only a passing phase in
Japan's capitalist development, the fabrication of an ideology of
distinctiveness proved to be far more enduring because it could
be pressed into service again in the changed circumstances of the
postwar world.

PERCEPTIONS OF EUROPEAN LABOUR RELATIONS IN THE 1960S/1970S

In some respects, Japan changed enormously under the impact of
the reforms introduced during the occupation from 1945 to
1952. In the field of labour relations, the biggest changes were
the USA's fostering of a mass union movement and the provision
of a constitutional framework within which union activity was
legalized. Japanese capitalists had no alternative but to accept
these changes to labour relations, since it was the US which
dictated policy and, indeed, which for several years blocked the
formation of an employers' federation dedicated to handling
labour problems until Nikkeiren was eventually permitted to
organize in 1948.

Faced with this new situation, Japan's capitalists reacted in the
only way that was open to them, which was to incorporate the
effects of the occupation's reforms into the notion of Japanese

distinctiveness, which they still found useful to employ. Distinctiveness was thus redefined so that, far from any longer castigating labour unions as an alien presence which conflicted with the essence of Japaneseness, the employers henceforth identified the type of enterprise union which emerged during the occupation as one of the hallmarks of Japaneseness. In fact, the enterprise union (along with the seniority/merit wages system and lifetime employment) came to be seen as one of the so-called 'three sacred treasures' which allegedly characterize Japanese labour relations. For example, Nikkeiren was quite typical when, in seeking to distinguish Japanese labour relations from those found in Western countries, it constructed its argument on the basis of the 'three sacred treasures':

> The peculiar [*dokuji*] labour relations of our country, represented by the seniority and merit system, lifetime employment and enterprise unions, are not to be found in European and American societies, which are strongly characterized by individual-centredness and the pursuit of efficiency (Nikkeiren, 1981: 656).

As this re-evaluation of the merits of labour unions demonstrates, capitalist ideology is truly a plastic product and the role of selective amnesia in manufacturing it should not be underestimated. As an appendix to the volume *Nikkeiren sanjūnen shi* [The 30-year history of Nikkeiren], which Nikkeiren published in 1981 to mark, somewhat belatedly, its first thirty years, there is a transcript of a discussion meeting involving leading capitalists and influential Nikkeiren officials. In the course of this discussion, Sakurada Takeshi, who was Nikkeiren's Chairman at the time, recalled:

> About the beginning of the Shōwa era [mid-1920s] we went to Britain to take a look at things and we understood just how many strikes British unions engaged in. However long we waited, the machines that we ordered just weren't ready. Even if they were a year late, they weren't bothered, were they? And if we say why, it was because if you went along to a factory there were generally 14 or 15 unions, because there was one for each industry (Nikkeiren, 1981: 703).

Sakurada delivered this damning criticism of British industry in the course of extolling the virtues of the postwar Japanese system, which has generally consisted of a single union organization in each major company. What he conveniently overlooked was that, at the time to which he referred, Japanese employers were uniformly anti-union, irrespective of whether there was one union or many in an enterprise. As this example clearly shows, the content of the distinctiveness argument has, in some respects, changed almost beyond recognition, but the use of distinctiveness as an ideological device has remained constant.

What about the train of thinking rooted in the notion of *backwardness*? Obviously, the experiences of defeat, occupation and the accompanying severe economic disruption combined to revive feelings of backwardness within the collective psyche of the capitalist class and among the population generally. Although by the 1960s the Japanese economy was booming and the highest annual growth rates in the world were consistently being achieved, the conviction that 'backward' Japan had to catch up the 'advanced' countries of the West was widespread and deep rooted.

Throughout this decade and up till the 'oil shock' of 1973–4, the slogan 'Catch up with Europe and overtake Europe' was regularly used by the employers and the unions alike (Asazawa, 1991: 17). At this stage of Japan's development, the United States still seemed out of reach, but matching European standards was a target to which both the employers and the unions could relate. When in 1963 Sōhyō, the largest union federation of the period, set itself the goal of achieving European-level wages, 'Europe' became a political football that was kicked back and forth between the employers and the unions as they maneouvred for tactical advantage. Sōhyō argued that Japanese wage levels were unreasonably low because productivity levels had already reached European standards and in some industries had surpassed them. Labour's share of national income, which then stood at about 50% in Japan, was also pointedly compared with the situation in a number of European countries, since it was well over 60% in France and West Germany, and was more than 70% in Britain.

Nikkeiren countered Sōhyō's arguments with an alternative interpretation of the economic statistics. It conceded that in the early 1960s wages were lower in Japan than in West European countries. Taking the average American wage in manufacturing industries as representing 100 on a comparative scale, other countries scored as follows (Nikkeiren, 1981: 462):

Britain	31.1
West Germany	25.3
France	17.8
Italy	15.9
Japan	12.9

However, it employed a variety of arguments to back up its claim that comparative wage levels revealed only part of the story. Nikkeiren insisted that productivity in Japan was lower than in its major competitors and accused Sōhyō of generalizing from unrepresentatively high pockets of productivity in Japan. Another favourite argument of Nikkeiren was that the exchange rates on which comparative wage calculations depended were unrealistic. According to this interpretation, if more realistic exchange rates were employed, real wages in Japan were already close to Italian levels in general and had surpassed both the Italian and French levels in the case of large enterprises (Nikkeiren, 1981: 462-3). Hence, Nikkeiren's conclusion was that:

> ... it is not possible in the short term to raise wages alone to European levels, as the unions contend. What is necessary is to eliminate our country's dual structure and to raise the level of national income to European standards (Nikkeiren, 1981: 466).

For the purposes of this paper, it is not necessary to adjudicate in this controversy, but merely to point out the extent to which this facet of labour relations was premised on the assumption of Japan's 'backwardness' relative to Europe. It was against this background that in 1970 Nikkeiren despatched its first postwar mission to investigate conditions in Europe and America. The reasons given for this initiative were that:

> In the ten years from 1960 to 1970, the growth in the world economy was amazing. As a result, in the advanced countries of Europe and America, a rise in productivity was brought about by such factors as the rapid development of technical change and changes in the structure of production. The other face of this was that new social and economic problems were brought about. In other words, problems such as shortage of labour power, wage rises outstripping the rise in productivity, decline in the rate of profit, the rise in inflation, pollution and environmental degradation started to come sharply into focus. Also, mechanization and the division of labour advanced apace, brought about by technical change, and, accompanying the rise in living standards, changes were brought about in workers' values and their views on work. Regarding the way in which work was thought about [kinrō ishiki] too, new problems were thrown up. The necessity for an approach which addressed the human side of things, including such factors as the so-called 'reinstatement of joy in work' and 'humanizing work', was strongly emphasized in Europe and America (Nikkeiren, 1981: 687-8).

Clearly, Japan's assumed 'backwardness' induced Europe and America to be seen through rose-tinted spectacles here, but, be that as it may, from 1970 top-ranking delegations were despatched by Nikkeiren to observe labour relations in Europe and America in order to learn from them. Typically, these tours would take in government departments, employers' organizations, national union centres and representative large enterprises. Discussions with top officials were held in each country and inspection visits were regularly included in the itinerary. In 1970 the first mission visited Sweden, West Germany, France and Britain (in addition to the United States) and the issues it selected for investigation in each country included 'social and economic problems arising under full employment' (these ranged from 'shortage of labour' to 'problems connected with work motivation' [kinrō iyoku]), 'the current state of labour-management relations' and 'methods, organizations and systems for fixing wages on the basis of rises in productivity' (Nikkeiren, 1981: 690-1). In Sweden the Nikkeiren delegation was impressed by negotiations between the employers' federation and the union confederation aimed at agreeing how to handle developments in the national economy. Likewise, in Germany's case, the three-way discussions between government officials, union representatives and employers in order to arrive at cooperative action impressed the delegation, as also did the incorporation of unions into the management's decision-making processes in industries such as coal-mining and iron and steel production (Nikkeiren, 1981: 690).

In retrospect, when one assesses the conclusions which the Nikkeiren delegation drew from its 1970 study trip, two points stand out clearly. One is that distinctiveness was relatively played down at this juncture, so that the similarity of the problems jointly affecting labour relations in Europe and Japan was forcefully recognized:

> ... with regard to the rapid advance of inflation, labour relations being poised at a turning point, or social welfare and work motivation, we realized that there were commonly experienced troubles which our country shared (Nikkeiren, 1981: 692).

Second, the feeling of 'backwardness' relative to the countries visited remained strong, both with regard to the organization of production and the provision of social infrastructure. Hence, in order to overcome the problems mentioned in the quotation directly above:

> ... we acutely felt the need, first, to strive to improve the quality

[*taishitsu*] of our enterprises and raise the efficiency of management and, next, to strive as a country to build up a sufficient stock of social capital, [means of] preventing pollution, investment in housing and so forth (Nikkeiren, 1981: 692).

Whether one examines the issues selected for investigation or the conclusions drawn, the image which emerges is that in this period Europe was being used as a laboratory for problems which Japan's employers either regarded as commonly shared or sensed as impending and wished to avoid. Europe seems to have been considered more relevant than the United States at this time because European practices of intervention were seen as closer to Japanese norms than the laissez-faire conventions that predominated in America.

It is not necessary to examine subsequent Nikkeiren study tours in as much detail as the 1970 mission, since there was much that remained the same. However, certain changes can usefully be noted. One is that gradually the number of countries visited was whittled down to West Germany, Britain and the US. Of the European countries, Germany and Britain seem to have been favoured because, from a Japanese perspective, they often stood at opposite poles. There was much in the West German experience with which Japanese employers could identify, including both its strong economic performance and its tradition of corporatism, while, at the other end of the spectrum, the numerous symptoms of the apparently intractable 'British disease' were an unending source of fascination for Japan's capitalists. While the US provided technical know-how, the countries of Europe were seen as a much richer source of lessons (particularly negative ones when it came to Britain) on labour problems and how to avoid them.

Second, although only a few years intervened between the first Nikkeiren mission in 1970 and the fourth in 1976, there is a striking contrast between the relative mixes of backwardness and distinctiveness that infused the thinking of the two delegations. It has already been noted that the first mission was despatched in a spirit of learning from the 'advanced' countries, but one of the conclusions drawn from the 1976 mission was that, from Japan's perspective, not all these countries were as 'advanced' as had previously been assumed. Thus:

... even though one talks about leading countries as though they were all the same, a difference in terms of economic power has emerged between America, West Germany and Japan, on the one hand, and Britain, France and Italy, on the other; from the angle of general economic management, a division has occurred into two polar opposites (Nikkeiren, 1981: 698).

While Japan was lumped together with America and West Germany in this assessment, a sense of being different from both these countries, not to mention Britain, France, Italy and elsewhere, was demonstrably on the ascendant by the latter half of the 1970s. This seems to have been one of the unanticipated results of the repeated missions abroad. Originally conceived as learning exercises, the Nikkeiren delegations were flattered to realize that often the boot was on the other foot and that capitalists abroad, conscious of the growth rates achieved in Japan throughout the 1960s and early 1970s, wanted to know more about Japanese-style labour relations and the part they played in economic success. Feelings of 'backwardness' rapidly evaporated in a climate where foreign capitalists increasingly sought to learn from Japan. Hence, a sense of pride in the achievements of Japanese capital was as palpable following the return of the 1976 mission as was the assumption that Japanese labour relations were truly distinctive. By this stage Nikkeiren was suggesting that:

> ... enterprise unions, which have been established on our country's traditional social foundations that expect harmony between the individual and the community, should be newly evaluated; and that Japan's unique practices of labour relations should be established on their own unique foundations. Starting with the visit to Japan of an OECD investigative team at the end of 1975 to examine labour relations, overseas interest in Japan's labour relations has been increasing. Bearing in mind this current tendency, perhaps we can say that these suggestions of ours have hit the nail on the head (Nikkeiren, 1981: 699).

Thus the changing economic circumstances of Japan in the 1960s/1970s altered the lenses of distinctiveness and back-wardness through which Japanese employers had habitually perceived labour relations.

PERCEPTIONS OF EUROPEAN LABOUR RELATIONS IN THE 1990S

In the early 1990s Japan was gripped by the most severe economic downturn since the Second World War. In the period 1992-4 economic growth virtually disappeared (the annual average growth rate was 0.4%) and, although it recovered to 2.3% in 1995, it shows every sign of long remaining below the 4.2% average of the 1970s and 1980s, not to mention the 10.6%

average of the 1960s (*Nikkeiren Times*, 1 January 1997). Evidently, this has severely dented the confidence of Japan's capitalist class, but nevertheless the country remains an enormously powerful player in the world economy, so that any reversion to a notion of Japanese *backwardness* would be out of the question. On the contrary, it is a self-image of *distinctiveness* that has characterized the efforts of Japanese capitalists to find a way out of their current economic difficulties. One expression of this belief in distinctiveness was Nikkeiren Chairman Nemoto Jirō's rallying call at the start of 1997 to construct a 'new Japanese model' for the economy.

In the field of labour relations, the Japanese model is presented as a 'third way', distinct from the 'European model' and the 'American model' (although occasionally the boundaries are arbitrarily redrawn in such a way that these last two are repackaged as the 'German-French model' and the 'Anglo-Saxon model' respectively). The purpose behind the construction of these ideological 'models' is evidently to persuade Japanese employees that, in contrast to the ways in which companies treat their workforces in other parts of the world, they are in a favoured position and hence should identify their interests with those of the enterprises that employ them. To this end, the 'European model' of labour relations was presented in a *Nikkeiren Times* editorial, following the April 1996 Lille summit of leading industrial nations, as one which delivers wage rises and maintains social insurance benefits, but which can do so only at the cost of phenomenally high rates of unemployment (*Nikkeiren Times*, 11 April 1996). Such an approach has been characterized by Nikkeiren as overly inflexible and involving widespread pain for many people. If anything, the 'American model' is portrayed even more negatively, since the costs attributed to it are limited social insurance, declining real wages and high unemployment (*Nikkeiren Times*, 22 March and 11 April 1996). Hence, given the fact that Nikkeiren is now able to work with Rengō, a far more pliable union federation than such predecessors as Sōhyō, Chairman Nemoto announced in March 1996:

> Labour and management are seriously searching for a way for Japan not to fall into the Western [*ōbei*] syndromes, such as the German (low growth and high unemployment) or the American (high unemployment and wage cuts) (*Nikkeiren Times*, 22 March 1996).

In contrast to the 'European' and 'American' models which

Japanese capitalists have constructed as bogies to scare their workforces, the 'Japanese model' is projected as far more solicitous of employees' interests. In his speech to the 49th Conference of Nikkeiren in May 1997, Chairman Nemoto described it as a 'third way', on the grounds that, '... while it continues to pivot on the relations of deep trust between labour and management, which are specific to Japan, and I think should take note of the resolute way in which restrictions have been loosened in the Anglo-Saxon model, at the same time regards it as important that an outlook based on social justice should not be abandoned (*Nikkeiren Times*, 23 May 1997). This ideological construct is nebulous in the extreme, but its purpose is revealed when its principal benefit of supposedly restricting unemployment is presented as being causally linked to the readiness of unions to exercise joint control over wages with the employers. This message is given added punch by virtue of the fact that unemployment in Japan, although apparently low by international standards (due consideration should be given to the fact that the Japanese authorities' definition of unemployment is not directly comparable to that used in most Western countries), has nevertheless been steadily increasing. Standing at 2.16 millions or 3.2% of the workforce in 1995 (*Nikkeiren Times*, 1 January 1997), unemployment has become a persuasive reinforcer of the employers' implied threat that, unless the unions maintain their cooperation over the control of wages, the 'Japanese model' could conceivably metamorphose into the 'European model' or something worse.

CONCLUSIONS

Whether in Japan or elsewhere, capitalism is a divided society which pits against one another classes that stand in a different relationship to the means of production. Employers and employees are two such classes, by virtue of the fact that they are buyers and sellers of labour power respectively. Buying and selling of labour power, as with any other commodity, is a zero-sum game. A better deal for the seller hurts the buyer, and vice versa. Since there is no escape from this conflict, which is built into capitalism wherever it exists, one device for handling it is to divert attention by pointing to other divisions which supposedly outweigh it. Throughout the existence of capitalism in Japan, this has been a major reason why the employers have directed attention to labour relations outside the country and have used a variety of arguments, ranging from the assertion that they lack *giri ninjō* to that they constitute fundamentally different 'models'. To the extent that Japanese employees have fallen for this and have had their attention deflected by external bogies, they have lost sight of the conflict that is built into the labour relations they experience as 'Japanese'.

Another way of putting this first conclusion which can be drawn from the study of Japanese employers' perceptions of European labour relations is that, as elsewhere, the maintenance of capitalism in Japan has been as dependent on ideological mystification as it has on achieving profits. This leads to a second conclusion, which is that, because Japanese employers studied European labour relations for an ideological purpose, their perceptions were continually clouded by whatever their immediate interests dictated. To an extent, employers' perceptions of Japanese labour relations as backward or distinctive were rooted in Japan's objective economic circumstances, but only to an extent. Concepts of backwardness and distinctiveness also served the ideological purpose of the hour and were switched on and off accordingly. As we have shown, examples of this are the ideological arguments employed at the time of the International Labour Conference in 1919 and during the 'social dumping' controversy in the 1930s. Perhaps what these cases highlight is an additional conflict that is also built into capitalism. Not only do class divisions produce conficts of interests, but the ideological management of those divisions leads to conflict with objectivity and truth.

BIBLIOGRAPHY

Asazawa, Makoto. 1991. 'Shin jidai no jinji rōmu' [Labour relations in a new era], *Nikkeiren kōenshū* [Nikkeiren lectures], 14. Tokyo: Nikkeiren.
Garon, Sheldon M. 1984. 'The Imperial Bureaucracy and Labour Policy in Postwar Japan', *Journal of Asian Studies*, 43(3): 441-57.
Gordon, Andrew. 1988. *The Evolution of Labor Relations in Japan: Heavy Industry, 1853-1955* (Cambridge, Mass. and London: Council on East Asian Studies and Harvard University Press).
——. 1991. *Labour and Imperial Democracy in Prewar Japan.* Berkeley, Los Angeles: University of California Press.
Marshall, Byron K. 1967. *Capitalism and Nationalism in Prewar Japan: the Ideology of the Business Elite, 1868-1941.* Stanford, Calif.: Stanford University Press.
Morita, Yoshio. 1958. *Nihon keieisha dantai hatten shi* [History of the development of Japanese employers' organizations]. Tokyo: Nikkan rōdō tsūshinsha.
Nihon kōgyō kurabu. 1972. *Nihon kōgyō kurabu 50 nen shi* [The 50-year history of the Japan Industrial Club]. Tokyo: Nihon kōgyō kurabu.
Nikkeiren. 1981. *Nikkeiren sanjūnen shi* [The 30-year history of Nikkeiren]. Tokyo:

Nihon keieisha dantai remmei.

Nikkeiren Times. Tokyo: Nikkeiren.

Wray, William D., ed. 1989. *Managing Industrial Enterprise: Cases from Japan's Pre-war Experience.* Cambridge, Mass: Harvard University Press.

NOTES

1. See, for example, Marshall (1967), Garon (1984), Gordon (1988), Wray (1989) and Gordon (1991).

7

Japanese Interest in the Ottoman Empire

SELÇUK ESENBEL

The history of the Japanese interest in the Ottoman empire during the nineteenth century reflects the motives, ideas and strategies entailed in Japan's entrance into the world of Great Power politics. After the Meiji Restoration of 1868, the new Japanese government sought to establish relations with the Ottoman Porte and started sending various missions to the Ottoman region that had territories which spread over the Balkans and the Near East. This paper is based upon the travel accounts and reports of the Japanese visitors to the region. It focuses on the character of the Japanese interest in the Ottoman empire, a declining old world empire which was once a formidable power in the sixteenth century, but now increasingly threatened by the involvement of the Great Powers in its affairs which was known as the Eastern Question.[1]

In terms of political history, one can detect two distinct phases in the development of the Japanese interest in the Ottoman empire. The first phase is during the years between 1868 and the 1890s that covers Japan's quest for gaining her full rights of sovereignty through treaty revision with the West. This is the period when the Japanese authorities are interested in learning from the Ottoman example in order to help their treaty revision policy because it was a non-Western polity which like Japan faced the problems of the 'unequal treaty' privileges that were conceded to the major Western powers. The main agenda of the Japanese and the Ottomans is to negotiate a treaty of trade and diplomacy that was mutually acceptable.

The Japanese and Ottoman relations of this period clearly represent the inflexible boundaries of such treaty privileges as extraterritoriality and the most favoured nation clause etc. that functioned as the 'international law of Western imperialism'. Imposed by the Western powers upon the Japanese and other non-Westerners as the international terms of trade and diplomacy, these treaty arrangements made it almost impossible for third parties outside of the Great Power circle to have formal diplomatic relations.

The second phase can be recognized to be the period that starts with the last decades of the nineteenth century until the outbreak of the First World War. This is when Japan as an ally of Britain due to the Anglo-Japanese Alliance of 1902 and the Ottoman government as an ally of Germany fall into conflicting camps. The second period contrasts with the earlier one as it entails the process of Japan's adoption of the posturing and strategies of being an imperialist Great Power *vis-à-vis* the Ottomans and the Anglo-Japanese Alliance appears to be an important turning-point. The Japanese contacts in the Ottoman world especially during this latter phase provides a window that reveals the numerous circles in Japan who competed with each other for access to influence in the domestic and international arena of Japanese imperialism and the rising agenda of Asianism. At this stage, such strategies as collaboration against Russia, an Asian solidarity against the Western empires, Japanese leadership in the world of Islam are different objectives that motivate the Japanese authorities in forming contacts with this 'European' power which had Asian roots.

JAPANESE IMPRESSIONS OF THE OTTOMAN WORLD AS PART OF THE WORLD OF ISLAM

The Meiji Japanese view of the Ottoman world and the world of Islam stems from the same process as that of the contemporary Western Powers, linking intelligence and information-gathering activities with cultural studies where knowledge serves the interests of power. Consequently, the late nineteenth-century rapprochement between the Japanese and the Ottomans is reflected in the frequency of the Japanese visits to the empire for information and intelligence gathering purposes that is also commensurate with the heightened awareness of the Japanese authorities of an immanent conflict with Russia and the requirements of empire-building. One can detect that the Japanese concern over the Russian expansion in East Asia was coupled with an avid interest in the conditions of the Ottoman empire and Persia that might help the interests of Japan. This perspective was also in agreement with the main British imperialist strategy of the late nineteenth century of containing Russian expansion to the south particularly in the Ottoman empire and Persia.

The Yoshida mission of 1880 is the best known among the Japanese efforts to collect first-hand extensive information about the conditions of the Near East. The Japanese Foreign Ministry, Gaimushō, organized a mission in 1880 led by Yoshida Masaharu of the ministry accompanied by the manager of the Imperial Hotel, Yokoyama Nagaichirō, Captain Furukawa Nobuyoshi of the army, two assistants, Tsuchida Seijirō and Asada Iwatarō, and some merchants. Known later as the Yoshida mission, the group arrived in the Persian Gulf that year with the battleship *Hiei* that is said to have been sent as a show of force. The Japanese team embarked upon a difficult land trek to 'Bushire' Peshwar and – according to their later accounts – arrived in Teheran after a horrifying journey. After staying on in Teheran for twelve days, the mission went on to the Caucasus region and in 1881 entered the Ottoman capital. The Ottoman Porte welcomed the Yoshida mission. Sultan Abdulhamid II encouraged the beginning of negotiations to sign a treaty between the two countries. Thereupon, the Yoshida mission went on to Romania, Budapest and finally reached Vienna where the mission split. Yoshida went on to St Petersburg while Yokoyama and the merchants went on to London, and Furukawa went back home via Italy.[2]

A noteworthy visit is that of the famous intelligence officer Colonel Fukushima Yasumasa for the Japanese General Staff, who accomplished a 488-day arduous land journey between the years 1892-3 on horse back through Central Asia. A visit to the Ottoman empire in such intelligence-gathering journeys was part of the Japanese aim to investigate the Russian designs to expand her influence towards the south. Fukushima left Tokyo in 1895 again and went on a difficult journey through Africa, Turkey, Ceylon, and India. The following year, in 1896, he entered Iran and went into Central Asia, turned south to Arabia, arrived in India, passed on to Thailand, Vietnam, and finally returned to Japan in 1897 whereupon he submitted a detailed report.[3]

Another similar intelligence-gathering visit of the time is that of Ienaga Toyokichi who travelled in Iran, Turkey, and India during 1899 in order to investigate the conditions of opium production so as to prepare a report for the colonial administration in Taiwan. Ienaga arrived in Peshawar in the Persian Gulf, took the same route as that of Yoshida to arrive in Teheran, and after travelling through Iran, emerged in Baku and Batum near the Black Sea coast, whereupon he sailed to Istanbul. From Istanbul, Ienaga embarked upon a land journey, the first Japanese to travel by land into the hinterland of Anatolia, in order to investigate opium production. Finally, he passed on to Syria, and after crossing into Egypt, went on to India. In 1900, Ienaga returned to Taiwan whereupon he submitted his report to the colonial authorities.[4]

The Japanese missions resulted in the preparation of reports about the region that reflect the Meiji Japanese perspectives about the peoples of the Eurasian continent including the world of Islam. As a result, there are at least eight well-known Japanese studies of the Ottoman empire and its region for this period. The number is quite prolific in view of the minimal degree of relations between the two countries despite numerous attempts to pursue treaty negotiations on the part of the Japanese that will be discussed below. The relatively large number of studies in addition to the Gaimushō communications and research on the area reflect the Japanese government's concern over the treaty question in the empire and the questionable future of the Ottomans as the famous Eastern Question of European diplomacy; the question was of particular interest to Russia and Great Britain that would share the territories of the empire in the Balkans and the Near East as spoils.

Some of these studies are the memoirs and personal accounts of visits of a diplomatic nature. The Kan'yū nikki [The diary of travels around the globe] of Kuroda Kiyotaka, of fame for the Hokkaido Colonization Board scandal who was probably a cabinet adviser at the time later to be the president of the Privy Council in 1887, includes an extensive account of his visit from Russia to Istanbul on his way to Italy. An early work is written by a Nakai Hiroshi, who appears to have been on duty in the London embassy, and travelled back to Japan via Ottoman Turkey. Nakai wrote the Man'yū kitei, [The account of travels] which was published in 1877. The diary of Ōyama Takanosuke who was a commanding officer of the Meiji naval visit to Istanbul stands out. The diary titled Toruko kōkaiki [The account of a sea voyage to Turkey] published in 1891, constituted an account of the visit to the imperial palace for an audience with

Sultan Abdulhamid II (Kuroda, 1887 [1987]; Nakai, 1877; Ōyama, 1890 [1988]).

Others are major works of the intelligence-gathering visits as that of Colonel Fukushima that contains a section on the Ottomans as part of the larger journey through Asia and Europe. Some of the well-known ones are those of Furukawa Nobuyoshi, *Perushia kikō* [The account of travels in Persia] written for the General Staff Head Quarters, the *Sambō honbu* in 1891, and Ienaga Toyokichi's work on Anatolia and the opium question which was submitted to the Taiwan colonial administration, later published as the *Nishiajia ryōkōki* [The account of travels in West Asia] (Furukawa, 1891 [1988]; Ienaga, 1900 [1988]).

An important classified report is that of the Foreign Ministry, the Gaimushō, on conditions in Turkey, titled *Toruko jijō*, prepared in 1911 by the Okada embassy. The Gaimushō report gives a detailed study of the ethnic configuration of the empire, probably translated from English sources, and deals with the problems of nationalism and decline, reflecting the Eastern Question approach. One of the interesting sections is when the report deals with the question of Albanian loyalty to the empire, considered for a long time as a supporting ethnic element in Abdulhamid's ethnic policies against Balkan nationalist currents. In another section, the prospects for Japanese business interests in developing cotton production in Iraq are evaluated in the event of direct British take-over of the territory from Ottoman rule.[5]

The Meiji Japanese perspective about the Near East and the world of Islam was generally critical and negative, a by-product of the Euro-American-based modernist agenda of the Meiji generations with a Westernist vision. Many of especially the early reports on the region carry the early impressions of the Japanese of Near Eastern polities and the world of Islam. Such Meiji statesmen as Prime Minister Itō Hirobumi and Foreign Minister Inoue Kaoru, who were bent on making Japan a Western-style Great Power, saw Islam and its peoples via the filters of the missionary and imperialist vision of contemporary Westerners. For example, Inoue Kowashi, the minister of education known for his contribution to modern education and drafting the constitution, is also purported to have upheld a critical evaluation of Islam in his so-called *Mohamettoron* [Mohamme-danism], which was one of the earliest offical policy statements about Prophet Muhammad and Islam. In contrast to his vision of

99

contemporary Western life, Inoue Kowashi apparently argued that Islam was an uncivilized religion in some respects and had little to offer to the modernist aspirations of the Japanese.[6]

The well-known arguments of the Meiji liberal intellectual Fukuzawa Yukichi for *datsua* – that young Japan had to 'leave Asia and enter the West' – generally dictated a rejection of Asia as a source of contemporary civilization and forms the foundation of this Westernist Meiji perspective on the world of Islam and partially influences the Meiji attitude toward the Ottomans. In *Bummeiron no gairyaku* [An outline of a theory of civilization] (1875), Fukuzawa provides an evaluation of the Ottoman state that is a standard liberal Westernist one of the age: the Ottomans, once a mighty power that was the foe of Europe, belonged to the semi-enlightened category of Asian nations together with China in a three-tiered view of the world. Japan needs to avoid the prospect of remaining in the Ottoman and Chinese category and should join the ranks of the enlightened world as represented by the West.[7]

Not surprisingly, the Japanese diplomatic and commercial contacts with the Islamic world entailed the prejudices and assumptions of the Meiji Westernist perspective. Furthermore, the initial historic encounter of the Japanese with the Islamic world is important for it created some themes and images that have survived as the 'code' words of the mainstream Japanese attitude of general disdain for Islamic culture and peoples as not sufficiently modern. Using a naturalistic argument, a main theme associated with the Japanese impression of the world of Islam was one of an arid and dry climate and the desert-like geography of the area which is not suitable to the sensibilities of the Japanese people. Other code words entail the notion of Muslim politics as corrupt governments and Muslim officials and peoples as unfriendly. An important argument that has survived to this day is that the Muslims are not secular because they are very strict about living according to the rules of their religion: this also reflects their unmodern character.

In a 1981 study, postwar Japanese scholars of Islamic studies criticize these early accounts, especially the famous Yoshida Mission to Persia in 1880, for their tone of exasperation and despair at the inscrutable behavior of Muslim Orientals. The authors note in hindsight that the early visitors to Persia appear to have experienced a traumatic 'cultural shock' at the alien environment that apparently worsened with the unfriendly reception of the local officials who were not particularly overjoyed at the sudden barrage of Japanese visitors to their country. Here, the Yoshida mission report was typical of the early Meiji alienation from the world of Islam as it described the conditions of the journey from Persia as having an arid and desert-like land with an unfriendly population. The same study also argues that the Japanese perceptions of the Muslim Near East demonstrated a much more ignorant mind-set than even that of the Europeans. Orientalist training may have induced a superior attitude among Europeans towards Muslims, but they also generally carried a deep admiration for the monuments and the cultural heritage of Islam and Ancient Near Eastern civilizations. On the other hand, the Meiji Japanese who at this point lacked the language training and the rigorous study of the local culture in the Orientalist manner, were cruder and more negative. Here what is fascinating to read is that the Japanese were considering themselves as completely alien to the conditions of the region as they perceived their own environment as a self-styled modern identity with a Western character.[8]

TREATY NEGOTIATION PROBLEM

In hindsight, the history of the Japanese interest in the Ottoman empire is part of the game of Great-Power politics from the political angle while it also provided for Japan a window to the world of Islam. Ironically, it shows how 'unfree' were the terms of the international law that was imposed by the West upon the countries of Asia with different traditions. The Japanese interest in the Ottoman empire begins with the problem of treaty revision in order to eliminate the 'unequal treaty' character of the 1858 Treaty of Amity and Commerce. It had brought home the legal foundation of Western imperialism to Japan due to the recognition of privileges especially of extraterritoriality, mandatory tariffs, and the most favoured nation clause to the Western powers. Like Japan, the Ottomans had remained distinct in the nineteenth-century history of imperialism and colonialism for while they were party to the system of treaty privileges given to the Western powers they were not colonized and had managed to remain a sovereign power. Furthermore, the Ottomans had entered into a nineteenth-century 'unequal treaty system' that defined Asian and Western relations relatively earlier than China and Japan in East Asia. Ottoman capitulation to foreign countries that derived from an early mercantilist form of trade during the sixteenth century, had evolved into a web of treaty privileges enjoyed by the Great Powers that had begun to expose the Ottoman realm to the economic and commercial forces of 'free trade'. Particularly the 1838 Anglo-Ottoman Treaty of Trade is seen to have opened the gates of the Ottoman economy to the transformative influences of Western imperialism, a few years before the 1842 Treaty of Nanking in China and the 1858 treaties of Japan which represented the entrance of Western imperialism in East Asia.[9]

The contacts between Japan and the Ottomans began in 1871 with the Iwakura Mission to the capitals of the West which hoped to revise the 1858 treaties. During the mission's visit to Europe, one of its secretaries, Fukuchi Gen'ichirō, was instructed by Prince Iwakura to visit Istanbul and study the Ottoman conditions of the capitulationist treaties that were similar to Japan's predicament under the 'unequal treaties'. There are reports about the practice of the treaties in the Ottoman empire, particularly the jurisdiction of the consular courts in terms of extraterritoriality that was a special concern of the Japanese authorities.[10] The accounts of Japanese-Ottoman relations conclude that the Fukuchi report of 1871 was considered unsatisfactory in terms of providing information about the conditions of the empire. Furthermore, the Japanese appear to have been interested in developing closer relations with the empire in line with their international interests. Presumably, this was the reason why in 1875 Foreign Minister Terajima Munenori instructed Ueno Kagenori, the Japanese minister for Great Britain, to initiate contacts with the resident Turkish ambassador for investigating the conditions in that country and for negotiating the possibility of signing a Trade and Amity agreement between Japan and Ottoman Turkey (Naito, 1931: 15).

It was already apparent that a formal diplomatic and commercial treaty would not be easy to formulate due to problems that the international law imposed upon both countries by the West entailed for either side. Ironically, the regulations of the treaties that Japan and Ottoman Turkey signed *vis-à-vis* the Great Powers in terms of extraterritoriality, mandatory tariffs and most favoured nation clause were supposed to enhance the globalization of trade and commerce in the name of 'free trade' between Asian countries and the Western powers albeit under 'unequal conditions' with the West. Now, the same regulations made it very difficult for the two interested parties to establish relations of mutual reciprocity.

Terajima's letter to Ueno indicates an awareness of the problem that will plague Japanese-Turkish relations into the twentieth century. Rather than a formal treaty Ueno formulated an alternative in colourful diplomatic language as:

> Turkey resembles our country in many respects (its mountains and rocks), if we dispatch an envoy or an observer to this country we may derive many advantages... With this in mind and although we do not yet have commercial relations with Turkey I would like you to approach the Turkish ambasador in London very discreetly in order to enact an agreement of friendship between our two countries (Naito, 1931: 15).

In addition to trade and commercial concerns, political motives also emerge as a factor in sustaining Japanese interest in the Ottoman empire. This was to be the strengthening of a regional line of containment against the threat of Russia, a policy encouraged by Great Britain in her concern about protecting the British empire, especially India. Despite the lingering treaty problem, Great Britain, Japan, and Ottoman Turkey appear to have shared the common concern for containing Russia that formed an incentive for forming closer relations. This was a strategy that was encouraged by Great Britain for whom the Ottomans, though weak, had remained to be important as a regional power against Russia since the 1854 Crimean War. Britain which was soon to see Japan as a rising new Asian power which would act as a bulwark against Russia with the Anglo-Japanese Alliance of 1902, appears to have encouraged contacts between Japan and Ottoman Turkey at all levels. The Ottoman government, for its part, expressed continued interest in developing relations with Japan particularly during the reign of the conservative modernist Sultan Abdulhamid II while sharing the general agenda of collaborating against Russia with a new concern for forming contacts with this successful modernizing power of the East.

When the *realpolitik* interest against Russia prevailed, already in 1876, certain British politicians approached the Turkish Grand Vizier Mithat Pasha, suggesting that the Ottomans establish close relations with Japan. In 1878 the Japanese battleship *Seiki* with naval cadets on board paid a twelve-day visit to Istanbul and was received with the due ceremonies (Takahashi, 1982: 128; Naito, 1931: 15; Naito, et al., 1942: 328-9; Matsutani, 1986: 19; Okazaki, et al., 1981: 169-70).

However, the official contacts between Japan and Ottoman Turkey continued to be plagued along the question of signing a treaty of trade and commerce with the Japanese side intent on learning about the existing treaty privileges in the Ottoman empire that they would also want to have. On the other hand, the Ottoman stance was to avoid at all costs any agreement that would reinforce the undesired practices of the existing capitulationist regime in trade which the Porte wanted to gradually abolish in the future. The negotiations continued in St Petersburg between the Ottoman ambassador, Sakir Pasha, and the Japanese ambassador, Yanagihara Sakimitsu. Yanagihara submitted a detailed questionnaire to Sakir Pasha on the judiciary, the legislative, administrative, and commercial systems of the empire, in particular to the application of the most favoured nation clause. A concern of the Japanese questionnaire was to find out about the practice of court litigation against foreigners and whether there were mixed courts of law. Both were issues which were hotly debated in Japan and in the treaty-revision negotiations of Japan with the Great Powers.[11]

Sakir Pasha's answers explained the official legal situation in the empire with the new legal reforms and the end to the most favoured nation clause due to the Treaty of Paris in 1856 after the Crimean War. Making use of their brief popularity with the West as the 'Grand ol' Turk' in the struggle of Britain against Russia, the Ottomans had managed to gain a foothold in the Ottoman aim for treaty revision, as the empire, for centuries a Turkish Muslim empire with a multi-ethnic population that had been the traditional foe of Europe, now was recognized as a 'European power with independence and integrity'. Most crucial, the Ottoman government was exempt from abiding by the most favoured nation clause in future treaty agreements with new countries, but it had to keep the existing treaty privileges with the major powers.

However, the memoires of Sait Pasha, the grand vizier of the time, reveals the existing state of affairs concerning the Japanese desire for a most favoured nation clause. In 1881, Sait Pasha notes in a frank manner the problems that the Ottomans faced with respect to the existing treaty practices. In his words, even though the Ottoman legal reforms of the nineteenth century had established a new framework with the adoption of European codes for commercial and administrative purposes which ensured mutual reciprocity and equality on principle, the *realpolitik* of great-power influence had continued to foster '... the unfortunate traditions in Turkey of the bad habit of resorting to Consular Courts for the litigations involving foreigners which was the accepted institutional rule'. Hence Sait Pasha concluded that although it was unacceptable, still it was understandable that Japan would want the same privileges as those accorded to the Great Powers in practice. Ultimately, he firmly declined the prospects for signing a treaty with Japan based upon the same argument as the above that conceding treaty-power privileges to Japan would injure the Ottoman government's partial liberation which had been gained with the 1856 Treaty of Paris from the treaty privileges (Sait, 1910: 37; Arik, 1989: 25; Naito, 1931: 31-5).

JAPAN AS AN ALLY OF GREAT BRITAIN

By the end of the nineteenth century, the anti-Russian agenda which had initially warmed relations between Britain, the Ottomans and the Japanese, began to exhibit a conflictual character due to the growing antagonism between Britain and the Ottoman Porte, over the emergence of British imperialist behaviour in the Balkans and the Near East that was considered to undermine Ottoman interests as the old ruler of the area. The antagonism also entailed a stronger ideological turn in a short period of time. On the Ottoman side, Sultan Abdulhamid II, gradually developed a pan-Islamist foreign policy in order to counter the standard argument of the Great Powers that justified their interference in the 'domestic' ethnic and religious problems of the empire by claiming the protection of its Christian subjects. Initially a measure with which to counterbalance the Russian hold over large populations of Turk Muslims, the Porte had begun to use the pan-Islamist twist to Ottoman foreign policy also against Britain with whom relations cooled off toward the end of the century. The real shock which troubled Ottoman-British relations had come in 1881 when Britain occupied Egypt, nominally a troublesome Ottoman territory that had already become effectively independent with the Muhammad Ali revolt in the early nineteenth century which had forced the Ottomans to seek British help in the first place. In the meantime, the institution of the British Raj in India with a large Muslim population, the systematic extension of British influence in the Arab world became serious problems as far as the Porte was concerned. By the twentieth century, British imperialist expansion in the Arab world was to erupt into a conflict between the two powers during the First World War of 1914 that was to lead to the British role behind the Arab revolt and the British Mandates over the former Arab territories with the dismemberment of the Ottoman empire at the end of the war (Zürcher, 1993: 85-6).

Officially, Japan was firmly in the camp of Great Britain in so far as world politics was concerned. Especially, after Japan's victory in the Sino-Japanese War, Britain and Japan became closer in terms of collaboration in the protection of their mutual interests. It is crucial to note that British leadership in the acceptance of treaty revision with Japan enabled her to abolish the 'unequal treaty privileges' by the end of the nineteenth century, before any other non-Western power. The pro-British stance of the Meiji officialdom continued to prevail in the nineteenth century. It had been formalized with the Anglo-Japanese Alliance of 1902.

The crux of the matter was that while Japan had become Britain's staunch ally in protecting mutual imperial interests in Asia, the Ottomans were dropping out of the British strategy to protect India from Russia. On their part the Ottomans were also not keen on reinforcing the existing practices of the treaty privileges for the sake of Japanese friendship. Feeling threatened by the British imperialist strategy in the Near East, the Ottoman diplomatic line was already collared with a more neutral stance *vis-à-vis* Britain that would not find strong support among the Meiji leadership of the day.

The above account of the main events that concern the political history of Japanese Ottoman relations is a good example with which to see the nature of the Meiji perspective on the world of Islam that was modified in the Ottoman case. Some of the above early impressions of the Japanese towards the Islamic world most likely infiltrated into the formulation of the 'cool' side to the Meiji foreign ministry towards the Ottomans insisting upon the concession of Great-Power privileges despite the official 'warm' diplomatic language of friendship. Naito Chishū, the best pre-war Turkish historian of Japan, attributes the insistance of the Gaimushō for treaty privileges, which resulted in the failure to establish relations between the two countries, to the *datsua* perspective of the Meiji élite. Inoue Kaoru who was the foreign minister at the time was not too keen on according an equal status to an 'Asian power' at the Ottoman empire that would undermine the treaty revision negotiations of Japan. Whether the *Bummeiron no gairyoku* or the *Mohamettoron* perspective cited above is responsible for the insistence of the Japanese authorities on getting Great-Power privileges from the Ottoman empire or not is hard to prove, but the critical rhetoric about 'superficial Westernism' will be important from now on in the evolution of the Japanese interest in the Ottoman and Islamic world.

THE *ERTUGRUL* NAVAL DISASTER: THE FIRST OTTOMAN VISIT TO JAPAN

While the treaty problem remained unsolved, the documents of the Japanese and Ottoman relations of the nineteenth century begin to exhibit a dual language of the early Meiji Westernist attitude that co-exists in time with a diplomatic language which exhibits the evolution of an Asianist Japanese identity. By the late decades of the nineteenth century, one can detect in the Japanese accounts of the Ottoman empire and the Turks in particular a formal language of warm friendship and solidarity among these two Asian powers that is used by both sides as the rhetoric for forming relations. This official rhetoric contrasts with the private language of cool *realpolitik* that is particularly apparent in the in house reports of both the Japanese Gaimushō as well as in the Ottoman Porte's evaluation of Japanese interest in the Ottoman empire.

The increase in meaningful contacts and relations between the Ottomans and the Japanese was to occur again in a decade after the treaty impasse in the 1880s, when the Asianist tendencies of Japanese foreign policy and the pan-Islamist overturns of Sultan Abdulhamid's foreign policy helped rekindle the interest of the two powers in each other and in a process giving birth to the development of the friendly official rhetoric of common Asian roots and martial camaraderie among the Turks and the Japanese befitting the political trends of the times.

The event which has had most influence in the construction of the amicable rhetoric of goodwill in Japanese-Turkish relations is the well-known calamity of the Ottoman imperial frigate, the *Ertugrul*, which sank along Japanese shores in 1890 after an arduous journey to pay a 'goodwill visit of friendship' (not an official diplomatic one obviously) to the emperor of Japan. After the treaty problem, the next important contact between the two countries was the visit of Prince Komatsu, the brother of Emperor Meiji and Princess Komatsu in 1886 during their trip to Europe. The royal couple arrived in Istanbul in the fall of 1887 and the occasion appears to have revived the desire to pursue closer relations (Naito, 1931: 36; Arık, 1989: 26).

Using the visit of the prince as an occasion to rekindle relations with Japan, Abdulhamid II launched a second attempt to form close relations with Meiji Japan, by now seen as the rising new star of the East in Ottoman public opinion. The government decided to send the imperial frigate *Ertugrul* with Commander Osman Pasha and his crew of 609 men to Japan. Osman Pasha was empowered to represent the sultan and delegated with extraordinary powers. The ship and her crew sailed out in March 1889 with the objective of paying a goodwill visit to the emperor of Japan in return for the visit in 1887 of Prince Komatsu. The voyage turned out to be a hazardous journey with recurring technical problems and mishaps. This was in part due to the fragility of the ship which was an old-fashioned wooden vessel and considered unfit for the journey by the British engineer who was a technical aid to the Ottoman navy. In hindsight the Turkish public opinion has also interpreted the disastrous journey as a typical reflection of the pathos of the last-ditch efforts of the Ottomans for a show of force. After sailing in Asian waters for more than a year which was full of various mishaps and difficulties, the *Ertugrul* arrived in Japan in June 1890. Osman Pasha and his crew managed to complete a successful visit with the authorities and the imperial family. On the return voyage, however, the Ottoman frigate, which had set out in September, sank on the eighteenth day due to a severe typhoon. She foundered on the dangerous sharp rocks off the coast of Wakayama in southwest Japan. Except for a mere 69 survivors, the waves of the Pacific Ocean claimed the pasha and his men. According to the official narratives of the tragedy, deeply saddened by the tragic event, the Japanese government sent the few survivors back to Istanbul with the Japanese frigates, the *Hiei* and the *Kongo*, together with the condolences of the Meiji emperor and the Japanese government. The Japanese visit which set out in October was to arrive in Istanbul on 2 January 1891 with Ōyama Takanosuke as the commander. The visit was to also bring Yamada Torajirō, who was going to be the first resident merchant, unofficial emissary of Japan in Istanbul for the next twenty years (Komatsu, 1992: 1-16; Mütercimler, 1993; Naito, 1931: 110-81).

The disastrous Ottoman voyage had had sober political ambitions, however, which reflected the ideological turn to pan-

Islam in recent years. Lately, Abdulhamid II had begun to use his title as the caliph of orthodox Islam (the Sunni sect) to advance a foreign policy of being strongly concerned with the welfare of the Muslim subjects of the Asian empires of the Western powers. Using his role as the caliph now as a foreign policy measure against the Great Powers, Abdulhamid had sent the *Ertugrul* mission to Japan in part to advance the pan-Islamist foreign policy of being strongly 'concerned' with the welfare of the Muslim subjects of the Asian empires of the West. The commander of the *Ertugrul* frigate, Osman Pasha, took the opportunity to meet with Muslim notables in each port of the British and French colonies in Bombay, Singapore, Saigon, and Hong Kong. Local Muslim papers gave major coverage that the ship of the caliph arrived in town and the crew of the Ottoman navy attended prayers with the local Muslim communities. On the other hand, the occasion proved to be a fruitful opportunity for the sultan for tailoring domestic opinion back home in his favour. During the voyage, the Ottoman papers of Istanbul reported at length about the path-breaking journey that spread the caliph's message to the Muslims of the world although it must be admitted that the London press had ignored this aspect in favour of the technical mishaps to the annoyance of the sultan.[12] In conclusion, while Japanese and Ottoman relations were encouraged in the context of the Anglo-Japanese Alliance by Great Britain, the Ottomans were sending a 'green light' to Japan as an ally in the world of Islam. So far as the Meiji authorities were concerned at the moment, however, the Japanese empire's interests were defined firmly in the terms of Great-Power politics with Britain, against Russia.

THE JAPANESE ASIANIST ROMANTICISM ABOUT THE TURKS

The account of the *Ertugrul* calamity written in Japanese by those who were involved in the aftermath such as Ōyama Takanosuke, the commander of the Japanese frigates that brought back the survivors, and Yamada Torajirō, the pioneer of Japanese-Turkish relations who settled in Istanbul, defines Japanese interest in the Ottoman empire and the Turks in terms of a new sense of Asian camaraderie, sharing a noble martial heritage. The most important visitor to the Ottoman realm in terms of establishing long-term personal contacts of more depth than previous brief contacts is Yamada Torajirō (1866-1957) the pioneer of Turkish-Japanese relations, and probably the first Japanese expert in Ottoman Turkish and culture. A young man of 23, Yamada arrived in Istanbul in 1892, one year after the Japanese frigates brought the *Ertugrul* survivors back home. He was sent on an official mission that was encouraged by the new foreign minister of Japan, Aoki Shūzō, who wanted to revive Japanese contacts with the Ottomans. Yamada was quickly accepted by the Ottoman Porte as the unofficial conduit for conducting relations between Ottoman Turkey and Japan. During the following decades he was to become the sole agent for trade with the Ottoman empire and acted as an unofficial consulate-general for Japanese visitors taking advantage of his congenial relations with the palace and the Ottoman élite circles who seem to have developed a liking for this young Japanese (for the details on Yamada and Turkish experience, see Esenbel, 1996).

While the *Ertugrul* affair was the subject of deep emotional bonding in official relations, during the years after 1891 the Japanese side still reattempted to negotiate a treaty of trade and commerce, and Yamada was to become the subject of some controversy as the Japanese authorities tried to use him as an example to push for the recognition of extraterritoriality and other privileges to Japan on par with the Great Powers. But the attempt floundered as the Ottomans were again to curtly refuse the issue. In a language that is a perfect example of 'oriental' inscrutibility at its best, the Ottomans explained that they were extending the benevolent 'protection' of the palace to Monsieur Yamada who was a good friend of the Turks and therefore did not need treaty privileges.[13]

It is clear that as the controversy over the treaty issue between Japan and the Ottoman Turkey died down, Yamada continued his career in Istanbul with the approval of the local authorities. He became an important conduit between the two governments during the Russo-Japanese War of 1904-05 and was free to fulfill a mission for the Japanese ambassador Makino in Vienna by reporting on the passage of the Russian Black Sea Fleet from the Bosphorus to join the battle in the Far East. He was to remain in the capital for almost twenty years and be witness to the history of the Hamidian era of conservative modernism and the subsequent dramatic transition to the constitutionalism of the 1908 Young Turk Revolution (Esenbel, 1996: 242). Yamada's account of his impressions of Istanbul and the inhabitants of this old world empire constitute a rich example of the new, friendly and admiring Japanese attitude towards the Ottomans that represents a romantic Japanese form of the 'friendly' version of an Orientalist perception of the Turks and their empire.

Yamada's friend, a Mr Sakitani who wrote the introduction, discusses the *realpolitik* character of the empire in a mode that exhibits the new Asianist emotions of Meiji Japan at the turn of the century. In contrast with the strategic reports of the Gaimushō, this account is imbued with the need to pay attention to the Turks because they represent an Asian power – more supportive in tone to the earlier Westernist arguments about the Ottomans because they had Asian roots. The Turks are a martial people who share a warrior tradition with the Japanese and they are important for their realm in Europe represents the extension of Asian power to the West. The new nationalist athmosphere of the Young Turk Constitutional Revolution of 1908 is a new element that is seen as reflective of the Turkish inspiration being drawn from the Meiji élan vital – an Asianist argument that advocated the Meiji Restoration as a revolutionary model for Asia (Esenbel, 1996: 247).

The best acknowledgement of this tug-of-war in hypothetical terms between the formal language of warm friendship that is constructed with the *Ertugrul* disaster between the Japanese and the Ottoman Turks and the language of great-power politics is illustrated in the text of the Gaimushō report prepared much later, in 1923, on a summary of the past history of Japanese-Ottoman relations that has been narrated so far.[14]

The report was prepared at a time when no formal relations existed between Japan and Turkey (these were to take place in 1925) following the Lausanne Treaty which abolished the capitulation and established treaty relations of mutual reciprocity and equality between the West and the young Republic of Turkey undergoing the Kemalist revolution. The analysis explains very well the previous problems of treaty revision between the Japanese and the Ottomans. The tone is curt with no recourse to the language of warm frienship and camaraderie due to common Asian roots that would be expressed in formal communiqués or in such private accounts as that of Yamada. It is a typical diplomatic in-house discussion that interprets the problems of the relations from the perspective of Japanese interest. There is a comment which reveals the extent to which this interest was defined in Japanese terms in the section on the history of the Ottoman-Japanese relations during the Russo-Japanese War of 1904-05. One would assume that since

111

Yamada's activities of local intelligence were allowed by the authorities in Istanbul, presumably this would have been interpreted as an act of a warm and friendly nature. Yet, the report concludes with a cool appraisal about Ottoman diplomatic policy towards Japan during the Russo-Japanese War as a policy of neutrality tinging on the unfriendly. The problem from the Japanese point of view was that the Ottoman authorities 'had not' allowed the Japanese to have a free hand in pursuing their activities of intelligence and propaganda within the territories of the empire. According to the report, this restrictive policy on part of the Ottomans was due to the diplomacy of neutrality during the conflict between Russia and Japan, carefully practised by the Sultan Abdulhamid (although he had sent the *Ertugrul* to Japan, during the war he practised a balance of power policy between Britain and Russia that entailed a shift to a line of neutrality which would not antagonize Russia). The report comments that this policy of neutrality was tinged with a pro-Russian slant due to the influence of the 'Russian clique', the *shinroha*, in the government.[15]

As far as the Gaimushō view of the late Ottoman history of Japanese-Turkish relations was concerned, the whole experience was one of failure because the Ottomans refused to concede treaty privileges to Japan, restricted Japanese intelligence activities, acted in a pro-Russian fashion during the Russo-Japanese War. The rhetoric of mutual admiration, the Turkish public's celebration of the rise of Japan as the star of the East, Asian camaraderie, the *Ertugrul* tragedy, are all absent from the analysis.

JAPAN AS THE SAVIOUR OF ISLAM

The history of the failure of Japanese and Ottoman formal relations remains as an instructive example of the Meiji government's Gaimushō perspective on the Ottomans. However, on the eve of the Russo-Japanese War and right after the dramatic Japanese victory that is acclaimed with enthusiasm in the anti-imperialist public opinion of Europe and Asia, one notices the formation of regular contacts between the Japanese and the Ottomans, outside of the top official circles, that is of an ideological nature aimed at a common anti-Western/imperialist agenda. The agents of these contacts are the Asianist expansionists in Japan, particularly linked to the *Kokuryūkai*, the Amur River Society, mostly known as the Black Dragons, and militant nationalists, activists among the Muslims in Russia, the Ottoman empire, and other countries particularly in Asia. The agenda of these contacts is the potential of activist Muslims to form 'the pro-Japanese network in the world of Islam'.

Ian Nish has noted that the charged athmosphere of Asianism and the demand for Japan's natural destiny as a new Asian empire fuelled the creation of new right-wing groupings whose adherents constituted a rival strata to the Meiji élite in power, with anti-Western views that justified the formation of an Asian empire which went hand-in-hand with the rising militant line against Russia (Nish, 1985: 95-6, 118, 153-4). In the context of the Asianism and Japanese imperialism at the turn of the century, the Japanese start to treat the Ottoman connection as part of a larger game plan to recruit like-minded friends and collaborators from Muslims to help the cause of the Japanese empire. No longer simply seen as a good environment of collaboration for reasons of obvious enmity shared against Russia as a traditional rival, the Ottoman world is now hoped to be 'used' by the Japanese authorities as sort of spring-board for making Japanese contacts with the politically engaged Muslims of Russia, Egypt, and Arabia who can be conveniently contacted through Istanbul, one of the main centres for intellectual and political activity of Muslims, to aid the interests of the Japanese empire.

From the numerous accounts of the Japanese activities among the Muslims which begins on the eve of the Russo-Japanese War, one gains the impression that the Japanese authorities were interested in forming pro-Japanese lobbies primarily from the activist political circles among the Muslims in Russia who were already in an ideological and nationalist opposition against the autocratic and pan-Slav tsarist regime. Sometimes, as in the case of Chinese Muslims, the Japanese strategic argument was that Muslims who were treated as marginal in a primarily non-Muslim environment had the potential to be sympathetic to the Japanese as a type of 'fifth column'. Soon there was also the view that Muslims in the Dutch Indies and British India who suffered under Western Christian rule would naturally be good candidates for collaborating with Japanese interests.[16]

The activities of colonel Akashi Motojirō, the military attaché of Japan in St Petersburg, who was the famous mastermind of Japanese intelligence and espionage in Europe, and his predecessor Tanaka Giichi of army intelligence, already trained as an expert on Russia and China, are a turning point in forming the Japanese network among Muslims just before the Russo-Japanese War. Akashi and Tanaka supported the anti-tsarist activities of Russian Muslims as part of their major strategy to fuel the revolutionary ardour in Russia. The Japanese strategy was to aid the opposition activities of such dissaffected groups as the anti-Russian Polish and Finnish nationalists, the Russian revolutionaries and the Cadet Party. The Russian Muslims, primarily of Turkish stock, were also on the stage as one of the opposition groups chafing under the strong-handed authoritar-ianism of the tsarist regime especially its recent pan-Slav policies. While Akashi comments in his memoirs, *Ryakka ryūsui*, that he still has not studied their situation in detail and that the Russian Tartars and the Muslims were at this point not good candidates for helping the aims of Japanese as they lacked a strong organization; still, circumstantial evidence indicates that he did support the political leaders of the Muslims in their propaganda activity and the organization of the All Russia Muslim Congress of 1905 which is considered to be a milestone in the emergence of nationalism among the Russian Muslims.[17]

The importance of the Japanese intelligence networking among militant Muslims at this time is that it will form the foundation for the activities of the Japanese authorities which will become more Asianist in its imperialism and militant in its expansionism after the First World War down the road to the Second World War. Accounts of Japanese intelligence activities in the Islamic world point to the early connection between Russia Muslims of Turkish origin during the terms of Akashi and Tanaka, who constitute a small core-group of pro-Japanese activists that, in later years, aid Japanese contacts and propaganda networks in the Muslim world.

In this context, from the Asianist imperialist point of view of intelligence activities around the turn of the century, now the Ottoman empire serves as as stage for the recruitmment of activist Muslims from Russia and the Near East for the Japanese cause. The life of Abdürresid Ibrahim (1854-1944) a Russian Tartar, a religious cleric (*imam*) and judge (*kadi*) well-known for his pan-Islamist and reformist ideas as a journalist and political activist, is a very meaningful example of these early contacts via Istanbul and St Petersburg during the Russo-Japanese War. Such contacts will mature into a wide network of Japanese intelligence activity geared towards the Muslim populations in later years. A maverick political figure and militant intellectual of the pan-

Islamism current at the time, Ibrahim is said to have become a close friend of Japan as the organizer of the All Russia Muslim Congress in 1905, whereupon he visited Japan through the help of Akashi and Tanaka. While his career spans over a good half of the twentieth century, Ibrahim's 'fated marriage' with Japan which began on the eve of the Russo-Japanese War, carried him to Tokyo first in 1906, then again in 1908 when he made contacts with figures in the bureaucracy, army, especially the ultra-nationalist *Kokuryūkai*, who were agitating the mood of Asianism in Japan.

Typical of many anti-imperialist, nationalist figures of Asia who were in admiration of the rise of Japan to power, Ibrahim continued to serve the Japanese authorities as one of their conduits in the world of Islam. He had prestige among the educated Muslim public in many countries due to his political and intellectual activism for the cause of Muslim emancipation around the world. Already in 1909, Ibrahim travelled back to Istanbul, with *Kokuryūkai* support, by taking a very long route back home that took him about a year as he stopped over in important Muslim communities in China and in the territories of the British and the Dutch empires to create a pro-Japanese public opinion.[18]

Ibrahim wrote a fascinating memoir of his travels in Japan and Asia during 1908 and 1909 on behalf of the *Kokuryūkai* and the *Ajia gikai* (an organization linked with the *Tōa dōbunkai*, which was formed in Tokyo by the Asianist Japanese and Muslims of many countries with Ibrahim as the main Muslim figure). The book is titled *Alem-i Islam Japonya'da Intisar-ı Islamiyet* [The world of Islam: The spreading of Islam in Japan] became a popular work favouring Japan's modernity, creating the image of Japan as the rising star of the East in the Turkish-speaking population of the Ottoman and the Romanov empires. Just like the Yamada work on the Turks, Ibrahim's memoir can be said to have become the first Turkish text with a vocabulary that has developed the full image of Japan as a friendly and familiar entity as an alternative Eastern model for modernity.

The continued contacts between Ibrahim and his Asianist Japanese friends is a story that takes him back to Japan for good in 1938 as the official head of the Japanese government organization for Islam, *Dai Nippon kaikyō kyōkai*, where he died in 1944. In the meantime, his career shows that the Japanese interest in the Ottoman empire during the rise of Asianism in

Japan carries a new ideological character: it is perceived as a convenient centre for spreading propaganda about Japan as the saviour of the Islam. While Abdulhamid II had striven to preserve the Ottoman empire with conservative modernism, the impact of nineteenth-century currents of Westernization, nationalism, and reform, the Ottoman cities had already become an important meeting ground for nationalist intellectuals and political figures from Russia such as the pan-Islamist Ibrahim, the new generation of Young Turk nationalists, whose travels back and forth in the region carried people and ideas through the press, the media, public lectures and the like that kindled nationalist and reformists movements. Thus, connections in Istanbul, had the potential to lead to others in Cairo, Beirut, Damascus, Mecca and Medina, for which the Asianist Japanese in Tokyo developed a strong interest.

This new phenomenon also engendered its typical Japanese experts, specialists on Islam and its way of life who became the agents of realizing the Asianist vision in the world of Islam. Here, the Japanese figures of this new network that was forming among Muslims start frequenting the Ottoman realm in the early years of the twentieth century and also constitute a new breed of Asianist activists frequently connected with the *Kokuryūkai* and army intelligence in some fashion. Many of them began to study languages such as Arabic and Turkish, the tenets and rituals of the Islamic faith, under Ibrahim and other pro-Japanese Muslim collaborators to become well-versed in Islamic ways in the manner of the Orientalist trained agents of the Great Powers such as Lawrence of 'Arabia'.

It is clear that right after the Russo-Japanese War that is followed by the tumultuous impact of the Young Turk Revolution in 1908 in the Ottoman world, the Asianist network for Japan in the world of Islam was in the making. The Russian Tartar Muslim Ibrahim again pioneered in this new policy of introducing Japanese Muslim agents into the Near East via the Ottoman realm. According to his memoirs, on his way back to Istanbul in 1909, Ibrahim meets with Yamaoka Kōtarō (1880-1959), a member of the Black Dragons whom he had known in Tokyo, in Bombay and accompanies him to Mecca and then to Istanbul. By now, Yamaoka who has already become 'Ōmer (Omar)' Yamaoka, the first Japanese Muslim convert, is introduced by Ibrahim to nationalist and pan-Islamist circles in Istanbul as a speaker. Yamaoka gave a number of conferences to the Istanbul audiences on the new Japanese policy towards helping the Muslim world and the importance of the *Ajia gikai* organization, which is now introduced as the Japanese Society of Islam. The Istanbul pan-Islamist press such as the *Sirat-i Müstakim* and the *Tearüf-i Müslimin*, owned and edited by Ibrahim after his return from Japan, published Ōmer Yamaoka's letters together with Ibrahim's pro-Japanese editorials. Significantly in Istanbul, Yamaoka addresses the Istanbul public, where pan-Turkist and pan-Islamist ideas are prevalent against the oppression of the Western empires, through conferences arranged by the Russian Tartar students organization – a connection to the world of Islam which the Japanese will continue to consider as important. In the meantime, Ibrahim's son disseminated Ibrahim and Yamaoka's conferences in the Russian Muslim world through the *Beyanül Hak*, of the Kazan region that appealed to the Tartar population of the Volga region.

It is also clear that Ibrahim aids Ōmer Yamaoka to make contact with Arab leaders in Mecca and Medina whereupon this Japanese Muslim also becomes the first Japanese pilgrim to visit the Holy Lands, which he duly uses to initiate contacts with the notables of the two cities and make publicity about the special attention of the Japanese empire regarding the plight of Muslims.[19] Traveling from Mecca in Arabia through Damascus, Beirut and Istanbul, Yamaoka was to return back to Japan and later continued a career of agitation and activism among the Chinese Muslims. In 1912, only a year after Ibrahim's book on Japan, he was also to publish an account of his experience in Arabia titled *Arabia jūdanki* [The record of the pilgrimage to Arabia] which probably was the first Japanese account of the Arabian world of Islam (Yamaoka, 1912: 1-2; Okazaki, et al., 1981: 173; Komura, 1988: 52-3, 360-7, 468-74).

Yamaoka's activities and impressions of the world of Islam signify the beginnings of a strong focus on the part of Asianists in forming a *kaikyō seisaku*, or Islam policy for Japan that becomes a major strategic line in the future for Japanese expansionism. In Yamaoka's account the Ottoman world is no longer the declining old empire of Meiji strategists, nor the romantic Orient of Yamada, it is the gate to the Arab Muslim world. As the first Japanese Muslim pilgrim to Mecca who went through the complete ritual of the pilgrimage in addition to formal contacts with local Arab leaders, Yamaoka advocates a strong Asianist line towards the world of Islam, and the focus appears to be no longer the Russia Muslims or the Ottoman Turks, but the Arab world and via the Arabs the Asian Muslims. Yamaoka's justification for conversion is also reflective of the combination of patriotism, Asianism, and imperialism that was the familiar mixture of that generation of Asianists. It will constitute the basis of the argument for training Japanese agents who will be active in the world of Islam through the Second World War. Yamaoka is very straightforward in the text that is appealing to the Japanese readers about his conversion. His argument is that it is justified as a patriotic duty for the emperor of Japan. Yamaoka argues that a global policy for Japan cannot be realized without incorporating a strategic policy towards the Muslim peoples suffering under the Great Powers.

In his introduction he discusses the importance for young Japanese to go out in the world and exert the pioneer spirit of the Japanese warrior ethos to help the pitiful people of the Orient and the Occident and to turn their gaze toward the region of western Asia. Significantly, the Westernist rhetoric which has been discussed above serves now as a scapegoat to justify the new Asianist perspective. In his introduction Yamaoka laments the superficial Westernism of the Meiji era as encouraging frivolity and demoralization. His daring journey to Arabia is presented as part of the duty to perfect the mission of the empire of the rising sun (Yamaoka, 1912: 1-2). It would seem as if Ōmer Yamaoka is taking the same road as Lawrence whose admiration for the Arabs served the British empire during the First World War. The political and military consequences of the activities of the Japanese enthusiasts and experts of Islam such as Ōmer Yamaoka is to become apparent later as Japan will embark upon her empire-building. The image of Japan as the saviour of Islam and *kaikyō seisaku*, an Islam policy will be used in the politics and propaganda of the Japanese expansionists and militarists who will come to power in the Second World War.

CONCLUSION

Neither Meiji Japan nor Ottoman Turkey could formalize their relations as long as either side was dependent upon the terms of extraterritoriality etc. which gave special privileges to foreign countries. The Japanese as well as the Ottomans were part of an agenda of imperialist interest in the terms set by the West, with Japan now adopting the posturings of a Great Power.

The political narrative about the Japanese interest in the

Ottoman empire shows the evolution of the Japanese idea of itself as a modern nation from a strictly Westernist definition of the early Meiji era to one imbued with a sense of Asian roots by the turn of the century. Stefan Tanaka has masterfully argued that the Japanese conceptualization of *tōyō*, the Orient, restored China and Asia in Japanese thought which 'provided the basis for a history [of the Orient termed] (*tōyōshi*) by which Japanese, as Asians, could compare themselves against the West, and at the same time, as Japanese, could measure their progress' (Tanaka, 1993: 18). For the first generation Meiji élite in power with a Westernist vision of the world, the Ottomans were simply the representation of the European-Western imperialist agenda of the Eastern Question of a crumbling 'semi-civilized' non-Western empire. For the young Meiji generation with a new sense of Japaneseness such as Yamada Torajirō, however, the Ottoman world was the object of romantic interest in the 'accessible Orient' of the Europeans which is off shore borders of Asia in Europe for Japan. It is a Japanese version of the contemporary Orientalist Western romantic image about the area. Unlike the Western Orientalist romantics, however, the Japanese romantic such as Yamada sought a personal identification within this Orientalizing image. For Yamada and his friends in Japan, the Ottoman Turks and the Japanese had much in common because of a martial warrior heritage and an Asian sensibility, and last but not least Meiji Restoration had been inspirational for the 1908 Young Turk Revolution as a modernist agenda.

The Russo-Japanese War was a breakwater in this story. The Muslims and other anti-imperialist peoples in the East as well as the West particularly against Russia, had suddenly created a world public opinion that enthusiastically admired Japan as the rising star of the East. Thus for the Japanese nationalists and expansionists as well as officials with a newly gained sense of confidence about Japan as a Great Power, the Ottoman empire as a polity is no longer simply the important bulwark against Russia; it was already the realm that could be 'exploited' in economic terms as in the case of the the 1911 report which pointed to the fertile lands of Mesopotamia. The Ottoman empire now became an arena where Muslim agents such as Ōmer Yamaoka would roam to spark off a militant Asianist line among Turks as well as Arabs and even Muslims of the world.

Given the imperialist motive of the Islam agenda for Japan, it

119

was however, obvious that there was a generational collaboration across national boundaries as well. Asianists of Japan who chafed under the so-called Westernism and prudency of the Meiji élite had found a common cause with the pan-Islamists such as Ibrahim, or for that matter the Young Turks who were also chafing under autocratic imperial regimes such as that of Tsar Nicholas and Sultan Abdulhamid; both sharing with their Japanese counterparts a militant combination of liberalism and nationalism that was deeply critical of the West. From now one, Muslims such as Ibrahim who appeared to be creating a militant defiance against the rule of Western imperialism will be convincing as potential collaborators in the quest for a Japanese Asian empire.

The late Meiji period interest in the Ottoman realm also created the words that will constitute the language that will be used within this political relationship among the Japanese and their Muslim friends. Towards the Ottoman Turks, the dual language of Japanese 'cool' diplomacy as a Great Power contrasted with the warm language of a shared cultural heritage illustrated the problematic very well. Furthermore, by the time Ibrahim brings Yamaoka to the Near East, Japan is not just the friend of the Turks with a shared martial heritage, but the saviour of Islam, a monolithic world of many nations for which the Ottomans provide only an entry and there is the need for Islam policy.

During the Cold War era, the political tone of this vocabulary especially toward the Turks was toned down as by gone became the political agenda of the past such as the treaty problem, Asianist politics, and great power politics. But some of the basic concepts have managed to survive to this day as the formal diplomatic language of Japanese-Turkish relations that stresses a shared cultural heritage with Asian roots. Since the end of the Cold War era it is intriguing to note the revival of some of the old vocabulary and perspectives of the prewar era in the new heightened Japanese interest towards the Turkish-speaking world and its consequences remain to be seen.

BIBLIOGRAPHY

Akashi, Motojirō. 1988. *Rakka ryūsui: Colonel Akashi's Report on His Secret Cooperation with the Russian Revolutionary Parties During the Russo-Japanese War.* Edited by Olavi K. Fält and Antti Kujula. Translated by Inaba Chiharu. Studia Historica, 31. Helsinki: Societas Historica Finlandiae.

Arık, Ümit, 1989. *A Century of Turkish Japanese Relations: Towards a Special Partnership*. Istanbul: Turkish Japanese Business Council.

Beasley, W. G. 1964. *The Modern History of Japan*. New York: Praeger.

Deringil, Selim. 1991. 'Osmanlı Imparatorlugu'nda Gelenegin Icadı, Muhayyel Cemaat, ve Panislamizm' [The invention of tradition, imagined community, and pan-Islamism in the Ottoman empire]. *Toplum ve Bilim*, 54: Yaz-Guz, 47-65.

Esenbel, Selçuk. 1995. 'Islam Dünyasinda Japon Imgesi: Abdürresid Ibrahim ve Geç Meiji Dönemi Japonları' [The image of Japan in the world of Islam: Abdurresid Ibrahim and the Late Meiji Japanese]. *Toplumsal Tarih*, 19(4): 13-8.

———. 1996. 'A Fin de Siecle Japanese Romantic in Istanbul: The Life of Yamada Torajiro and His Toruko Gakan'. *Bulletin of SOAS*, 59/2: 237-52.

Fukuzawa Yukichi. 1875 (1970). *Bummeiron no gairyaku* [An outline of a theory of civilization]. In *Fukuzawa Yukichi zenshū*. [Collected works of Fukuzawa Yukichi], 4. Tokyo: Iwanami shoten.

Furukawa Nobuyoshi. 1891 (1988). *Perushia kikō* [Persia travelogue]. Tokyo: Sambō hombu. In *Meiji siruku rōdo tanken kikōbun shūsei*. [A collection of Meiji period Silk-road expedition travelogues], 2. Tokyo: Yumani shobō.

Gaimushō [Ministry of Foreign Affairs]. 1911. *Toruko jijō* [Conditions in Turkey]. Tokyo: Gaimushō seimukyoku dainika.

———. 1923. 'Tai-to jōyaku teiketsu keika' (Ōshū taisen mae). In Gaimushō, Documents on Japanese-Turkish Relations, Taishō 12 file. Library of Congress, Microfilm, MT11212.

Harries, Meirion, Harries, Susie. 1991. *Soldiers of the Sun*. New York: Random House.

Ibrahim, Abdürresid. 1910/1911 (Islamic 1328 and 1329). *Alem-i Islam ve Japonya'da Intisar'ı Islamiyet* 2 volumes. Volume 1 Ahmet Saki Bey Matbaası (Ahmet Saki Bey Printing) 1910; Volume 2 Kader Matbaası (Kader Printing) 1911.

Ienaga, Toyokichi. 1900 (1988). *Nishiajia ryōkōki* [The record of the travels to west Asia]. Tokyo: Minyūshi. In *Meiji shiruku rōdo tanken kikōbun shusei*. [A collection of Meiji period Silk-road expedition travelogues], 16. Tokyo: Yumani shobō.

Jansen, Marius. B. 1975. *Japan and China: From War to Peace 1894-1972*. Chicago: Rand-McNally.

Komatsu Kaori. 1992. *Ertugrul faciasi: Bir dostlugun dogusu* [The Ertugrul calamity: The birth of a friendship]. Ankara: Turhan kitabevi yayinlari.

Katsufuji Takeshi, Naiki Ryōichi and Okazaki Shōkō. 1981. *Isuramu sekai: Sono rekishi to bunka* [The world of Islam: Its history and culture]. Tokyo: Sekai shisōsha.

Kokuryūkai. 1930. *Kokuryūkai jireki* [The Kokuryūkai records]. Tokyo: Kokuryūkai.

Komatsu Kaoru and Komatsu Hisao, 1991. *Caponya* [Japan]. Tokyo: Daishokan.

Komura Fujio. 1988. *Nihon isuramu shi senzen senchū rekishi no nagare no naka ni katsuyōshita Nihonjin musurimutachi no gunzō* [Japan and the world of Islam the group of Japanese muslims who were active in the process of the history before and during the war]. Tokyo: Nihon isuramu yūji remmei.

Kuroda Kiyotaka. 1887 (1987). *Kan'yū nikki* [Journey around the world]. In *Meiji ōbei kemmonroku shūsei*. [The collection of the accounts of the Meiji study missions to the United States and Europe], 6. Tokyo: Yumani shobō.

Matsutani Hironao. 1986. *Nihon to Toruko: Nihon Toruko kankeishi* [Japan and Turkey: the history of Japanese-Turkish relations]. Tokyo: Chūtō chōsakai.

Muramatsu Masumi and Matsutani Hironao. 1989. *Toruko to Nihon* [Turkey and Japan]. Tokyo: Saimuru shuppankai.

Mütercimler, Erol. 1993. *Ertugrul faciasi ve 21 yüzyila dogru Türk-Japon ıliskisi* [The Ertugrul calamity and Turkish-Japanese relations towards the twenty-first century]. Istanbul: Anahtar kitaplar.

Naito Chishū. 1930. 'Toruko shisetsu Osman pasha raichō no shimei' [The mission of the Turkish envoy Osman Pasha to our monarchy]. *Shigaku*, 9(4): 575-86.

———. 1931. *Nitto kōshō shi* [The history of Japanese-Turkish relations]. Tokyo: Izumi shoinban.

Naito Chishū, Kotsuji Setsumi and Kobayashi Hajime. 1942. *Seinan Ajia no shūsei* [Trends of southwest Asian history]. Tokyo: Meguro shoten.

Nakai Hiroshi. 1877. *Toruko Girisha oyobi Indo man'yū kitei* [Account of travels in Turkey, Greece and India]. Tokyo.

Nish, Ian H. 1976. *The Anglo-Japanese Alliance: A Study of Two Island Empires*. Westport: Greenwood Press.

———. 1985. *The Origins of the Russo-Japanese War*. London: Longman.

Okazaki Shōkō, Naiki Yoichi and Katsuzo Morita. 1981. *Isuramu sekai: Sono rekishi to bunka* [The world of Islam: Its history and culture]. Tokyo: Sekai shisōsha.

Office of Strategic Services. Research and Analysis Branch. 1942. 'Japanese Infiltration Among the Muslims Throughout the World'. R&A. No. 890. Washington DC: National Archives.

———. 1944. 'Japanese Infiltration among Muslims in Russia and Her Borderlands'. R&A. No. 890.2 National Archieves. Washington DC: National Archives.

Ōyama Takanosuke. 1890 (1988). *Toruko kōkai kiji* [The record of the sea voyage to Turkey]. In *Meiji shiruku rōdo tanken kikōbun shūsei*. [A collection of Meiji period silk-road expedition travelogues], 10. Tokyo: Yumani shobō.

Sait Pasha. Sait Paşa'nin Hatirati, 2 volumes, Sabah Matbaası, Istanbul, 1328 (1912), pp. 37-38; Arık, Naito Chishu, Nitto kosho shi, pp. 31-35.

———. 1912 (Islamic/solar calendar 1328) *Sait Paşa'nın Hatıratı* (The memoirs of Sait Pasha), 2 volumes. Istanbul: Sabah Matbaası (Sabah Printing).

Shaw, Stanford J. and Shaw, Ezel Kural. 1977. *History of the Ottoman Empire and Modern Turkey*. Cambridge: Cambridge University Press.

Takahashi Tadahisa. 1982. 'Türk Japon Münasebetlerine Kısa bir Bakıs' [A brief look at Turkish-Japanese relations]. *Türk Dünyası Arastirmalari Vakfı Dergisi*. 18 June, 124-8.

Tanaka, Stefan. 1993. *Japan's Orient: Rendering Pasts into History*. Berkeley, Los Angeles: University of California Press.

Toyama ō shashinden kankōkai. 1935. *Tōyama ō shashinden* [A photographic biography of the venerable Toyama]. Tokyo: Tōyama ō shashinden kankōkai.

'Toruko oyobi Ejiputo ni aru ryōjikan saiban no ken' [The collection of the drafts of translations for the Meiji government, concerning the consular courts in Turkey and Egypt]. 1986. *Tsūyaku shūsei daiichi hen* of *Meiji seifu tsūyaku sōkō ruisan*, 5. Tokyo: Yumani shobō.

Uçar, Ahmet. 1995a. 'Japonların Islam Dünyasındaki Yayılmaci Siyaseti ve Abdürresid Ibrahim' [The expansionist policy of the Japanese in the world of Islam and Abdürresid Ibrahim]. M.A. dissertation, Selçuk University.

———. 1995b. 'Japonların Islam Dünyasındaki Yayılmaci Siyaseti ve Abdürresid Ibrahim' [The expansionist policy of the Japanese in the world of Islam and Abdürresid Ibrahim]. *Toplumsal Tarih*, 20 August, 15-17.

Yamaoka Kōtarō. 1912. *Sekai no shimpikyō Arabia jūdanki* [Mystery of the world; the record of the pilgrimage to Arabia]. Tokyo. Hakubunkan.

Zürcher, Erik J. 1993. *Turkey, A Modern History*. London: I. B. Tauris and Co.

NOTES

1.   For a general history of the Ottoman Empire and Modern Turkey in English, see Shaw and Shaw 1977, and Zürcher, 1993. There are many terms which are historically used for the country known as Turkey today. The paper will use some of them as it fits customary use. The Ottoman empire (1299-1923) is the standard term which is used for the polity that was formally abolished in 1923 after the First World War and the foundation of the Republic of Turkey. In European languages it was customary to refer to the Ottoman empire as Turkey, or Ottoman Turkey, and the Ottoman government as the Sublime Porte or simply the Porte from the term *Bab-ı Ali*.
 The works of Naito Chishū – the pioneer of Turkish studies in Japan – give the best pre-war account of Turko-Japanese relations. See Naito, 1931: 15, for the above; Naito, et al., 1942: 327-34; Naito, 1930; Takahashi, 1982: 128 for the above and for an overview in Turkish; Arık, 1989: 19, to be used with caution for citations (see the Japanese translation of Arık's work which has correct citation of Japanese sources). For a recent appraisal of Turkish-Japanese relations, see, Matsutani, 1986.
2.   On the Yoshida and Furukawa missions, see Katsufuji, et al., 1986: 169-71; Naito, 1931: 15; Naito, et al., 1942: 328-9.
3.   See Katsufuji, et al., 1986: 170-2. Komura, 1988: 46-8, gives accounts of the above Japanese visits to gather intelligence information explained from a 'pro-Islamic' perspective. The author, originally an intelligence officer in Inner Mongolia during the Second World War is one of the active figures among the few Japanese converts to Islam.
4.   Same sources as the above.
5.   See Gaimushō, 1911: 105-18, for Albanians; 100-4, 246-48, for Japanese interest in acquiring economic and commercial interest in the Basra area such as land for cotton cultivation.
6.   See Komura, 1988: passim, for a general account of early Meiji publications on Islam that convey the standard Western missionary critical perspective. See also ibid.: 45, for Inoue Kowashi, *Mohammettoron*, his policy which claimed Islam was not very suitable for a civilized religion.
7.   See Fukuzawa, 1875 (1970): 16, for a three-tiered view of the world: the unenlightened world of primitive peoples such as in Africa, next is Asia which belongs to the semi-enlightened category (that has the potential for full enlightenment). The second category should be rejected by Japan which has to join the ranks of the enlightened world represented by the West.
8.   See Katsufuji, et al., 1986: 169-73, for an account of the early Japanese visits to the Near East and their negative impressions.
9.   Beasley, 1964: 57-76, on treaties and politics; Jansen, 1975: 84, 197, 206, 214; for the Anglo-Japanese Alliance of 1902, see Nish, 1976, 1977. For Ottoman treaties with the West, see Zürcher, 1993: 49-50, 58-69, 78-88 for an overview of the Küçük Kaynarca Treaty of 1774 after the defeat of the Ottomans to Russia that forced the Porte to recognize diplomatic equality with the Europeans, impact of the French Revolution and nationalist rebellion in Greece and Egypt, 1838 Anglo-Ottoman Treaty of Trade that brought the nineteenth-century 'unequal treaties' home by opening the empire to 'free trade', and the history of Westernization and reform as a corresponding process.
10.   'Toruko oyobi Ejiputo ni aru ryōjikan saiban no ken' [The collection of the drafts of translations for the Meiji government, cincerning the consular courts in Turkey and Egypt], in *Tsūyaku shūsei daiichi hen* of *Meiji seifu tsūyaku sōkō ruisan*, 5. Tokyo: Yumani shobō, 1986.

11. See Naito, 1931: 23-5, for the questionnaire, ibid.: 28, 31-5, for problems with the treaty; Arık, 1989: 20-2, for the English translation of the questionnaire.

12. See Naito, 1931: 182-252, for an extensive treatment of the pan-Islamism of Abdulhamid II; Mütercimler, 1993: 151-2; Deringil, 1991: 47-65.

13. I am grateful to Selim Deringil for documentary information on the negotiations concerning the diplomatic and trade treaty between Japan and the Ottoman Porte. See, Basbakanlık Arsivi, Yıldız Mütenevvi Maruzat, 198/122 Daire-i Hariciye no. 436, for comment about special protection from the palace.

14. See 'Tai-to jōyaku teiketsu keika' (Ōshū taisen mae), in Taishō 12 file, Gaimushō, documents on Japanese-Turkish Relations, Library of Congress, Microfilm, MT11212.

15. In 'Tai-to jōyaku teiketsu keika' one reads: 'torukokoku nai ni wa shinrōha no seiryoku. . .'. The comment is interesting because it is quite unfeasable from the Turkish point of view to imagine a pro-Russian clique in the Turkish politics at the time in view of their historic rivalry. See Takahashi, 1988: 241-4, for a detailed account of Abdulhamid's balance of power strategy between Russia, France, and Great Britain which was behind the official policy of neutrality during the Russo-Japanese War.

16. For detailed account of these activities see, 'Japanese Attempts at Infiltration Among Muslims in Russia and Her Borderlands' August 1944, R&A, No. 890.2, Office of Strategic Services, Research and Analysis Branch. I am grateful to Tamamoto Masaru for bringing these invaluable sources to my attention. The material on the nationalist Japanese and their strategy in the world of Islam is part of this author's research in progress for a book on the subject.

17. See, 'Japanese Infiltration Among Muslims in Russia and Her Borderlands', for extensive coverage of Akashi and Russian Muslims who helped the Japanese cause; Akashi, 1988: 28, mentions briefly help to Tartars and Russian Muslims; Harries and Harries, 1991: 80, 92.

18. Part of work in progress to be published as Japan and the World of Islam. There are many sources on Ibrahim's activities in Japanese, Turkish, English and Russian. A basic bibliography has been published as part of a special file on Ibrahim which is made up of a collection of articles in Turkish in the journal *Toplumsal Tarih*, 19, July 1995; 20, August, 1995; Esenbel, 1995. Major sources are 'Japanese Infliltration Among the Muslims Throughout the World', OSS, R&A, No. 890, 1942, in addition to the OSS. No. 890.2 report cited above. See also Kokuryūkai, 1930: 17, 21, for references to Ibrahim and his son Münir; Tōyama ō shashinden kankōkai, 1935: 55, for a photograph of Ibrahim with Tōyama Mitsuru, the spiritual head of the *Kokuryūkai*. For Ibrahim's memoir, see Ibrahim, 1910, 2 vols. The first volume is on Japan and has been translated in Japanese, see Komatsu and Komatsu, 1991.

19. For the letters and conferences by Ōmer Yamaoka and Ibrahim about the *Ajia gikai* society, see newspapers published in Istanbul, *Tearüf-i Müslimin*, 17, 13 October 1910: 278; 22, 17 November 1910: 358; 23, 24 November 1910: 363; 32, 1 February 1911: 125; *Sırat-ı Müstakim*, 4(83), March 1909: 53-6; March 1910: 66-74; 5(133), March 1910: 42-45. For the dissemination of articles in the Russian Muslim press, see Uçar, 1995a, 1995b:15.

Japan and Eastern Europe

8

Major Fukushima Yasumasa and His Influence on the Japanese Perception of Poland at the Turn of the Century

EWA PALASZ-RUTKOWSKA

Major Fukushima Yasumasa (1852-1919) was one of Japan's most brilliant military officers of the Meiji era (1868-1912). He is an important personage not only for someone like the present author, who is researching the history of Polish-Japanese relations, but also for any student of Japan's modern history. Fukushima was the first representative of the new Japan to travel across Polish territory with his lonely horse ride across two continents and to become acquainted with the history of Poland and to get in touch with some Poles – unofficially, because Poland still did not exist as a country. He provided the Japanese army with valuable information on Europe and Russia and made Poland and its tragic history known in Meiji Japan.[1]

THE FIRST INTELLIGENCE AGENT OF THE MODERN JAPANESE ARMY

Born as the eldest son of Fukushima Yasuhiro, a samurai from the Matsumoto *han* in Shinano province, he was educated from his youngest years as a soldier of the new, modern era. He studied not only tactics from a Dutch in Edo but also, after the restoration of power to Emperor Mutsuhito (1852-1912), at the Kaisei school [*Kaisei gakkō*].[2] After spending a year in the Ministry of Justice as a translator in 1874 he was transferred to the Army Ministry and in 1878 to the newly established General Staff. He visited the United States, Mongolia, China, Korea and India. In 1887 he was promoted to the rank of major and appointed as a military attaché in Berlin. The reason was that the

General Staff had decided to study the strategies of strong European countries. By this appointment Fukushima became the first intelligence agent of the modern Japanese army acting in Europe. Speaking five foreign languages fluently, he made friends with many foreigners, including Poles. His contacts with the latter were probably especially frequent as he could get valuable information from them concerning Russia.

One of the main aims of the Japanese authorities at that time was the creation of an army that was strong and modern in the Western sense, since the Japanese government felt that only such an army would be able to ensure the security and sovereignty of Japan.[3] In order to be able to plan a general strategy, the country needed information on the strategies of other states, particularly Japan's most powerful and most dangerous neighbour, Russia.

This is why, during his five-year stay in Berlin, Major Fukushima, in addition to gaining detailed knowledge on the Prussian army which constituted the model for the modernization of the Japanese Army, also visited several European states, England, Denmark, Sweden and Finland, the Netherlands, Belgium, France, Spain, Portugal, Italy and Switzerland, but also went to the European part of Russia and the Balkan Peninsula. Probably at this time Fukushima also visited several times territories of the then divided Poland, where he established contacts with Poles (Shimanuki, 1979, 1: 146). He felt that it was only the so-called Polish patriots [*Pōrando gishi* or *shishi*], who were staunchly opposed to Russia and striving to gain independence for Poland through arms, who could supply him with the most important information on Russia as a whole. This information was passed on to the Japanese General Staff, which in turn formed the basis of his rationale for his great, solitary journey. For he wanted to see with his own eyes what he had heard from his informers. For strategic reasons, he was interested in the Trans-Siberian Railway which was under construction. It is obvious that the Poles, among whom were those who had experienced exile, were able not only to supply him with information on Siberia, but also help in establishing contacts with compatriots there.

FUKUSHIMA'S LONELY EXPEDITION BY HORSE AND REMINISCENCES FROM POLAND

On 11 February 1892, on the day of the *Kigensetsu*, when the anniversary of the establishment of the empire by the legendary

Emperor Jimmu in 660 BC is celebrated in Japan, Fukushima left on his favourite horse, *Gaisen* ['triumphal return'] from Berlin on a solitary journey back to Japan. He travelled for 488 days – across two continents, through non-existing Poland, Russia, Siberia, Mongolia and Manchuria, covering 14,000 km. He sent the reports from his travel to the General Staff. Some parts of the reports were published by the *Osaka Asahi shimbun* as *Fukushima chūsa tanki enseiroku* [Lt. Col. Fukushima's records concerning his lonely expedition by horse]. Soon, however, the newspaper had to stop publishing these articles as the authorities felt that Fukushima's journey should remain secret in the period in which its agent was active on their behalf. For this reason, his reports were considered secret military documents (Shimanuki, 1979, 1: 2). The majority of them were destroyed following Japan's failure in the Pacific War. Luckily for historians and the descendants of Fukushima himself, some documents remained after his death, including *Tanki ensei* [The lonely expedition by horse] (Fukushima, 1941: 1-225), on the basis of which the course of Fukushima's travels can be reconstructed in a fairly detailed manner and his impressions and opinions, including those of Poland, can be known. Regarding the latter, he wrote:

> The country has died, only mountains and rivers have remained. Lost in trees and grass, the castle laments the traces of a lost fatherland. . . . At sunset, on a suburb of the former capital, Warsaw, I think of the days of the uprisings past by and my heart is seized with sorrow. I lament the many unburied heroes' souls and I am completely unable to control a deep feeling of eternal hatred in me. Though, 200 years ago Poland was the great monarchy of Central Europe, stretching from the Baltic to the Black Sea (Fukushima, 1941: 13-4).

But he also wrote:

> Horrible wars intensify in Europe, unable to imagine the Japanese living for years in peace. . . . The fact that peace has reigned in Japan until today is great luck for her. It was possible because Japan is surrounded by sea and was far from the external enemy. Today one can clearly see that in the near future it will be possible to arrive quickly in Japan, due to the railroad tracks being built from Europe to the east. . . . And then the luck of living in the peace distant Japan will become cause for misfortune. This is why it is necessary to prepare quickly for war now, because it will be too late once the enemy attacks us (Fukushima, 1941: 10).

In these reports, Fukushima not only sincerely sympathized with Poles, but on the basis of the Polish tragedy he strove to warn the

Japanese of possible loss of independence, and hence the need for effective defence of their country. It should be added that on the basis of Fukushima's reports Ochiai Naobumi (1861-1903), a Japanese poet, wrote a long poem, *Kiba ryokō* [journey on horse back], a part of which, called *Pōrando kaiko* [Reminiscences from Poland] (Ochiai, 1960: 114-15) became a very popular soldier's song sung even by children. It is precisely due to this that the Japanese heard of Poland and its history.

FUKUSHIMA'S RIDE ACROSS POLISH TERRITORY

Due to the above reports it is also known what Fukushima saw and thought while travelling across Polish territory. On the basis of them, a fairly detailed travel itinerary can be reconstructed (Fukushima, 1941: 8-19; cf. Shimanuki, 1979, 1: 202-20).

On the third day of his journey, Fukushima reached Kostrzyn at the mouth of the Warta and Odra rivers. He knew that it was formerly a city at the Polish border but was now situated in the German partition and had lost its strategic importance and hence collapsed. On the next two days, covering a distance of 150 km, he observed fortified bases and roads rebuild by the Germans in case of conflict with the Russians.

On 15 February he reached Poznan, close to the Russian partition border. It was the largest city of this region, and not surprisingly had been made the headquarters of the German Army in this region. His arrival in Poznan was awaited and he was greeted warmly. As he had already travelled 260 km, he decided to take a rest and treat both his own and his horse's wounds. Fukushima travelled in the winter, and the temperature then was approximately 10°C below zero. Luckily for him, there was no wind, which is especially hard for travel by horseback. In these conditions, if the trip is brief, one can cover 100 km a day. On trips of many months, the optimum distance is 50 km a day. Fukushima tried to maintain this pace.

As a result of five days of observations, Fukushima claimed that the Germans were very well prepared for a possible war with Russia. Both the state of the roads and the railway testified to this, particularly in the border area, as well as efficient telecommunication devices, both for the civil population and the military, and the rapid transfer of information.

On 18 February Fukushima left Poznan and on the next day entered the territories of the Russian partition. He was surprised by the rudimentary border controls, explaining to himself that it was a relatively newly demarcated border. For he knew that this had been Polish land until quite recently. He quickly settled the border formalities and for two kilometres was accompanied by a soldier stationed at the border, and was then accompanied by a young Cossack who had come to greet Fukushima on his father's – an officer from Konin – wishes. (We have to remember that officially, on the territory of the Russian partition of Poland, he was meeting with Russians, primarily from the army.) In Konin, in the square in front of the train station, approximately fifty cavalrymen greeted him with an orchestra. The greeting party crossed the city with Fukushima and took him to a base twenty km away. After a one-day rest, Fukushima left on 20 February for a longer trip to Kolo (present-day Kutno) where a gunner regiment was stationed. A young officer awaited Fukushima at the border of the city and accompanied him on his way to the garrison. There the commander-in-chief of the regiment took care of the guest. Fukushima was invited to the wedding party of one of the non-commissioned officers which was taking place that day in the officers' canteen. The Japanese officer was shocked by the fact that, although he had heard of strict compliance to class divisions, both the commander-in-chief and other officers, all from the aristocracy, sat at one table and enjoyed themselves in the company of low-ranking officers and soldiers.

On 22 February Fukushima left for Lowicz, and on 24 February reached Warsaw, the orderly, buzzing and animated – as he wrote – capital of the once free Poland. The Royal Castle in particular impressed him, testifying not only to the sacredness of the former Polish kingdom, but also to the high culture of Poles. He also saw, however, much evidence of the tragedy which the city had experienced in the line of battle of the uprisers against the partitioners. Fukushima decided to stay longer in Warsaw as he had to rest from having travelled 550 km and prepare for the longer, much more difficult stages of the journey that would involve more intense cold and more snow.

It could be assumed, on the basis of what he wrote about the so-called Polish patriots, that in his preparations for the journey across the specific Russian territory, and mainly Siberia, Fukushima also met with Polish activists in the conspiracy movement and with those who had been sent to Siberia. For he knew that there were some secret Polish political organizations whose aim was to regain Polish independence. Their head-quarters, and branches as well, were located in most cases beyond the borders of the former Poland, in England, France, Germany and other states, in order for them to safely gather capital, arms, equipment, etc. Activists in these organizations frequently cooperated with the secret service of a given country, wishing to use this cooperation in order to regain Polish independence. Thus, it is very probable that the secret agent of the Japanese General Staff, a country just beginning to explore the sphere of intelligence in the international arena, sought assistance and professional guidance, particularly among those experienced in gathering information on Russia. Remarks on Russia and contacts with Poles were also important for Fukushima as he established the route of his journey across Russian territory. He probably selected places recommended by Polish independence activists, those in which he could make contact with their colleagues and obtain additional information which his superiors in Tokyo required.

On 25 February Fukushima visited the headquarters of a cavalry brigade, where for the first time since his arrival in Warsaw he met with the commander-in-chief and other soldiers stationed here. As cavalrymen, they all were experts on horses and so the Major decided to make use of their remarks and experience in riding horses in deep snow. Instead of the road to Dyneburg (Dangavpils), covered by three metres of snow, they recommended he use the road leading to Kaunas as safer and less snowy. He readily accepted this proposal, thinking that he would also have the opportunity to see the military equipment on the border.

On 28 February Fukushima left Warsaw in the company of the commander-in-chief of the brigade, young cavalry officers and an orchestra which accompanied him for six km outside the border of the city. In accord with the cavalrymen's suggestions, he took the road to the northeast towards Kaunas. The next day he stopped at the garrison of a regiment in Ostroleka and on 2 March reached Lomza where he had occasion to watch part of a five-day field exercise of the unit stationed there. In observing the behaviour of the soldiers in the frost, their effectiveness and resistance, he claimed that the Russian army is used to harsh winter and is well trained in battle in such conditions.

Travelling farther north, in the direction of the border of the Russian partition and East Prussia, Fukushima came to the conclusion, on the basis of observations of the border installations, the size and the training of the military, that the border region to the east, closer to historically Russian territory, was better protected than the length of the border to the west which he crossed at the start of his journey.

On 5 March having travelled 267 km from Warsaw, through Szczuczyn and Augustów, Fukushima reached Suwalki and then Mariampol. Two days later he stopped in Kaunas, on 9 March in Wilkomierz (Ukmerge), and then in Uciana (Utena), in the home of a rich Pole who he had known earlier from the Berlin days. Further, through Dyneburg, on 13 March he arrived in Lucyn, the last city on his route which was still part of the Poland prior to the partitions. Now a trip through the core of the Russian Empire awaited him, which exceeds the scope of this work.

However, it is worth quoting a fragment from the unpublished memoirs of Stanislaw Kazimierz Kossakowski, then resident of Wilkomierz, who writes on Fukushima's stay in this city and of his travels:

> In the first half of March 1892 a major of the Japanese General Staff, Fukushima ... came through Wilkomierz, riding from Berlin, through Warsaw, Kaunas, Dyneburg, Petersburg, Moscow, Kazan, Szkutek, Vladivostok. Fukushima made the entire journey by horse, and in addition to the regard he deserved for his trip through the above-mentioned cities, for his pleasant manner, quick thought and intelligence, he also stirred up admiration for his exceptional persistence with regard to the difficulties he faced on the journey which lasted, without a break, for 16 months.
>
> Fukushima was received by Commander-in-Chief Nord and his officers, one of which, Aleksander Newiandt, described the stay of the above mentioned 'Japanese Moltke'[4] in one of the Russians papers.
>
> ... Who would have thought, then, that such a short, bright-eyed Japanese man, personally dressing the legs of his mount ... a few years later as a general at the head of a Japanese division, would reach the walls of Peking, and even later would have managed to be perceived by the world as the 'Japanese Moltke', one of the creators of the plan of war against Russia. Who would have then thought that this journey by a lone Japanese through the immense space of Russia would play a role in the history of the Russo-Japanese War. Still, then he was received hospitably, almost sincerely (Kossakowski).

CONCLUDING REMARKS

The Russians were aware of the fact that the fundamental aim of Fukushima's journey was to gather information on Russia, its military arrangements, the number of units in various points of the country and the Trans-Siberian Railway. They felt, however, that this was not threatening activity because of

Japan's modest international position. Russia did not yet consider Japan a threatening enemy, hence Fukushima was treated warmly and he was provided with assistance along the entire route. He was highly respected for his ability as a rider, his bravery and persistence.

On the basis of Fukushima's report it follows that he established contacts on Russian territory as well with Polish opponents to the empire, which were used a few years later by Akashi Motojirō (1864-1919), on the eve of and during the Russo-Japanese War.[5]

Fukushima reached Vladivostok on 12 June 1893, after sixteen months of solitary travel. Upon his return to his country he was recognized as a hero and warmly welcomed both in Tokyo and other cities. The General Staff decided to use his intelligence capacities and knowledge in this field. This is why in 1899 he was given the function of chief of the intelligence section of the General Staff, which he held until 1906, hence also during the Russo-Japanese War. Then again – though still unofficially – he had the chance to talk with Poles about cooperation against Russia.[6]

BIBLIOGRAPHY

Akashi Motojirō. 1988. *Ryakka ryūsui. Colonel Akashi's Report on His Secret Cooperation with the Russian Revolutionary Parties during the Russo-Japanese War*. Edited by Olavi K. Fält and Antti Kujala. Translated by Inaba Chiharu. Studia Historica, 31. Helsinki: Societas Historica Finlandiae.

Bandō Hiroshi. 1995. *Pōrandojin to Nichiro sensō* [Poles and the Russo-Japanese War]. Tokyo: Aoki shoten.

Deacon, Richard. 1990. *Kempeitai. The Japanese Secret Service Then and Now*. Tokyo: Charles E. Tuttle Company.

[Fukushima Yasumasa]. 1941. *Fukushima shōgun iseki* [Documents left by General Fukushima]. Tokyo: Tōa kyōkai.

Hata Ikuhiko, ed. 1991. *Nihon rikukaigun sōgō jiten* [Comprehensive dictionary of the Japanese army and navy]. Tokyo: Tōkyō daigaku shuppankai.

Inaba Chiharu. 1992. 'Polish-Japanese Military Collaboration during the Russo-Japanese War'. *Japan Forum*, 4(2): 229-46.

——.1995. *Akashi kōsaku* [Akashi's maneuverings]. Tokyo: Maruzen raiburarii.

Komori Takuji. 1968. *Akashi Motojirō*. 2 vols. Tokyo: Hara shobō.

Kossakowski, Stanislaw Kazimierz. *Wspomnienia 1837-1905* [Memoires 1837-1905] (unpublished).

Lerski, Jerzy. 1959. 'A Polish Chapter of the Russo-Japanese War'. *Transactions of the Asiatic Society of Japan*, III/7: 69-96.

Nihon kindai shiryō kenkyūkai, ed. 1971. *Nihon rikukaigun seido, soshiki jinji*, [The system, organization and personnel affairs of the Japanese army and navy]. Tokyo: Tōkyō daigaku shuppankai.

Ochiai Naobumi. 1960. 'Pōrando kaiko' [Reminiscences from Poland]. In *Otakebi* [War cry]. Tokyo: Kaikōsha, 114-5.

Palasz-Rutkowska, Ewa. 1990. 'Changes in the Japanese Army after the Meiji Restoration'. *Rocznik Orientalistyczny*, 46(2): 137-41.

——.1995. 'Kontakty Polaków i Japonczyków w czasie wojny japonsko-rosyjskiej (1904-1905)' [Polish-Japanese contacts during the Russo-Japanese War]. *Japonica*, 5: 65-83.

Palasz-Rutkowska, Ewa, Romer, Andrzej T. 1996. *Historia stosunków polsko-japonskich 1904-1945* [History of Polish-Japanese Relations, 1904-45]. Warszawa: Bellona.

Shimanuki Shigeyoshi. 1979. *Fukushima Yasumasa to tanki Shiberia ōdan* [Fukushima Yasumasa and his lonely horse ride across Siberia]. 2 vols. Tokyo: Hara shobō.

NOTES

1. Fukushima was promoted to general in 1914. For more details on his life and activities, see Shimanuki, 1979; Hata, 1991: 123; Deacon, 1990: 67-80; Palasz-Rutkowska and Romer, 1996: 20-8.

2. After unification with the Tokyo School of Medicine [*Tōkyō igakkō*] in 1877 it was transformed into the Tokyo Imperial University [*Tōkyō teikoku daigaku*].

3. On the modernization of the Japanese army see, for instance, Hata, 1991: 466-83; Nihon kindai shiryō kenkyūkai, 1971: 412-25, Palasz-Rutkowska, 1990.

4. Helmuth Count von Moltke (1800-91), Prussian general, head of the General Staff of the Prussian army 1857-88. His reorganization of the army was largely responsible for Prussia's victories over Denmark, Austria and France.

5. For more details on Akashi and his activities, see Komori, 1968; Akashi, 1988; Inaba, 1995.

6. This is treated more extensively in, for instance, Bandō, 1995; Inaba, 1992; Lerski, 1959; Palasz-Rutkowska, 1995.

9

Japan's Enlightened War: Military Conduct and Attitudes to the Enemy during the Russo-Japanese War

ROTEM KOWNER

Four decades after the outbreak of the Pacific War, historians have started to reveal the full scale of one of the most salient components of the Pacific War, namely the strong racial attitudes both the Japanese and the Allies held towards each other (Shillony, 1981; Dower, 1986). On the Japanese side, one finds not only the demonization of the enemy, but harsh treatment of captured combatants as well as civilians (e.g., Kerr, 1985; Hicks, 1994; Daws, 1995). The Pacific War was the second full-scale war Japan waged against a Western state. Earlier, in 1904, Japan attacked the Russian fort at Port Arthur in a similar fashion to that of Pearl Harbor. In an effort to protect its interests in the Korean Peninsula from the encroaching Russia, Japanese forces landed in Korea and attacked Russian positions in neighbouring Manchuria. The ensuing war was fought for a year and a half with a total manpower close to two million strong (Nish, 1985; Duus, 1995).

Due to the strategic implications and moral significance this war had for Japan, one may expect to find some similarities in the combat actions and attitudes to the enemy between the Russo-Japanese War and the Pacific War. Likewise, one may presume that the attitudes Japanese and Russians had for each other served as a precursor to the attitudes revealed in the next major confrontation between Western and Asian powers. Nevertheless, and despite the search for continuity, historical evidence offers only little support for these hypotheses.

   This chapter seeks to examine Japanese attitudes to the enemy on the front-line and in the rear, in an attempt to show that there was only limited affinity between the two wars. The war chronicle I found is in fact rather surprising since it reveals much mutual compassion and respect. True, it was a dreadful war, with hundreds of thousands of casualties, but it was conducted with a certain fairness and *naïveté* that were lost in subsequent 'total' wars. On the Japanese side especially there was no indiscriminate massacre of civilians, or extensive attacks on non-military targets, or casual killing, or even deliberate mistreatment of prisoners captured in battle. Precisely because of what we do not find in this merciful conflict, the Russo-Japanese War may have a value within a broader historical perspective regarding human behaviour in battle. It may illuminate some of the causes of the escalation into racial conflict during the Pacific War and even offer ways to avoid such conflicts in the future.

BEHAVIOUR IN BATTLE

A major part of the Russo-Japanese War was fought around heavily guarded forts and fortified lines. It was a slow war and advance was frequently measured in metres (Great Britain, 1907,1908; Hoyt, 1967; Connaughton, 1988). While combatants of both sides depicted the war in their memoirs as relentless and fierce (e.g., Sakurai, 1907; Tretyakov, 1911; Taniguchi, 1981), non-partisan observers were often astonished by sights of benevolence and concern for one's enemy. A typical testimony to the spirit of the conflict was written by Lieutenant-General lan Hamilton, the top British observer at the front, who followed the siege on Port Arthur from the Japanese side. Hamilton witnessed several incidents where bloody confrontation ended with compassion, and soldiers on both sides helped and bandaged each other (Hamilton, 1905).
   Some of the stories he reported regarding the benevolent relations between the Japanese and Russian soldiers at the front seem utterly bizarre, especially in light of the bitter and vindictive combat behaviour so notorious during the Pacific War (e.g., Cameron, 1994). In one of his reports, Hamilton mentioned a cave which was occupied by the Russians at night and by the Japanese in the dayime. When the Russians left the cave in 'a very dirty condition', the Japanese soldiers wrote a note 'asking that their mutual abode might be kept cleaner. Before leaving the cave in the evening, they left the note

together with a bottle of brandy. Next morning they found the cave clean, and a rouble was lying on the ground to pay for the brandy (Hamilton, 1905, 2: 292-3).

Such a friendly gesture between the combatants was not unique. During the siege of Port Arthur, soldiers in one Japanese position near the Twin Dragons Fort were surprised to see a stone thrown from the Russian side land near them. Attached to it they found a note from a Russian soldier, asking them to telegraph his mother, and let her know he was alive and well. With the note there was also a ten-rouble note to defray expenses. The Japanese fulfilled the request, and informed the soldier by the same method that the money was not sufficient. Minutes later, they received another rock with the additional money attached (Ashmead-Bartlett, 1906). Other war correspondents were also surprised at the apparent friendliness of the two armies, and that 'hostile men and firearms could have such consideration for one another' (McCormick, 1907, 1: 127).

The manifestations of camaraderie between soldiers of both sides were even less restrained when combat actions ended. One such occasion was the capitulation of Port Arthur. While the commanders of the two armies, General Nogi Maresuke and Lieutenant-General Anatolii Stoessel, were holding their first meeting, the soldiers of their escorts fraternized outside 'in the most friendly manner' (Ashmead-Bartlett, 1906: 400). Around Mukden as well, a few months later, special relations were frequently established between soldiers of the two armies. When Field Marshal Ōyama Iwao and General Alexei Kuropatkin exchanged a communication their officers fraternized over Russian and foreign wines, and later when the Russians rode down to see the Japanese they came without a white flag and were 'well received' (McCormick, 1907, 1: 330).

TREATMENT OF THE WOUNDED AND DEAD

While fierce and violent combat behaviour is an inevitable outcome of any war, the treatment of the enemy's wounded and dead soldiers reflects the emotional and moral environment of a war. During the Pacific War the cruel Japanese treatment of their prisoners became notorious (MacKenzie, 1994; Moore and Fedorowich, 1996), and also Allied troops, concluded John Dower, 'participated in or at least witnessed the killing of helpless, wounded, or captured Japanese' (Dower, 1986: 66).

In the Russo-Japanese War none of these manifestations was

evident. While some sporadic killing of surrendered enemy soldiers may have occurred (e.g., Wincelberg, 1976), the common attitude towards enemy soldiers was respectful and civilized. Such an attitude is evident in *Nikudan* [Human bullets], the most popular Japanese book about the war. Two years after the war the author of the book, an army officer named Sakurai Tadayoshi, was still moved by the traumatic memory of the death of his unit's first captured Russian soldier from his wounds, which 'brought out tears of sympathy to our eyes'. Sakurai assured his readers that every soldier '. . . was honourably buried under a cross and Chaplain Toyama offered Buddhist prayers' (Sakurai, 1907: 35). The Japanese acted in a similar fashion also after battle over the 'heaven-reaching' pass. Russian bodies were scattered everywhere. A slip of paper was attached to one of the bodies begging the Japanese to care for the dead. The Japanese not only complied with this request, but put flowers upon the Russian graves (Hamilton, 1905).

On the naval front as well compassion on the side of the Japanese was common. When the Russian cruiser *Rurik* was sunk the Japanese '. . . used utmost endeavour to rescue the crew who were floating about on mattresses, wooden articles, and swimming, all boats having been destroyed' (McCully, 1977:186). A similar report was written by a British war correspondent, who observed the naval operations from the Japanese side. He noted on the manner in which the crew of his boat picked up weak and wounded Russian sailors from their sinking *Rurik*:

> Our doctor immediately proffered his services, which were gratefully received. Our sentry at the gangway saluted, the Russian officer returned. The Russian sailors were assisted up the gangway by the Japanese . . . and one of the Russian wounded kissed the Japanese sailor who was assisting him. . . . We supplied them with everything they asked for (Wright, 1905: 72).

Once the Japanese had carried Russian wounded soldiers from the battle scene, they transferred them to field hospitals where they received careful medical treatment. Ethel McCaul, a representative of the British Red Cross who served as an inspector for the Japanese Red Cross, was impressed by the Japanese medical treatment of Russian soldiers during a visit to one such hospital at the front. 'If anything', she remarked on the living conditions of the Japanese and Russian wounded, the latter 'were in more comfortable quarters'. One of the Russians was very ill, and upon meeting her he burst in tears. McCaul was 'much impressed' by the medical officers' tender and kind treatment, and found the Japanese staff to be on 'quite friendly terms with them all' (McCaul, 1904: 122).

The conscientious medical treatment given to the captured Russians continued after their arrival at prison camps in Japan. At the largest Red Cross hospital in Matsuyama, McCaul was surprised to see that each Russian patient had a room for himself. 'Flowers', she noted, 'had been most generously given, and many sacred prints so dear to the Russians, hung upon the walls.' Some of the prisoners told her 'they were sorry to leave'. The situation at the adjacent military hospital was not much different: 'The surroundings were of the cleanest, and there was an air of European comfort everywhere pervading.' One Russian officer told her that '. . . they were all doing well, and were thoroughly well looked after' (McCaul, 1904: 195-6). One of the Russians wounded in the hospital received a letter from the Japanese Navy Minister expressing sympathy for him, recognizing the Russian fighting spirit, and wishing him a quick recovery (Seaman, 1905: 63).

The civil attitude to the enemy was also apparent at the rear, and stemmed partly from the approach of the government. One such occasion was at the death of the Russian Admiral S. Ossipovitch Makarov, the commander of the Pacific Squadron, with about eight hundred of his men. Makarov's demise at the early stages of the war, when his ship hit a mine, was no doubt detrimental to the war effort of the remaining crews of the squadron. The Japanese did not celebrate the loss of their naval foe and his flagship. In Tokyo, a statement was issued by the Japanese Naval General Staff which mentioned Makarov's scientific achievements, and described his death as a loss for every navy in the world (Kostenko, 1906, cited in Diedrich, 1978: 201).

TREATMENT OF POWS

The most prominent difference in attitude to the enemy between the Russo-Japanese War and the Pacific War can perhaps be found in the treatment of combatant and civilian prisoners. In the early stages of the Pacific War, Japanese troops were notorious for their atrocities against Allied troops who surrendered as well as non-combatant civilians captured in the cities of southeast Asia. In numerous cases Japanese soldiers bayoneted, drowned, or decapitated their prisoners, and raped, tortured, and killed captured civilians (e.g., Russell, 1958). The Allies were often not more merciful to Japanese soldiers, and despite reasonable treatment in POW camps, instant killing of surrendered Japanese troops became a common feature. None of this happened in the Russo-Japanese War. This difference is remarkable, especially since the Russians captured relatively few prisoners whereas the Japanese were burdened with tens of thousands of POWs, soldiers from the captured fortress of Port Arthur and other battles as well as sailors from sunk and surrendered warships. This numerical imbalance suggests that the fair treatment the Japanese provided to their 80,000 Russian POWs was not aimed at mitigating the enemy's treatment of the 2000 Japanese POWs in Russia (Hata, 1996).

With the outbreak of the war the Japanese government issued regulations regarding the humane treatment of enemy prisoners, and established a POW Information Bureau in the Army Ministry (Hata, 1996). These rules were followed strictly, especially in light of the international uproar after the massacre at Port Arthur in 1894 (Villiers, 1895; Lone, 1994). Both Russian POWs and foreign reporters testified during and after the war to the considerate manner in which the Japanese treated their captured enemy. This Japanese attitude to their enemy did not alter even though a squadron of three Russian cruisers from Vladivostok were causing havoc on the Japanese coast. In one of their attacks, the Russian warships sank the transport *Hitachi maru* carrying troops to the battlefield. The funeral for the 631 soldiers who perished was held in Tokyo with an immense crowd attending. Almost on the same day, 601 prisoners captured from one of the attacking cruisers arrived in Japan. Two of the prisoners who died of their wounds were buried in a military ceremony (Lensen, 1967).

The civilized treatment accorded to Russian prisoners became more apparent following the capitulation of Port Arthur, a position the Japanese army relentlessly fought for for ten months with the sacrifice of innumerable human lives. The most famous episode of the surrender, perhaps, was the delicate manner in which General Nogi dealt with the surrendering commander of the fort, General Stoessel. The day after the capitulation General Nogi dispatched one of his assistants, Captain Tsunoda, into Port Arthur to arrange a meeting with Stoessel. Tsunoda conveyed his respects to the general and his wife, and asked if anything could be done for their comfort. On

4 January 1905 Tsunoda returned with a present for Mrs Stoessel, consisting of chickens, bottles of champagne, and bottles of claret (Ashmead–Bartlett, 1906).

At the first meeting between the two commanders, they shook hands and then presented their respective staffs to one another. General Nogi expressed great pleasure at shaking hands with General Stoessel and the latter reciprocated (Ashmead–Bartlett, 1906). Nogi gave Stoessel a special room to receive his staff officers, who were allowed to wear their swords, and there he gave them his last orders. The Russian officers were given the choice of being sent to Japanese prison camps along with their troops or returning to Russia with the pledge not to participate in the war. Stoessel chose Japan. On his departure, Japanese posted only a guard of honour at the station, while leaving the main bulk of their troops a mile away. Nogi's commitment to Stoessel did not end with his departure. He also wrote to the governor of Nagasaki and requested that General Stoessel 'shall be treated with special consideration during his brief stay in the port' (Baelz, 1932: 338).

A day after the departure of the Russian garrison, the Japanese army entered Port Arthur. One of the most conspicuous features of the arrangements was the apparent attempt of the Japanese Headquarters Staff to avoid humiliating their foes. For this reason General Nogi had refrained from entering the town until after the departure of General Stoessel and most of his officers. The rule Nogi set himself was rigorously enforced on others, so that the divisional and brigade commanders were obliged to remain outside the town with their troops, and gaze for a period of twelve days on the 'promised land beyond' (Ashmead–Bartlett, 1906: 406).

The Russian POWs were sent to 29 camps in Japan, the biggest of them located in the city of Matsuyama on the island of Shikoku, where a decade earlier Chinese POWs were kept (Saikami, 1969). The Japanese were happy to show their facilities and demonstrate their generous hospitality. Visitors to the camp attributed the fine mental condition of the prisoners to the Japanese treatment, and described the Russian prisoners as cheerful and happy (McCaul, 1904: 201; Seaman, 1905: 62). Testimony of Russian prisoners indicates that the conditions in Matsuyama were not only a show for visitors. The prisoners had expected cruelties, but '... were astonished to find themselves surrounded by what they were pleased to call paradise'. Many of them attested that 'they have never fared better in their lives' (Seaman, 1905: 62-3, 60).

The Russian count Constantine Benckendorff, who served as a young naval officer at Port Arthur, has provided an excellent first-hand account of the life in a Japanese POW camp. According to the terms of Port Arthur's 'honourable surrender', as Benckendorff called it, officers were allowed to keep their swords, and '. . . to have the unprecedented, at least in modern times, privilege of choosing between becoming a prisoner of war, or returning home on parole not to take part in active service until the end of the war'. Benckendorff, like the majority of the officers, chose to go with his men to Japan. With other junior officers, he made the voyage from Manchuria to Matsuyama aboard a passenger steamer, where he was '. . . free on board as any passenger in normal circumstances'. At Matsuyama, the quarters the prisoners were assigned to were inside the local temple. They were surprised to receive good bedding, and food was plentiful, '. . . containing about twice as much meat as the Japanese soldier ever saw'. The prisoners could even supplement their provisions by anything they fancied from the shops in town, '. . . which we could visit ourselves three times a week, under escort of a private of the guard, invariably sympathetic and helpful' (Benckendorff, 1955: 70-4).

The rumours regarding the favourable conditions of imprisonment in Japan reached the front and had a demoralizing effect on the Russian troops. As news on the surrender of Port Arthur reached the heroic Colonel Nikolai Tretyakov and his officers, there was tremendous commotion in the room and soon they started to debate the conditions of the surrender. Tretyakov supported their return to Russia rather than going to Japan. First, he argued that officers would be separated from the rank and file and thus the presence of the former would not lessen the hardship of the latter. Second, Russia badly needed officers in other frontiers. And finally, he argued, '. . . people in Russia might think that we officers became prisoners of war in order to spend a pleasant time in beautiful Japan, free from all duty and hardship, at a time when disturbances are taking place in the centre of our own country. . .' (Tretyakov, 1911: 299). The Japanese army was not oblivious to the demoralizing effect of these rumours. Near Mukden, it flew large kites into the Russian lines bearing photographs of the temples of Japan and letters from Russian prisoners (McCormick, 1907, 2: 327).

Another aspect of the chivalry and respect Japanese combatants displayed during the war was their appraisal for the Russian fighting spirit. 'We cannot but admire', Japanese officers stated, 'the stubborn courage with which the Russian Generals and soldiers defended their post under circumstances of extreme difficulty and suffering.' On the Russian attempts to recover Kenzan, Sakurai wrote:

> Their tenacity of purpose is truly worthy of a Great Power and deserves our admiration. Just as we have our loyal and brave *Yamato-damashii* they have their own undaunted courage peculiar to the Slav race. . . . Each of the contending parties had a worthy foe with which to compare its strength (Sakurai, 1907: 89-90).

During the campaign around Taipo-shan the Japanese were attacking and the Russians were in the defence. A group of Japanese officers evaluated the battle: 'The enemy is certainly brave', said one of them. 'Yes, they are fighting hard', said another, and Sakurai concluded that they were 'beginning to feel that the Russian strength came not only from their mechanical provisions, but also from their intrepid behaviour.' As Taipo-shan was taken over after 58 hours of incessant fighting, Sakurai admitted that 'our hearts involuntarily hated our opponents', but he was quick to rationalize: '. . . those who have had experience in actual fighting will easily sympathise with this sense of hatred . . . of course it is a silly thing! and we do all admire without stint their valor and perseverance' (Sakurai, 1907: 135, 144-5).

In almost every battle or encounter where the Russians fought relentlessly, their Japanese rivals were quick to manifest their deference. After the battle of the Yalu the Japanese were loud 'in their praises of the bravery of the Russians here'. Similarly, after the battle of Chia-a-tzu, '. . . all the Japanese taking part in the action, from staff officers to private soldiers, agreed in praising the individual courage and bearing of the Russian soldiers, whose admirable fighting qualities were completely negatived by the Russian general in command not having provided an adequate protection on the right flank' (McKenzie, 1905: 155, 207). Within the Japanese navy as well, officers often expressed their feeling that the Russian sailors were '. . . better men, stronger, more intelligent and more highly trained than their soldiers' (Hamilton, 1905, 2: 307).

The sympathy for the enemy was also common among the

142

highest echelon of the Japanese command. General Nogi, for example, expressed empathy towards his arch-rival. In an interview he admitted that he was thinking often of General Stoessel. He confessed:

> To be frank, I think of him every day. When I go to bed at night and when I get up in the morning, and often between times I wonder about him, how hard his position must be, and how well he defends it, and if he is really injured as we have heard (Barry, 1905: 145-6; cf. Villiers, 1905: 114).

Nogi retained his admiration for Stoessel even after the surrender of the latter, and at the first meeting between the two generals both of them praised the bravery of the troops of the other (Ashmead-Bartlett, 1906).

While it is possible that some of the opinions mentioned above were a mere courtesy or manifestation of modesty before foreign observers, there is enough evidence regarding the genuine sentiments the Japanese felt for the rivals (e.g., Tamon, 1927; Taniguchi, 1981). Although not all shared such high esteem for the Russians, the common opinion was far from the demonized image of the allies so prevalent four decades later. Many Japanese combatants were not involved in judging the Russian army, yet they expressed keen interest in the Russians, their customs, and beliefs (see Irokawa, 1970; Ōe, 1988; Zama shiritsu toshokan, 1990-94).

JAPANESE PUBLIC ATTITUDES TO THE ENEMY

The high public morale in Japan was partly a reflection of the rising loyalty of the people to the emperor and the state. But more than anything else, Okamoto Shumpei contends, it was '... the glorious news of the progress of the war and the numerous promises about the outcome of the war that the press was making with convincing unanimity' (Okamoto, 1970: 129). After years of constant fear of the Russian giant, the reports of successive victories, followed each time by the nationwide, lantern march celebrations, had an intoxicating effect upon the Japanese.

The growing literacy towards the end of Meiji era contributed to the expansion of the reading public, and during the war newspapers were sold in unprecedented numbers. The educated echelon followed the siege of Port Arthur and the advance of the Russia's Baltic fleet through agitated and offensive 'extras' editions (Watanabe, 1963). The common people were also dependent on popular media to characterize the enemy, and much of the information came in graphic form. The most popular format for war prints was *nishiki-e* triptychs, which like newspaper accounts manifested the epitome of Japanese bravery.

Triptychs from the period of the Russo-Japanese War, noted art historian Elizabeth Swinton, conveyed three primary messages. The most common type celebrated the chivalry and achievement of the Japanese military and showed the Russians with no special sentiment, albeit in defeat. A second, infrequent category of prints was those which denigrated the Russians as either cowardly, weeping, and trembling soldiers or as a cruel enemy. It is important to note, however, that the Russians were never shown with animal-like faces as the Chinese had been depicted a decade earlier. Finally, certain prints portrayed the Russians, notably Vice Admiral Makarov and General Kuropatkin, as heroic figures and most importantly as worthy adversaries. This type of print was instrumental in demonstrating the technological advance of Japan as capable of defeating a powerful enemy (Okamoto, 1983; Swinton, 1991, 1995).

While the common people supported the government and the military in their management of the war without much hesitancy, the élite was divided into two groups. One group, consisting mainly of intellectuals and certain industrialists, advocated a resolution of the war, even though Japan had not won a decisive victory. Their motives were either because of the fear of Russia, the rising human losses, or the intimate knowledge of the limit of Japan's economic capabilities. The second group, whose influence grew steadily during the war, demanded a protracted war until Japan gained a decisive victory over Russia. The failure of Japan to force Russia to recognize its victory was one of the reasons for the rising popularity of the second camp. In May 1905 public opinion in Japan strongly supported the continuation and even the expansion of the war, believing that only the destruction of the Russian army in the east would compensate their nation for the sacrifice made (Okamoto, 1970).

These ardent public attitudes to the war notwithstanding, the common people treated Russian POWs in a humane and courteous manner. An American visitor who saw some Russian POWs upon their arrival at Kobe, noted in his diary that

... the town is full of soldiers returning from the war. Trainloads of

> Russian prisoners arrive during the day, generally loads of from 500 to 700. . . . The Japanese attitude towards them is one of quiet, respectful reserve. They look at them as they march through the streets and the Russians, as they pass, say *Sayonara, sayonara* (Manthorpe, 1986: 185).

These indifferent if not warm attitudes were particularly apparent at the end of the conflict. After the armistice had been signed Russian POWs in Matsuyama anticipated their evacuation and were at liberty to move about in the town and to freely contact the local population. Benckendorff was tired of the communal life and rented a house. On the very day he settled in, two Japanese offered him their services – a cook and a rickshaw driver. Benckendorff consented and stayed there for the next six months until his evacuation to Vladivostok (Benckendorff, 1955).

STILL . . . WAR IS WAR

To say the Russo-Japanese War was conducted on 'civilized' lines, does not mean that misconduct beyond 'normal' battle behaviour and even sporadic atrocities did not occur. Moreover, various observers and reports on both sides suggest that most of the aberrant incidents of war conduct and maltreatment occurred on the Russian side. One of the most shocking events of the war was the brutal attack made by the three cruisers of the Vladivostok squadron on several Japanese transports. The accounts of the sinking of *Hitachi maru*, for instance, show some discrepancies, but is certain that the Russians did not allow non-combatants much chance to escape. They opened fire on the ship at short distance and continued shelling even after it stopped. About 1000 people were killed or drowned (Cassell, 1905, 1: 387-99). This and similar incidents, however, did not affect Japanese chivalrous conduct towards Russian captives on the naval front, as survivors of the fiasco at Tsushima attested (e.g., Novikoff-Priboy, 1937).

The unyielding siege of Port Arthur provided much opportunity for violation of the Geneva Convention to which both parties were committed. During the fierce attacks against the Russian fortifications at the northern slopes of Port Arthur (the 'Eagle's Nest') in August 1904 thousands of soldiers, most of them Japanese, were left wounded and dead between the trenches of the two sides. The Japanese were agitated about the fate of their soldiers lying on the battlefield, since it was impossible to collect them. Yet, the proximity of the hostile lines, and the desire to keep one's arrangement of positions as secret as possible, rendered any discussion of a temporary armistice out of question (Ashmead-Bartlett, 1906). While the Russians did not let the Japanese enter the area, they attempted to gather the wounded. The Japanese were furious at what they considered breach of military decorum and opened fire on some of the Russian burial parties, forcing them to withdraw. Under these circumstances, about 7000 dead and wounded Japanese, not counting the Russians, were left exposed on this small area of ground between the lines. Eventually, many others were rescued, but hundreds lying higher up the mountain, closer to the Russian lines, were left to die slowly (Great Britain, 1908, 3: 51).

In the heat of the struggle for Port Arthur, a place which both sides recognized as crucial to their success in the war as a whole, mid-level commanders deliberately abandoned the Geneva Convention. Both parties ignored the Red Cross, and made no effort to conclude armistices for collecting the wounded and burying the dead. The reason for this state of affairs, a contemporary observer explained, '... was to be found in the long and determined nature of the struggle, in unavoidable misunderstandings, and in the fear that any concession to the suffering might lead to the exposure or capture of important positions in the chain of defence' (Ashmead-Bartlett, 1906: 189-90).

The final months of the siege of Port Arthur were the watershed of Russian misconduct. In certain cases the Japanese army responded severely, though locally, to Russian atrocities. The Cossacks from the Caucus, for example, were notorious for robbery and murder. The Japanese army charged them with many outrages against the laws of civilized warfare. The army asserted that owing to their murder of the Japanese wounded and prisoners and the robbing of the wounded and dead, it was compelled to wage 'a war of extermination against them' (McCormick, 1907, 1: 266-7). Still, Russian misconduct did not affect the overall Japanese attitude and often were treated strictly by the Russian high command due to Japanese complaints (Kinai, 1907, 2: 193-4).

JAPAN'S WARS WITH THE WEST: ACCOUNTING FOR THE ATTITUDINAL DIFFERENCES

The circumstances that led to the outbreak of the Russo-

Japanese War were similar in many aspects to those of the Pacific War. In both cases Japan's expansionist policy encountered the ambitions of an adversary expansionist nation: Tsarist Russia in the former and the United States in the latter. Both wars were preceded by a deep sense of vulnerability on the side of Japan, which feared that its recent conquests and international recognition were doomed and that it may slide back to the rank of the so-called less developed nations. Both wars were also fought against foes that were objectively stronger and were perceived as such; finally, both wars began with a surprise Japanese attack.

These similarities notwithstanding, there are several substantial differences between the Russo-Japanese War and the Pacific War which may account for the relatively restrained antagonism Japan manifested to its Russian foe, as compared with the brutal attitudes displayed to the Allied forces.

The first difference lies in the international circumstances. In the Pacific War Japan fought against most of the major Western states, whereas in the Russo-Japanese War the West was on Japan's side or at least not against it. As a whole, the West in 1904 was Japan's audience, whereas in 1941 it was Asian peoples who became Japan's desired audience and reference group. Further, during the Russo-Japanese War Japan was still attempting to enter the 'club' of the developed and civilized nations, thus behaving according to the highest perceived requirements of that club. By the eve of the Pacific War, however, Japan was just a disappointed and embittered 'honorary member' of the club, conscious of its inability to join as an equal member.

The international circumstances were reflected in Japan's willingness to adhere to international codes of conduct in battle. Prior to the Russo-Japanese War, Japan adopted the obligations determined in the first Geneva Convention (1864), the Brussels Declaration (1874), and the Hague Convention (1899) dealing with land warfare and human rights of POWs. Japan followed the rules and boasted of its fair play, acts that led to its temporary recognition as a 'civilized nation'. In 1929, however, it refused to adopt the new Geneva Convention, claiming that the differential approach to POWs would impose duties only on Japan (Hata, 1996). Refusing to follow Western conventions, Japan thereupon embarked the path of fanaticism, at least in the eyes of West.

Nationalism also played a role in shaping Japanese attitudes. In the early years of the twentieth century, ethnic nationalism [*minzokushugi*] began to appear in 'powerful if still inchoate form' as Doak (1996: 82) has pointed out, yet the Russians were not conceived as the ultimate 'other' in the Japanese self-identity. In the years which preceded the Pacific War, however, ethnic nationalism turned into ultra-nationalism. This course had a pervasive impact on the attitudes to the enemy in the eventual struggle with the West, since it meant full indoctrination of the youth about the divine mission of Japan, blind conformism, and lesser ability to see the human side of the other camp (Maruyama, 1963; Iritani, 1991).

In the Russo-Japanese War, the presence of foreign observers – journalists, military attachés, and Red Cross representatives – from nations Japan wanted to emulate certainly helped to prevent local atrocities. Moreover, there were only a few civilians involved in either side in that war, and their absence offset the 'natural' tendency to escalation. During the Pacific War, in contrast, the killing or maltreatment of 'innocent' civilians, either in the Philippines or by the Allies' city bombing, was an important factor in the escalation. Finally, although both parties in the Russo-Japanese War employed large armies of more than one million soldiers, this conflict cannot be defined as a total war, and it was unquestionably far from the scale – either in duration, manpower involved, or human suffering – witnessed during the Pacific War.

All the above factors led to an increasing dehumanization of the enemy in the Pacific War, while the Russo-Japanese War was characterized by increasing respect for each other by the two sides. While the Japanese were determined to engage in civilized warfare from the outbreak of the war, their capacity to maintain their conduct depended on their rival. Certainly, the Japanese did not operate in a vacuum. Although Russian combatants acted occasionally in a more savage manner than the Japanese, the Russian military as whole fought within the contemporary civilized guidelines. The Russians, and especially the rank and file, who entered the war with quasi-racial contempt for the Japanese soon changed their attitudes. As the war progressed, even Russian generals could not mistake the admiration they gradually came to feel for the Japanese soldiers (e.g., Baring, 1905; Kowner, 1998). Consequently, the ability and especially the desire to prevent escalation in combat misconduct became notable in this war; a decade later, during the Great War in

Europe, it began to vanish. In this sense, the Russo-Japanese War was the first 'civilized grand war' and perhaps also the last.

BIBLIOGRAPHY

Ashmead-Bartlett, Ellis. 1906. *Port Arthur: The Siege and Capitulation*. Edinburgh: William Blackwood & Sons.

Baelz, Erwin. 1932. *Awakening Japan: The Diary of a German Doctor*. Edited by Toku Baelz. Translated from German by Eden and Cedar Paul. New York: Viking Press.

Baring, Maurice. 1905. *With the Russians in Manchuria*. London: Methuen.

Barry, Richard. 1905. *Port Arthur: A Monster Heroism*. New York: Moffat, Yard & Co.

Benckendorff, Constantine A. 1955. *Half a Life: Reminiscences of a Russian Gentleman*. London: The Richards Press.

Cameron, Craig M. 1994. *American Samurai: Myth, Imagination, and the Conduct of Battle in the First Marine Division, 1941-1951*. Cambridge: Cambridge University Press.

Cassell. 1905. *Cassell's History of the Russo-Japanese War*. 4 vols. London: Cassell and Co.

Connaughton, Richard Michael. 1988. *The War of the Rising Sun and Tumbling Bear: A Military History of the Russo-Japanese War, 1904-5*. London: Routledge.

Daws, Gavan. 1994. *Prisoners of the Japanese: POWs of World War II in the Pacific*. New York: W. Morrow.

Diedrich, Edward C. 1978. *The Last Iliad: The Siege of Port Arthur in the Russo-Japanese War, 1904-1905*. Ph.D. dissertation, New York University.

Doak, Kevin M. 1996. 'Ethnic nationalism and romanticism in early twentieth-century Japan'. *Journal of Japanese Studies*, 22, 77-103.

Dower, John W. 1986. *War without Mercy: Race And Power in the Pacific War*. New York: Pantheon.

Duus, Peter. 1995. *The Abacus and the Sword*. Berkeley: University of California Press.

Great Britain, Historical Section. Committee of Imperial Defense. 1908. *Official History of the Russo-Japanese War*. 5 vols. London: General Staff.

Great Britain, War Office. 1907. *The Russo-Japanese War: Reports from British Officers Attached to the Japanese Forces in the Field*. 3 vols. London: General Staff.

Hamilton, Ian. 1905. *A Staff Officer's Scrap-Book during the Russo-Japanese War*. 2 vols. London: Edward Arnold.

Hata, Ikuhiko. 1996. 'From consideration to contempt: The changing nature of Japanese military and popular perceptions of prisoners of war through the ages'. In *Prisoners of War and Their Captors in World War II*, edited by Bob Moore and Kent Fedorowich. Oxford: Berg, 253-76.

Hicks, George. 1995. *The Comfort Women: Japan's Brutal Regime of Enforced Prostitution in the Second World War*. New York: W.W. Norton.

Hoyt, Edwin. 1967. *The Russo-Japanese War*. London: Abelard-Schuman.

Iritani, Toshio. 1991. *Group Psychology of the Japanese in Wartime*. London: Kegan Paul International.

Irokawa Daikichi. 1970. 'Nichiro sensōka no heishi no kiroku: Ōzawa jōtōhei senchū nikki' [A soldier's chronicle of the Russo-Japanese War: Private Ōzawa's diary during the war]. *Jfimbun shizen kagaku ronshū* (Tōkyō keizai daigaku), 24 (November), 195-290.

Kerr, E. Bartlett. 1985. *Surrender and Survival: The Experience of American POWs in the*

Pacific 1941-1945. New York: William Morrow & Co.

Kinai, M., ed. 1907. *The Russo-Japanese War: Official Reports.* 2 vols. Tokyo: Shimbashido.

Kowner, Rotem. 1998. 'Nicholas II and the Japanese Body: Images and Decision Making on the Eve of the Russo-Japanese War'. *The Psychohistory Review,* 26, 211-52.

Lensen, George Alexander, ed. 1967. *The d'Anethan Dispatches from Japan, 1894-1910.* Tokyo: Sophia University.

Lone, Stewart. 1994. *Japan's First Modern War: Army and Society in the Conflict with China, 1894-95.* New York: St. Martin's Press.

MacKenzie, S. P. 1994. 'The treatment of prisoners of war in World War II'. *Journal of Modern History,* 66, 487-520.

Manthorpe, Victoria, ed. 1986. *Travels in the Land of the Gods (1898-1907): The Japan Diaries of Richard Gordon Smith.* New York: Prentice-Hall Press.

Maruyama, Masao. 1963. *Thought and behavior in modern Japanese politics.* London: Oxford University Press.

McCaul, Ethel. 1904. *Under the Care of the Japanese War Office.* London: Cassell & Co.

McCormick, Frederick. 1907. *The Tragedy of Russia in Pacific Asia.* 2 vols. New York: The Outing Publishing Co.

McCully, Newton A. 1977. *The McCully Report: The Russo-Japanese War, 1904-05.* Annapolis, MD: Naval Institute Press.

McKenzie, Frederick Arthur. 1905. *From Tokyo to Tiflis.* London: Hurst-Blackett.

Moore, Bob and Fedorowich, Kent. 1996. 'Prisoners of war in the Second World War: An overview'. In *Prisoners of War and Their Captors in World War II,* edited by Bob Moore and Kent Fedorowich. Oxford: Berg, 1-18.

Nish, Ian H. 1985. *The Origins of the Russo-Japanese War.* London: Longman.

Novikoff-Priboy, A. 1937. *Tsushima, Grave of a Floating City.* New York: Alfred A. Knopf.

Ōe Shino'o, ed. 1988. *Heishitachi no Nichiro sensō: 500 tsū no gunji yūbin kara* [The soldiers' Russo-Japanese War as seen from 500 military letters]. Tokyo: Asahi shimbunsha.

Okamoto, Shumpei. 1970. *The Japanese Oligarchy and the Russo-Japanese War.* New York: Columbia University Press.

——. ed. 1983. *Impressions of the front: Woodcuts of the Sino-Japanese War, 1894-95.* Philadelphia: Philadelphia Museum of Art.

Russell, Edward Frederick Langley (Lord Russell of Liverpool). 1958. *The Knights of Bushido: A Short History of Japanese War Crimes.* London: Cassell & Co.

Saikami Tokio. 1969. *Matsuymama shūyōjo: Horyo to Nihonjin* [Prison camp Matsuyama: The captives and the Japanese]. Tokyo: Chūō kōronsha.

Sakurai, Tadayoshi. 1907. *Human Bullets: A Soldier's Story of Port Arthur.* Tokyo: Teibi Pub.

Seaman, Louis Livingstone. 1905. *From Tokio through Manchuria with the Japanese.* New York: D. Appleton & Co.

Shillony, Ben Ami. 1981. *Politics and Culture in Wartime Japan.* Oxford: Clarendon Press.

Swinton, Elisabeth de Sabato. 1991. *In Battle's Light: Woodblock Prints of Japan's Early Modern Wars.* Worcester, MA: Worcester Art Museum.

——. 1995. 'Russo-Japanese War triptychs: Chastising a powerful enemy'. In *A Hidden Fire: Russian and Japanese Cultural Encounters, 1868-1926,* edited by Thomas Rimer. Stanford, CA: Stanford University Press, 114-32.

Tamon Jirō. 1927. *Tamon Jirō Nichiro sensō nikki* [The diary of Tamon Jirō from the Russo-Japanese War]. Tokyo: Fuyo shoten.

Taniguchi Jinkichi. 1981. *Nichiro sensō jūgunki* [A record of the front-line in the Russo-Japanese War]. Fusō chō (Aichi ken): Taniguchi Saburō.

Tretyakov, Nikolai Alexandrovitch. 1911. *My Experience at Nan shan and Port Arthur with the Fifth East Siberian Rifles.* Translated by A. C. Alford, edited by F. Nolan Baker. London: Hugh Rees.

Villiers, Frederic. 1895. 'The Truth about Port Arthur'. *North American Review*, March, 325–30.

——.1905. *Port Arthur: Three Months with the Besiegers.* London: Longmans Green.

Watanabe Kazuo. 1963. *Jitsuroku gōgai sensen* [The authentic chronicle of the battle of the extra (editions)]. Tokyo: Shimbun jidaisha.

Wincelberg, Shimon and Anita. 1976. *The Samurai of Vishogrod: The Notebook of Jacob Marateck.* Philadelphia: The Jewish Publication Society of America.

Wright, Seppings H. C. 1905. *With Togo: The Story of Seven Months' Active Service Under His Command.* London: Hurst and Blackett.

Zama shiritsu toshokan, ed. 1990-94. *Nichiro sensō jūgunki* [A record of the front-line in the Russo-Japanese War]. 2 vols. Zama shi (Kanagawa ken): Zama shiritsu toshokan.

10

Japan and Russia: Mutual Images, 1904-39

YULIA MIKHAILOVA

INTRODUCTION

I t has been widely recognized that the images people of one
nation have about others are quite instrumental in mobilization
of public opinion which, in its turn, is an important factor in
international relations. The Russian and Japanese images of each
other in the past still have an impact on people's mentality today,
and often function as psychological barriers on the path to political
rapprochement. Recent academic works discussing mutual
Russian-Japanese perceptions focus mainly on individuals or
separate groups of individuals (Itō, 1990; Akizuki, 1990; Togawa,
1990; Mikhailova, 1993; Molodiakov, 1996). In our era of
globalization when contacts between people at grassroots level are
rapidly increasing, it is especially important to know what images
and perceptions underpinned relations between Japan and Russia
on the level of mass consciousness, what political and cultural
mechanisms were involved in their creation and how stereotypes
of the past have influenced popular opinion in later years.

This article first examines some popular images of the
Russians and Japanese during the Russo-Japanese War (1904-
05), that is, when contacts between the two nations involved
people on a large scale for the first time in history. The
development of these images is traced through into the 1930s
when military clashes on Lake Khasan (Chengkufeng incident,
1938) and the River Khalkhin-gol (Nomonhan incident, 1939)
took place. The creation of images of Self and Other is analyzed
in relation to perceptions of national identity and race in modern
Japan and the Soviet Union.

The article is based on political cartoons, satirical stories and articles published in magazines aimed at the general public, children and soldiers of the Red Army. Particular attention is given to visual forms of representation which, more than verbal ones, appeal to people's emotions, more easily turn into identifying icons and serve as effective propaganda tools. At the same time graphic images not only influence and create public opinion, but also reflect the existing mood of a society and may serve as a gateway for understanding the psychology of relations between Japan and Russia.

PRECEDING FIRE AND SWORD

Before the Russo-Japanese War both the Russians and Japanese already had certain images of each other. In Japan, the image of Russia comprised several, often contradictory, notions: a northern threat, a vast country, an empire of wise rulers, a friendly land of generous people, a country less advanced than other Western states. In cartoons Russia was usually represented as a bear or a tiger, animals more known for their strength than their wits (Yoda, 1928; Shimizu, 1994).[1]

The dominant image of Japan in Russia, like everywhere else in the West, was a heart-warming image of a country inhabited by polite doll-like people. After the Sino-Japanese War (1894-95) – and especially after the Boxer Rebellion (1900) – the Russians began to realize, not without surprise, the ability of the Japanese to transform their country into a modern industrial state. Some Russian philosophers, like Vladimir Solov'iov, sensed the potential might of Japan and warned that it could become a threat to European civilization. He even predicted the invasion of Russia and Europe by the Japanese and the Chinese hordes (Solov'iov, 1914: 193-7). However, until the beginning of the Russo-Japanese War, his prophesy was disregarded in Russia as the imagination of a decadent poet and mystic. In Russian public opinion Japan presented no danger and was even viewed as Russia's ally in the Far East. Discourse on the 'yellow peril' and on the superiority of the 'white race', which had developed by that time in the West, was less popular in Russia, partly because of Russia's own ambiguous identity – half-European and half-Asian – and partly because of the realities of the Russian Empire which incorporated ninety-five ethnic groups.

Representatives of a school of thought called *Vostochniki*, 'Easterners', viewed Russia as a harmonious part of Asia and maintained that the Russians and the Asians were united by the same spirit, the same mystical character and even blood. They saw Russia's move to the East not as political occupation, but as cultural assimilation and claimed that Russia's historical mission was to merge with the East by incorporating the latter into the Russian Empire and 'become the leader of the East' (Ukhtomskii, 1900: 31). After the Boxer Rebellion in China, when Russian troops occupied Manchuria, even the term *Zheltorossia*, 'Yellow Russia', was used in the nationalist press which actively tried to install this new notion into the Russian mentality. In essence this was nothing but a Russian version of the ideology of imperialism.

RUSSIA IN THE JAPANESE MIND DURING THE WAR OF 1904-05

What transformation did these images undergo with the beginning of the war? Naturally, war became the main topic of newspapers, journals and magazines. It also stirred a boom in political cartoons. The Japanese had already begun using actively political cartoons for political propaganda purposes during the Movement for Freedom and Popular Rights [*Jiyū minken undō*] (1874-89). The most popular weekly magazine, which contained numerous caricatures on contemporary events was *Marumaru shimbun* founded in 1877. Its first issue had circulation of 5000 (Shimizu, 1991: 55). New forms of satirical magazines appeared consisting mainly of stories in cartoons with captions, some of them quite long. Such magazines included *Kokkei shimbun* (founded in 1901), *Nipponchi* (founded in 1904), *Tokyo pukku* (founded in 1905).

The war with Russia was popular in Japan and people were thirsty for war news. Although telegraph lines had been opened, they were not easily available for reporters and detailed accounts of life in battle had to be delivered by mail or by hand (Huffman, 1997: 280). Photography was not yet widely used. Besides, the Japanese public wanted to hear only about the victories of its army and navy which did not always correspond to reality. Consequently, stories had to be made up, and cartoons opened up enormous possibilities as the genre allowed exaggeration and invention. So, stories in cartoons did not necessarily carry information about the real facts of war, but rather conveyed the feelings and emotions of authors who knew well how to satisfy the expectations of the public. While at the beginning of the war the Japanese were watching events with apprehension and tension, the defeat of the Russian army at Liaoyang and Mukden, the capitulation of Port Arthur and, at last, 'the great victory' in the Tsushima Straits brought a feeling of relief and the Japanese began to express themselves openly, making fun of the Russians.

Three main topics stand out in the Japanese cartoons and the satirical stories which accompanied them: their authors wanted to show that Japan was waging a war of justice against Russia-the-aggressor; they denigrated the Russians as silly cowards who underestimated the Japanese; and they depicted Russia as a country torn apart by internal strife.

Despite the fact that it was Japan, not Russia, which launched the first attack on 8 February 1904, Japanese cartoonists blamed Russia for igniting the fire of war, which was viewed as an expression of ambitions of a 'devilish man-eater'. This image of Russia was represented, for example, in a cartoon 'Man-eating Russia' [*Hitokui Rokoku*], published during the first month of war (see fig. 1). The caption to it read:

> At the time it was put down by Japan, Russia, like a devilish man-eater, severely abused people of all countries it had swallowed: [the devil] eats some tendon and starts sneezing, he bites some meat, but starts coughing, he pinches something and becomes itchy, he thrusts somewhere and farts. But in the end he throws up everything he has eaten (Yoshino, 1993: 117).

The devil in this cartoon had the face of the Russian Emperor Nicholas II whose sinister look and rapacious grin left no doubt among readers about his greed and cruelty, and the artist depicted people of different nationalities imprisoned in his stomach. In the era of imperialism when the power of states was measured against the size of their territorial possessions, Japan, which itself carried out a policy of territorial expansion, perceived Russia as its rival in the Far East and, in reality, probably envied the huge size of the Russian Empire.

From the time Russia defeated the Tartars in the fourteenth century and formed a unified state, successfully repelling subsequent attacks of various invaders, the Russians thought of themselves as the best warriors in the world, courageous and heroic. The overwhelming victory over Napoleon in 1812 made Russia the most powerful state in Europe. It was this very image that horrified the Japanese. What a triumph it was for them to realize that their formidable northern neighbour was not that strong. It was a double triumph to poke fun at the Russian military men. *Kokkei shimbun* ran the cartoon 'Russian soldiers: A

人 食 ひ 露 國

Figure 1: Man-eating Russia (unknown artist)

bunch of cowards' [*Rokoku-no gunjin: Koshinukezoroi*], which used a traditional Japanese design style *hitomoji* (characters written in human figures) to write the word 'Russia'. This made it possible to expose the Russians in various humiliating postures: trembling with fear and cringing before the Japanese (Yoshino, 1993: 139). In another cartoon 'Firing a volley' [*Isshin shageki*], the Russians were lying on their backs, defeated by the Japanese, and trying in vain to beat the enemy off with their heels (Yoshino, 1993: 139). This cartoon claimed that the Japanese spirit *Yamatodama* was superior to the Russians', pejoratively named them *Rosuke*, a word consisting of the syllable *ro* for 'Russia' and the suffix *suke* which is used in names and has a pejorative connotation. Newspapers and magazines widely advertised the medicine *seirogan*, a stomach pain-reliever, replacing the character *sei* (justice) with *sei* (overcome), thus turning its meaning into 'subjugation of Russia'. Numerous cartoons and stories made fun of the commander of the Russian army General Kuropatkin, who allegedly left the army on the eve of the battle for Mukden. In reality he was dismissed by the czar, but decided to remain in the army as an ordinary officer till the very end of the war and was glorified for his personal courage in Russia.

Figure 2: Morning of the Russian Tsar biting his navel (Kitazawa Rakuten)

The Russian czar was among the favourite objects of the Japanese satire. The front cover of the inaugural issue of *Tokyo pukku* represented a huddled figure of Nicholas II 'trying in vain to bite his own navel' (see fig. 2). The artist, the famous cartoonist Kitazawa Rakuten, intended to convey a message that the Russian czar was not very bright and had realized the power of Japan too late (Shimizu, 1986: 5). Another cartoon depicted the czar's frightened face and small figure struggling with waves in the Sea of Japan and begging the American president for help (Haga and Shimizu, 1985: 24). In contrast, the Japanese

157

portrayed their own soldiers with impressive appearance, full of dignity and pride. The desire of the Japanese to contest the image of them as doll-like people and to assert themselves against the Russians is obvious. The fact that the Russians did not live up to the reputation they boasted about facilitated this.

Actually, the Japanese proved able to find the most vulnerable points of the Russians. This is not to say that individual Russians lacked courage or valour. But the war on the whole was unpopular in Russia. Russian soldiers and sailors were morally and psychologically unprepared to fight a war. They did not exhibit much resourcefulness or ingenuity, automatically following instructions of their commanders, who were often ineffectual. As a result the Russians lost one battle after another. The lack of a unifying national lodestar in the war deprived people of the martial spirit and this predestined the failure.

The defeat of the Russian army speeded up the revolution at home. On 9 January 1905 a peaceful demonstration of workers with families walked up to the czar's palace in St Petersburg only to be shot down by order of the czar. Strikes broke out throughout the country and in June the famous uprising on the battleship *Potemkin* horrified Russian authorities. All these events were reflected in Japanese cartoons. One of them represented a larger-than-life figure of the war hero Marshall Ōyama Iwao, triumphantly looking at a crumbled building of the Russian church, the symbol of the Russian monarchy (Kitamura, 1985: 7-8). Another depicted a Russian *muzhik* tearing off the crown from the czar's head (Kitamura, 1985: 27), still another a sailor in a hand-to-hand struggle with an officer (Haga and Shimizu, 1985: 31).

War-time cartoons, like woodblock prints, often aimed at demonstrating Japan's progress (Swinton, 1995: 122-3). The Japanese depicted themselves wearing modern uniforms and armed with modern weapons, treating Russian prisoners-of-war with delicious Western food and so on. However, for the Japanese, as Confucians, 'civilization' also had traditional connotations, meaning preservation of harmony and order in society. Russia, torn apart by internal strife, was uncivilized in the eyes of the Japanese. This kind of propaganda added to the Japanese public self-assurance and belief in success.

On the whole, Japan waged the war to achieve equality with the West and achievement of this goal depended, both military and psychologically, upon putting down Russia, which claimed to be one of the strongest states in the international club. Thus, Russia was to play the role of Japan's Other at one of those moments which were critical for the development of a national identity in Japan. In their aspiration towards equality with the West the Japanese were anxious not to be accepted as representatives of the 'yellow race' and were outraged when they were called 'the yellow peril'. The appraisal of the war as 'the first victory of the yellow race over the white race' was not emphasized by the Japanese at that time.

WAR IN THE RUSSIAN EYES

Russian journalists and cartoonists were confronted with a more difficult task than their Japanese colleagues. They had to sing the praises of deeds when hardly any victories existed in reality. They also had to find persuasive arguments to mobilize the public for the war effort in the absence of tangible national goals. One way out was found in using the time-honoured images of a Russian epic hero and *muzhik*. Both were depicted as larger-than-life and contrasted with exaggerated small figures of the Japanese. From the Russian viewpoint, it was obvious that these tiny doll-like people were predestined to fail in their attempts to contest the Russian giants. The efforts of Japan to strive for equality with great Russia seemed childish, Japan's courage and impertinence looked funny, her modern technology and borrowing of Western culture were superficial and lacked any merit. Russian cartoonists and satirical writers claimed that the Japanese were swindlers, robbers and dirty pillagers who could win only by conniving whereas Russians were 'simple, but honest fellows'.

Caricatures in Russian newspapers often depicted Japan as a *geisha*, although with masculine facial features, exerting herself to the utmost in a futile attempt to raise a huge stone to the top of a mountain.[2] This was meant to symbolize the inability of Japan to carry the burden of war. Other cartoons depicted a thin-legged Japanese soldier trying in vain to crack a huge nut – a metaphor for Japan's failure to take the Russian fortress Port Arthur by storm. 'Firm as a nut' is a Russian colloquial phrase often used to praise someone's valour, obviously, that of the Russians in this case.

Knowing that the Japanese authorities did not easily allow reporters to get direct information from the battlefield, the Russians claimed that Japan's reports on its victories were nothing but canards. Cartoonists drew pictures of ducks flying over the Sea of Japan, as in Russian the word *utka* for 'duck' has also a meaning of 'false rumour' and is used slightly ironically.

In contrast to the pre-war period, one of the main tools of the Russian war-time propaganda came to be racism. The Russo-Japanese War was seen not as merely a war between two countries for the domination over territories, but as '... a necessary consequence of the awaking of the yellow race from its long dream'. One author wrote:

> Japan is a representative of the idea of pan-Mongolism – the unification of the people of that [yellow] stock against the white race ... Russia is an obstacle for the realization of the Japanese government's plans. ... Russia must stay on guard to preserve the European interests from the encroachment of the yellow race (Voronov, 1904: 78).

Another pamphlet claimed: 'The yellow race found its organizers and leaders [in Japan], and pan-Mongolism is in the process of change from dreams to pragmatic politics' (Slonimskii, 1904: 762). Strikingly racist was a lecture given by a professor of Kiev University. He declared that in contrast to many other wars fought for territories or new markets, the present war 'was a racial war and an important biological event'. He emphasized that the Russian mission was the biological sanitation of the Mongol stock (Sikorskii, 1904: 11).

If articles in journals, pamphlets and lectures were meant for a rather well-educated public, the brainwashing of ordinary people was made mainly through graphic forms of representation. Here the so-called 'popular prints', lithographs which were based on a traditional Russian art form *lubki* (Mikhailova, 1998), and political cartoons in popular magazines were most instrumental. The years 1903-07 was a relatively liberal period for the Russian press. Numerous satirical magazines mushroomed in St Petersburg and Moscow at that time and quickly picked up the war as a topic.

One example of this is the cover of the popular magazine *Budilnik* which ran a cartoon poking fun at the commander-in-chief of the Japanese navy, Admiral Tōgō Heihachirō, who was shown as an ugly hairy ape sitting on a tire tube and writing telegrams with 'four hands' (see fig. 3). His face had a silly expression and the caption claimed that only 'macaco' brains could use rumours for the sake of salvation, that is, to produce false reports in order to get the financial help of Western countries (Sviridenko, 1904). In the Russian language the expressions 'to write on water' or 'to write with pitchforks on water' are colloquial sayings for casting doubt on something.

Figure 3: The main 'macaco' of the Japanese navy (U. Sviridenko)

Another cartoon of this magazine put 'the civilized yellow-skinned Japanese' below 'the barbarian Africans' (see fig. 4). A Japanese soldier, although dressed in modern uniform, was endowed with beastly features and depicted sneaking like a foul thief in the night, while a leader of an African tribe was represented holding a declaration of war.[3] He looked like a noble warrior straightforwardly confronting his enemy (Budilnik, 1904: 14). The cartoon referred to the surprise attack of the Japanese navy on Port Arthur on 8 February 1904 which, from the Russian viewpoint, was against the norms of international law. It is interesting, though, that in the cartoon called 'Yellow peril', [*Zheltaya opasnost*] (*Budilnik*, 1904: 38) which represented Japan as a witch frightening the European community with some potion in a pot, the witch had Semitic,

161

not Asian, features.[4] It is well known that the Jewish pogroms took place quite often in central Russia at this time. So, the author of the picture appealed to anti-Semitism to kindle hostility against the Japanese.

Figure 4: How they start the war (unknown artist)

By the end of the war the Russians began to present themselves as protectors of Europe from the 'yellow peril' in order to draw the sympathies of the West. The topic was gaining more and more popularity. In this way Russia was giving up the 'Asian part' of its identity it had claimed earlier and, on the contrary, was emphasizing its membership in the European club of nations.

Russian graphic representations of war in cartoons and the accompanying satirical captions incorporated many features of the national folklore and popular humour and accentuated the most primitive instincts of people. Quite often the existing stock phrases were used and images of the Japanese were inserted into them which, in turn, gave birth to many jokes about the Japanese. All this made war-time images easily acceptable by ordinary people and helped to promote the war-time perception of Japan into the future. Alhough many of the Russian intelligentsia criticized these caricatures for their vulgarity or racism and were even ashamed of them, their influence may be seen in the graphic representations of the Japanese in later Soviet posters and political cartoons.

ON THE PATH TO CONFRONTATION

In October 1917 a new state, Soviet Russia, came into being as the result of the socialist revolution. Its ideology of Bolshevism was directed against capitalist states, Japan included. In 1918 under the direct leadership of Lenin the so-called International Communist League, Comintern, was established in Moscow with the purpose of carrying out a world-wide socialist revolution. With the help of the Comintern the Communist Party was organized in Japan. In 1918 the Japanese government, together with other capitalist states, initiated intervention into the Soviet Far East to suppress the Russian revolution, but had to withdraw in 1922.

Under these circumstances mainly two types of attitude towards the Soviet Union developed in Japan. The dominant attitude on the part of the government was the vision of the Soviet Union as an enemy. The old territorial rivalry between Japan and Russia was aggravated by the ideological confrontation. From the second half of the 1920s until 1945 the Japanese government pursued a policy of repression against the left, arrested and put into jail nearly all members of the Japan Communist Party and a system of strict censorship was introduced. In the 1930s the Kwantung army started fostering plans for war with the Soviet Union. It collected intelligence information against its northern neighbour in Manchuria and the Soviet Far East and after the Manchurian incident of 1931 instigated numerous clashes on the border between Manchuria and Mongolia.[5]

An additional reason for this activity was the rivalry between the army and the navy over their share of the national budget. In contrast to the army, representatives of the navy purposely belittled the Soviet menace and even supported the Japanese-Russian Association which aimed at development of friendly relations between the two countries. In 1937-38 domestic problems in the Soviet Union, such as purges organized by Stalin and difficulties in the supply of consumer goods, all well-reported in Japanese newspapers, created an impression that the northern neighbour was not very strong, although the Soviet Far Eastern army increased from 42,000 men in 1929 to 290,000 in 1937 and was equipped with modern technology (Hirai, 1992: 40-1). At this time some members of the Department of Strategy came up with the so-called 'theory of the reconnaissance of the Soviet military might' and started planning a limited attack on the Soviet Union. This plan eventuated in the military clashes on Lake Khasan and the River Khalkhin-gol, both of which ended with Japan's defeat.

In contrast to the official anti-Soviet policy, many of Japanese intellectuals experienced infatuation with the Soviet Union. Some of them were enchanted by Russian literature, music, theatre or arts. Others exhibited sincere interest in the ideas of Marx, Plekhanov and Lenin, and in the Soviet experiment of implementing those ideas in practice.

How were these attitudes of the political and intellectual élite reflected in graphics and other publications designed for mass consumption? Nothing similar to the boom in political cartoons of the Russo-Japanese War took place in Japan. Occasionally, caricatures appeared accusing the army of imperialistic aspirations and glorifying the Soviet Union. They were probably drawn by those who belonged to or sympathized with the left wing. Such was, for example, the cartoon *Manshū ni heiwa o!*, 'For peace in Manchuria', by Inagaki Kogorō which depicted the United States, Great Britain, Chinese militarists and Japan as aggressors eager to take over parts of Manchuria while the Soviet Union had the image of 'a peaceful industrial land' (Inagaki, 1931).

Mainstream trends in popular propaganda regarding to Russia may well be seen in literature for children. One of the most popular magazines for children was *Shōnen kurabu*, which promoted patriotic and military indoctrination of the youth. There could hardly be any better means of doing so than using images of the Russo-Japanese War and the thirtieth anniversary of the battle in the Tsushima Straits came in handy. Every issue of *Shōnen kurabu*, published in the middle of the 1930s, contained photographs of heroes of war, their short biographies, explanations about their deeds and contribution into the Japanese victory. Children were taught to draw simplistic portraits of Admiral Tōgō Heihachirō together with portraits of Saigō Takamori, the hero of the Meiji Restoration, and

Hayashi Senjurō, a contemporary military leader. Reminiscences of the war as well as real and fictitious stories with illustrations were published in abundance, conveying to the young generation the atmosphere of the time when the Japanese were anxiously awaiting the capitulation of Port Arthur and the coming of the Baltic fleet, the excitement they felt when General Anatolii Stoessel opened the gates of Port Arthur or when Russian ships went to the bottom. The war was remembered with pride and nostalgia.

For example, on the occasion of the foundation in 1936 of Cossack regiments in the Red Army, *Shōnen kurabu* published a double-page size picture of galloping Cossacks with the following commentary: 'Doesn't it seem to you that the cavalry troops called Cossacks who bravely attacked our army during the Russo-Japanese War, stir up sweet memories for us?' (Kawashima, 1936).

Figure 5: A tachanka *squad of the Soviet army (Itō Kikuzo)*

The old inimical image of Russia as a threat or as a country which cannot be trusted was however also presented. In 1937 *Shōnen kurabu* ran a double-page size picture of a Soviet *tachanka*, a machine-gun put on a horse-drawn cart (see fig. 5). It explained that it was very effective in attacking enemies, that the Soviets were very proud of this weapon and concluded: 'The evening sun casts a gloomy light from beneath the low clouds. A tachanka squad rushes quickly into the wilds. What country does it aim at?' (Itō, 1937). The picture is significant in many ways. Low dark clouds, bodies of horses in disarray, ruined buildings in the background produce an ominous impression on the viewer as if saying that no good can be expected from these troops. It hints that the enemies of the Soviets may be the Japanese. But the picture could also be interpreted as revealing the weakness of the Red Army armed with a horse-drawn machine gun in the era when tanks were already in use. The same message was conveyed through a cartoon ran by the *Tōkyō pukku* in 1934, when a drawing of Stalin was accompanied by the following message: 'The one who is afraid of war wants to look fearful. He puts on the skin of a lion as if frightening others, but at heart he is frightened to death himself.' (Shimizu, 1986: 5).

It may be suggested that for the popular consciousness of the Japanese who were brought up with the idea of the greatness of Japan's victory over Russia in 1905 and who did not possess any true information on the Red Army, the defeat at Lake Khasan and at the River Khalkhin-gol was a shock no less strong than the occupation of the Kuril Islands in the last days of World War II. Since the end of the thirties the Japanese had enough reasons to view the Soviet Union as 'a mysterious country which had great military power' (Hirai, 1992: 42), Japan's policy towards the Soviet Union became more cautious, and distrust towards the northern neighbour increased.

BUILDING THE SOVIET IDENTITY

The Soviet Union made it widely known through the mass media that it regarded the Khasan incident as 'the impudent aggression of Japanese militarists on the sacred Soviet land'. From 3-8 August 1938 the main Soviet official newspapers *Pravda* and *Izvestia* published information about numerous meetings held at various plants, factories or collective farms citing extracts from resolutions accepted there. Stock phrases such as 'we condemn impertinent provocative actions of Japanese military cliques', 'hold up to shame the mean fascist bandits', 'express indignation about the bloody massacre', etc appeared in every newspaper. The events became instrumental in setting the Soviet propaganda machine into motion. The ideas of Soviet patriotism, Soviet spirit, glorification of the Soviet motherland, Soviet heroes, the greatness of Stalin, the 'symbol of the Soviet victory', and the Soviet Army were expressed, criticizing and denigrating the

Japanese. From that time until the beginning of *perestroika* organization of similar meetings became an essential feature of life. The government would inspire them every time it needed the so-called 'mass support and approval' of its policy, be it engagement of troops in Czechoslovakia or Afghanistan. Word clichés did not undergo much change, except that the Japanese were replaced by German fascists during the Great Patriotic War (1941-45) and by American imperialists after the war.

Whereas Soviet newspaper articles carried out mainly ideological propaganda criticizing imperialist Japan, caricatures suggested that the Soviet propaganda was not free from racism. For example, a magazine published for the soldiers of the Red Army ran a story in cartoons under the title 'A story about a "bave" samurai' [*Skaz o 'khrabrom' samurae*] (Smolnyi, 1939), with the word 'brave' within quotation marks. It depicted a figure of a small Japanese soldier attempting to attack territories of neighboring states, China and the Soviet Union. His aggressive intentions were conveyed through his wide open mouth with shark-like teeth, hugged beastly claws and wildly glittering eyes. The caption written in primitive verse expressed the message straightforwardly: the Japanese are pickers and stealers, bandits and greedy pillagers. Treachery is their inherent quality; their sole desire is to grab territories of other states. It also stated that in contrast to the Japanese, the Soviet people would never even think of an aggression, but would neither give up a single inch of their own land. This phrase would also become a cliché deeply ingrained into the Soviet mentality.

The Japanese soldier was depicted in this and many other cartoons as small, undersized or weak. On the contrary, his adversary was huge and strong, with large guns, rifles and airplanes. To emphasize the might of the Soviet military men, the angle that looks from below, creating a sense of distance and scale, was often used by the artists (Efimov, 1938). The cartoonists and writers stressed that the Japanese were frightened by the Soviet military technology, they were amazed, even hypnotized by the outstanding strength and courage of the Russians, by their height, even by the size and beauty of their boots. Physical differences, primarily differences in size, were what the Soviet cartoonists appealed to first of all.

The Soviet caricatures on the Japanese produced in the 1930s, like those of the Russo-Japanese War, endowed the Japanese with animal features and dehumanized them. They belittled the enemy soldiers physically and spiritually, depicting them as mentally and emotionally stunted. One story published in the magazine *Krasnoarmeets* portrayed the Japanese as constantly crying or depressed and the following phrases were used to characterize them: 'Sergeant Akamatsu was angry. His eyes became red and full of tears...'; 'Aikura noticed on the dirty face of Lieutenant Matsunobe a bright tear'; 'tears were running along the commander's face', etc. (Ryklin, 1939). This story claimed that it was based on the book *Fourteen Days of Struggle with the Red Army* by the Japanese author Hara Shirō which was based on reminiscences of Japanese soldiers injured at Lake Khasan and issued as a warning against the formidable northern neighbour.

The Japanese were also represented as children, students who had to be taught. One of the cartoons showed an impaired Japanese soldier sitting at a school-desk with two sheets of paper in front of him: 'Lesson no. 1 – Siberia, 1922; lesson no. 2 – Lake Khasan, 1938' (Sashin and Ganf, 1939). Another carried the message: 'Thirty five years ago: we [the Japanese] marked Mukden, Port Arthur, Tsushima on the map. The present: we [the Russians] mark Volochaevka, Spask, Khasan on the map' (Gench, 1939).[6] It is clear that the Soviet victory over Japan in 1938-39 was viewed as revenge for the defeat in the Russo-Japanese War. Still, Khasan, and the even larger victory at Khalkhin-gol, were seen as minor military achievements in comparison with the Russo-Japanese War. The day the Russian men of the older generation had waited for forty years, as Stalin would put it, came in September 1945 (Nimmo, 1994: 29).

The Soviet propaganda campaign of the 1930s was especially successful in inspiring anti-Japanese feelings because here ideological goals – Japan = imperialist country = enemy – were supported by the traditional Russian racial hostility against the Japanese. It is possible to refer, in this regard, to the words of John W. Dower about the American attitude to the Japanese during World War II. He suggests that it is easier to kill dehumanized enemies, and no moral or legal justification was required to take the land of those who were inherently treacherous, greedy, or who looked like dogs or undeveloped children (Dower, 1986). It is in these attitudes that the roots of the Soviet postwar policy towards Japan seem to lie.

Russo-Japanese confrontation has revolved around the issue of land ownership and land, more than anything else, was related to national feelings which always added vigour to the dispute. It is instructive to learn, for example, that the Soviet anti-Japanese propaganda of the late 1930s used the victory at Khasan much more than the one at Khalkhin-gol which was, however, larger in scale. Moreover, the victory at Khalkhin-gol was glorified through an appeal to the memory of the heroes of Khasan which took place one year before. The explanation lies, probably, in the fact that Lake Khasan was the Russian territory while Khalkhin-gol was in Mongolia. But even on the eve of the final attack at Khalkhin-gol the appeal to Soviet soldiers claimed: 'Comrades! On the border of the Peoples Republic of Mongolia we defend our own land from Baikal to Vladivostok.'

CONCLUSION

The Russo-Japanese War was a milestone in modern Japanese history and an important event in shaping Japan's identity. The convincing military victory over the formidable northern neighbour and a bitter sense of humiliation after the Portsmouth Treaty brought forth complicated feelings – pride, hatred, fear, vanity, irony, respect and admiration at the same time. Russia became the enemy against which the young modern state of Japan measured its successes and failures. Because the war was so important, it had a great impact on the mentality of contemporary Japanese and stereotypes created at that time lingered on.

Military clashes of the 1930s, though definitely of a smaller scale than the Russo-Japanese War, were the first tests of the military might of the Soviet Union after the end of the civil war and since the power of Stalin had been established. They were the first tests of the Soviet propaganda machine which aimed at creating the image of 'Soviet patriots defending their motherland from aggressors'. This time it was Japan which was destined to play the role of the Other for the Soviets. The thorny history of relations between the two countries unfortunately created a favourable climate for Japan to become the Soviet adversary. Thus, it may be concluded that two events of different historical epochs – the Russo-Japanese War and military clashes at Lake Khasan and River Khalkhin-gol – played a somewhat similar role in the historical development of each country. The fact that Japan and Russia lived through the negative experiences in mutual relations during the most crucial periods of their histories probably explains why hostility and distrust are not quick to fade away.

BIBILIOGRAPHY

Akizuki Toshiyuki. 1990. 'Edo jidai ni okeru Nihonjin no Roshia kan' [Japanese views on Russia in the Edo period]. In *Nihon to Roshia* [Japan and Russia], edited by Yasui Ryohei. 2nd ed. Tokyo: Nauka, 1-12.

Budilnik. 1904. 'Kak nachiaynut voinu' [How do they start the war], 1904 (14): 1.

Dower, John W. 1986. *War Without Mercy: Race and Power in the Pacific War.* New York: Pantheon Books.

Efimov, Boris. 1938. 'Vysota u ozera khasan'. *Krasnoarmeets,* 20: 1.

Gench, L. 1939. 'Tridtsat piat let nazad. Teper' [Thirty-five years ago. The present]. *Krokodil,* 3:3.

Haga Tōru and Shimizu Isao. 1985. *Nichiro sensōki no manga* [Cartoons of the Russo-Japanese War]. *Kindai manga* [Modern manga], 4. Tokyo: Chikuma shobō.

Hirai Tomoyoshi. 1992. '30 nendai Sobieto kyōi ron no kōzō to dainamizumu' [The structure and dynamism of the theory of the Soviet threat in the 1930s]. In *Proceedings of Symposium on Russo-Japanese Relations.* Tokyo: Sophia University, 38-42.

Huffman, James L. 1997. *Creating a Public. People and Press in Meiji Japan.* Honolulu: University of Hawai'i Press.

Inagaki Kogorō. 1931. 'Manshū no heiwa o!' [For peace in Manchuria]. *Tōkyō pukku,* 20 (11): 5.

Itō Kikuzo. 1937. 'Shingeki suru Sobietogun no tachanka butai [A tachanka squad of the Soviet army on attack]. *Shōnen kurabu,* 4: plate 3.

Itō Mayumi. 1990. 'Japanese perceptions of the Soviet Union'. *Acta Slavica Iaponica,* 8: 165-82.

Kawashima Katsuichi. 1936. 'Kozakku kihei no shūgeki' [An attack of Cossack cavalry]. *Shōnen kurabu,* 8: plate 2.

Kitamura Masamitsu, ed. 1985. *Fukkoku Tōkyō pukku* [Tokyo Puck in reproduction], 1. Tokyo: Ryūkei shōsha.

Mikhailova, Yulia. 1993. 'The Image of Japan in Russo-Soviet Japanese Studies'. *Japanese Studies Bulletin,* 13(2): 59-74.

——. 1998. 'Images of Enemy and Self: Russian "Popular Prints" of the Russo-Japanese War'. *Acta Slavica Iaponica,* 16: 30-53.

Molodiakov, Vassily. 1996. *The Image of Japan in Europe and Russia, 1860-1918.* Moscow: Institut Vostokovedeniya RAN.

Nimmo, William F. 1994. *Japan and Russia. A Reevaluation in the Post-Soviet Era.* Westport, Conn: Greenwood Press.

Ryklin, N. 1939. 'Dvenadtsat mesyatsev spustya' [Twelve months later]. *Krasnoarmeets,* 3(4): 27-9.

Sashin, Yan and Ganf, Yu. 1939. 'Rasskaz o stranakh, armiyakh i litsakh, chuzhim dobrom mechtavshikh pozhivit'sha' [A story about countries, armies and people enriching themselves at others expense]. *Krasnoarmeet,* 3(4): 54-5.

Shimizu Isao. 1991. *Manga no rekishi* [A history of manga]. Tokyo: Iwanami shoten.

——. ed., 1986. *Tōkyō pukku* [Tokyo Puck]. *Manga zasshi hakubutsukan* [Museum of Cartoon Magazines] 5, Tokyo: Kokusho kankōkai, 5.

Shimizu Isao and Yumoto Gōichi, 1994. *Gaikoku manga ni egakareta Nihon* [Japan represented in foreign cartoons]. Tokyo: Maruzen bukkusu.

Sikorskii, L. 1904. *K kharakteristike chernoi, zheltoi i beloi ras v svyazi s voprosom o Russko-Yaponskoi Voine* [On characteristics of the black, yellow and white races in relation to the Russo-Japanese War]. Kiev: Tipografiya Tovarischestva I.N.Kushnerev i Ko.

Slonimskii, L. 1904. '"Zheltaya opasnost"' [Yellow threat]. *Vestnik Evropy*, 4: 762-76.

Smolnyi, G. 1939. 'Skaz o "khrabrom" samurae' [A story about a 'brave' samurai]. *Krasnoarmeets*, 1: 26-7.

Solov'iov, Vladimir, 1914. *Sobranie Sochinenii* [Collected Works], 10. 2nd ed. St Petersburg: Prosvescheniye.

Swinton, Elizabeth de Sabato. 1995. 'Russo-Japanese War Triptychs: Chastising a Powerful Enemy'. In Thomas Rimer, ed., *A Hidden Fire: Russian and Japanese Cultural Encounters, 1868-1926*. Stanford: Stanford University Press, 114-32.

Sviridenko, U. 1904. 'Glavnyi "makak" Yaponskogo Flota' [The main 'macaco' of the Japanese navy]. *Budilnik*, 12.

Togawa Tsuguo. 1990. 'The Japanese View on Russia Before and After the Meiji Restoration'. In Nakamura Yoshikazu, ed., *Roshia to Nihon* [Russia and Japan], 2. Tokyo: Waseda daigaku, 32-48.

Ukhtomskii, Esper. 1900. *K sobytiyam v kitaye. Ob otnosheniyakh zapada i rossii k vostoku* [On the events in China. On the attitudes of the West and Russia to the East]. St Petersburg: Vostok.

Voronov, L. 1904. *Borba Zheltoi i Beloi Rasy* [The struggle of the yellow and white races]. Moscow: Universitetskaya Tipografiya.

Yoda, Shuichi, ed. 1928. *Manga Meiji Taishō shi* [History of cartoons in the Meiji and Taishō periods]. Tokyo: Chūō Bijitsusha. 'Zheltaya opasnost' [Yellow peril]. 1904. Budilnik: 38: 1. Tada Shuichi, 1928.

Yoshino Takao, ed. 1993. *Kokkei shimbun* [Comic newspaper], 14. Tokyo: Yumani shobō, 117.

FOOTNOTES

1. The image of a tiger, probably, had its origin in traditional Far Eastern imagery, whereas representation of Russia as a bear was borrowed by the Japanese from Western pictures and cartoons.

2. This study is based on political caricatures published in Russian newspapers in 1904-05 taken from the collection of the Section of Prints of the Russian National Library in St Petersburg. It consists of four albums with more than two hundred cuttings from the newspapers *Peterburgskii Listok, Peterburgskaya zhisn', Svet, Birzhevyie Vedomosti* and also includes postcards and pictures of cigarette packs. The compiler of the collection is unknown.

3. This was a reference to a rebellion of a local tribe in Namibia against the German colonizers which took place at the same time and was reported in Russian newspapers.

4. I am thankful for this observation to Dr Phyllis M. Senese of the Department of History, University of Victoria.

5. With the foundation of Manchukuo (1932), which was a client state of Japan, and conclusion of the Treaty of Mutual Help between the Soviet Union and the People's Republic of Mongolia the Soviet Union and Japan actually faced each other over the long border between Manchuria and Mongolia.

6. Volochaevka and Spask were famous in the Soviet Union as places where Communist partisans crushed the Japanese army during the Japanese expedition against Soviet Russia in 1918-22.

11

'How Could You Fear or Respect Such an Enemy?' The End of World War II on Sakhalin

MARIYA SEVELA

E very nation chooses its heroes, its anti-heroes, its victims. Just as it decides to make some immortal, it condemns or erases others. This is how the numerous Japanese POWs whom the Soviets sent to labour camps in Siberia are seen as victims, remaining far from forgotten in their native country today. These are the 450,000 military and 125,000 civilians, captured in August 1945 after a rapid conflict between the two countries, that was central to the 'Soviet Far Eastern Campaign'.[1] While many of the internees did not survive, those who did were allowed to return home in the late 1940s and 50s to an historicized welcome. By contrast, however, the fate of the Japanese colony of Karafuto, the southern half of Sakhalin Island that was part of the same theatre of war, has largely fallen into obscurity. Although vividly remembered by its actors, it has, paradoxically, a far less significant place in Japanese national history. This article explores that imbalance.

In order to reconstruct the last days of Karafuto and to understand how two former wartime enemies relate to their common past across shifting terrains of history and memory, the end of the Cold War is our springboard. The opening of the Soviet archives has provided us with accounts of how the conquerors interpreted events. In turn, the Japanese witnesses, long since conquered and departed, feel more at ease sharing their impressions, now that Russia has emerged from its long isolation. Their perception of the Russians as *enemies/conquerors* and *neighbours/friends* has followed them across the Sōya Strait and stayed with many of them for good. Over the last several years I have collected oral histories of this significant period of 'cohabitation' in Russo-Japanese history, and compared the participants' narratives against popular national myths and archival sources.

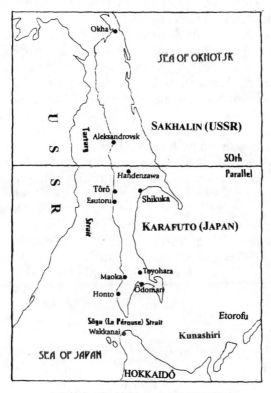

1. *Sakhalin Island before the August 1945 War.*

FROM JAPAN TO RUSSIA

Sakhalin is located at the crossroads of the Russian Far East and Japan. 'Discovered' nearly simultaneously by the Russians and the Japanese in the mid-seventeenth century, the island witnessed – partially or entirely – several shifts of rule between 1855 and 1945.[2] Following Japan's victory over Russia in 1905, the Treaty of Portsmouth divided Sakhalin at the 50th parallel. While the northern part remained Russian, the Japanese colony of Karafuto was established in the south. Starting from 1942

173

Japan incorporated Karafuto into the 'home islands' [*naichi*], and no longer administrated it through the Ministry of Colonization. Karafuto thus lost its colonial status and was becoming gradually an integral part of Japan. The Soviet military invasion put an end to Karafuto in August 1945. By then its population was nearly half a million people, consisting of Japanese, Korean labourers, White Russians, Poles, and the island's indigenous peoples – Ainu, Nivkhi and Ul'ta (Wakatsuki, 1991).

Acting upon the Yalta Agreement, the USSR declared war on Japan on 8 August 1945, breaking the neutrality pact with Japan signed on 13 April 1941. Compensation for fighting the Japanese in Manchukuo, Karafuto and Chishima promised to be highly lucrative – South Sakhalin and the Kurile Islands were going to become Russian once again.

The Soviet attack on Karafuto, as part of the 'Far Eastern Campaign', began on 9 August. The war continued until 25 August, when the Red Army took over Karafuto's capital Toyohara, ten days after Emperor Hirohito announced Japan's capitulation and seven days after the Imperial Headquarters in Tokyo had ordered all Japanese forces to cease fire. Despite these facts, Japanese military resistance continued, while the civilians, confused and terrified, cowered under the relentless bombardments and artillery fire that went on for days. A large portion of the population – primarily women, children and the elderly, altogether some 100,000 – managed to escape from the island across the Soya Strait during the first days of the war, while the remaining ones streamed towards Toyohara from all occupied locations (Stephan, 1971).

This short war left thousands of dead on both sides; over 18,000 Japanese were taken prisoner and some 300,000 civilians were kept on the island by Soviet forces.[3] The days of the forty-year old Japanese settlement known as Karafuto were numbered (Nakayama, 1995).

The battles over the Kurile Islands were finished on 3 September. It was the end of the war with Japan and also the end of World War II. Now began a 'confused epoch' on the island of Karafuto/Sakhalin – that of *when Japan became Russia*.

Whereas Manchuria and Korea remained foreign territories where the Soviet presence could only be temporary, Sakhalin and the Kurile Islands were to be incorporated into the Soviet Union. For this reason, measures to be taken towards the local residents – who were considered part of the deal – were meticulously prepared (Nimmo, 1988). The Soviet goal was clear: First to use the Japanese and the Koreans as the main workforce in transforming Karafuto into a Soviet land, then to persuade them to stay and form a 'Japanese region' on the island, joining the family of Soviet republics. The treatment of civilians was therefore distinctly better than that in other Soviet-occupied areas.

The next few years that followed the official beginning of Karafuto's occupation by the Russians were chaotic. A military government was established. The publication of the local press was banned, but was resumed shortly with the *New Life* [*Shinseimei*], a Soviet Japanese-language newspaper. Radio sets and cars were confiscated, telephone and mail services were stopped; a curfew was imposed. Each household was issued a 'resident permit' without which one could not move around. The military were sent to labour camps on either the continent or on North Sakhalin.[4] Karafuto's governor, Ōtsu Toshio, was placed under house arrest and eventually transferred to a prison near Khabarovsk. The élite – bureaucrats, publishers, company managers, and other community leaders – would eventually depart for the camps as well, but not before serving as advisers to the new government in the process of rebuilding the acquired land the Soviet way, using Japanese hands and know-how (Karafuto shūsenshi kankōkai, 1973).

In September 1945, the Civil Administration Department of South Sakhalin and the Kuriles [*Minseikyoku*] was created in Toyohara under the supervision of Colonel Dmitrii Kriukov, with eleven branches throughout the island. Former Japanese bureaucrats, working under a Russian supervisor, were now responsible for the smooth process of Sovietization of their fellow *Karafutojin*.

The archives show that the decision to use the Japanese as a workforce was taken at once. A document dated 15 September 1945, states:

> Considering the fact that we can neither bring on immediately the necessary labour force for the local industry, nor create acceptable living conditions for them at the present moment, we must temporarily use the Japanese administration, their engineers and workers. Otherwise the economy of this region will be completely ruined. It should also be noted that many of the Japanese already express their wish to stay on South Sakhalin and start working (*GASO*: f. 171, o. 1, d. 4, l. 23).

It is hard to say whether many Japanese wished to stay on the island and further the Soviet cause. But they were, without doubt, willing to work and get paid – on a 'no work-no eat' basis.[5]

Some of those who escaped earlier on to Hokkaidō, now wanted to *return* to Sakhalin. Colonel Kriukov's letter to Anastas Mikoyan on this matter, of October 1945, was rather perplexed:[6]

> People keep asking us to allow them to bring their families back from Hokkaido where they escaped in August. Although we gave no such permission, this month already 253 persons, arriving from Hokkaido, were caught by our guards. What should we do with them? Should we let them stay and give them work? By the way, those who were caught say that in spring all fishermen who worked on Sakhalin and the Kuriles in the past are planning to come back (*GASO*: f. 171, o. 1, d. 5, l. 41).

2. A. Mikoyan, on a familiarization tour, meets Japanese civilians in Ōdomari (September 1945)

We do not know if Kriukov ever received an answer to these questions, but it is clear that many matters were taken care of personally by him and managed quite brilliantly. This is what he writes thirty years later in his memoirs:

> I had first invited the Governor Ōtsu Toshio to come and see me at the end of September. ... He was permanently accompanied by six bodyguards, in order to be sure that no secret contact was made between him and other Japanese. In reality he was under arrest, but was told that it was for his own protection. ... Originally, he had held the status of the first-rank councillor and had the right to meet with the *Mikado*. ... He was fluent in English and German. ... I asked him not

to bow, shook his hand, and said, sort of jokingly, that this 'ceremony' was sufficient. . . . He smiled nodding his head, introduced himself, sat at the table and wrote something down in his elegant notebook. . . . I told him through a translator: 'We'll have to meet quite often from now on. You'll govern on behalf of the military government like your Mikado governs on behalf of MacArthur.' He bowed. I asked: 'Do you agree to do so of your own free will?' He repeated 'Yes' several times, adding that he does it 'out of honour and respect for the people'.

I continued: 'Then let us start with our matters. We have decided to change the administrative division of South Sakhalin and the Kuriles. . . .' He studied the map, made a few suggestions and approved. Then I familiarized him with the instruction concerning the control over banks, etc. . . . and also with the one on 'the immediate reinstallation of all industrial and public enterprises'; I asked him to explain the above to his people and make sure that all the orders were executed. He listened and said that the Karafuto Office did not interfere in the activities of firms. To this I answered: 'Many enterprises can start work today, but they don't. Workmen don't get wages and are badly off. We will start giving them food, but for money, otherwise they can't get it. From the firms' side, it looks rather like a sabotage. . .'. He listened very attentively. I looked at his face – it was changing all the time. I thought to myself: 'Funny, one says that they stay cool in any situation. . . .' When our meeting was over . . . I asked him if he had any wishes. He kept silent for a moment, then said: 'None, I am just grateful for everything. We will do our best.' Then I asked him to sign all the instructions. . . .

. . . Everywhere on the territory of South Sakhalin and the Kuriles we allowed free commerce of food and personal belongings. For this purpose, markets were organized in towns and villages. . . .

Precisely on 25 October, as planned, Ōtsu Toshio came to see me and reported that the harvesting was completed [by the Japanese peasants] and gave figures (Kriukov, 1993, 1: 25-8).

The island was to be renamed, rapidly reorganized and re-settled. Its past was to be erased, its history rewritten.[7] The new rulers were busy installing their administration and settling their own countrymen, the new colonists, with a fierce efficiency. In the meantime, the fate of the Japanese residents remained in suspense.

The Soviet government officially replaced the rouble with the yen in March 1946. By June that year all towns, villages and streets had been given new names. The newly created Japanese newspaper, *Shinseimei*, published a full list of these changes, offering its Japanese readers the new Russian equivalents in *katakana*.[8] Russian-Japanese conversation dictionaries were printed with the help of translators – Karafuto's White Russians, known to be bilingual, or those trained in the Soviet Union.

Schools underwent a rapid and efficient transformation. The teaching of social sciences was replaced by a new subject: 'Introduction to Marxism-Leninism for Young Communists'. Japanese children were singing songs praising Stalin, and adults were struggling to learn Russian to avoid being detained or accidentally killed due to a lack of language proficiency. The so-called *transition* and *cohabitation* had started: the forced cohabitation of two cultures, two races, the conquerors with the conquered. The cohabitation was literal, since the Japanese were not only forced to share their land but also their housing, with those who were arriving from distant lands, intending eventually to take their place (Sevela, 1995).

It goes without saying that the policy was to keep the badly-needed Japanese labour force in place for as long as possible. Moreover, since the spring of 1946, rumours were circulating that military conflict between the United States and the Soviet Union would be inevitable. Red Army officers advised the Japanese to be ready to fight on their side instead of contemplating departure.

Due to the American pressure, however, the repatriation of the Japanese was finally announced in October of 1946. It took place in mass numbers through December 1948, continuing at a slower pace until 1950.[9] The Soviet authorities nevertheless made particular efforts to delay the process: the permits to leave were hard to obtain and were often bought or acquired through 'private connections' (SCAP, 7 May 1946).

For those waiting for weeks to board a ship, a special transit camp was established in Kholmsk (formerly Maoka), in what used to be a high school. Among the archives of the civil administration that could be consulted, there is a file containing some hundred pages assembled under the general title: 'The collection of statements of Japanese repatriates at the transit camp no. 379 for the period from 15 April until 24 July 1947'. Numerous individuals, as well as group representatives, were forced to express their gratitude before leaving the island: to the Red Army for having defeated Japan, to the Communist Party for having given them work, and to Generalissimo Stalin for making it all possible. Some of them were also wondering how to keep themselves busy once in Japan, but then came up with the answer: They were going to 'try and make Japan as democratic as the Soviet Union' (GASO: f. 4, o. 1, d. 306, l. 162).

More than 200 ships crossed the Sōya Strait to the ports of Hokkaidō, transporting nearly 313,000 people. Practically the only Japanese civilians who remained on Sakhalin were those who missed the last ship to Japan or those married to Koreans who were forbidden to leave the island with their spouses (Takagi, 1990: 53).[10] But there were also others who expressly *asked* to stay. Here is one such petition:

> I was born on South Sakhalin in 1919. I know nothing of Japan and have never been there. My husband died and I am alone with two children. At the moment all Japanese are leaving this place. But I consider South Sakhalin as my homeland and have no desire to leave. I wish to stay and always work with Russians (GASO: f. 4, o. 1, d. 306, l. 222).

Possessions were left behind; neither Japanese nor Soviet currency could be carried across the border. The same rules applied to photographs and printed material, the only exception being the Soviet Constitution brochures that upon arrival were confiscated by the Americans.

Consequently, Karafuto residents reached post-war Japan literally empty-handed. After receiving a modest one-time stipend, they were to start new lives in a homeland that many of them had never seen before.

Meanwhile, on the ground in Karafuto, Soviet geographers created a new 'South Sakhalin region' (February 1946), which later turned into the 'Sakhalin region' in January 1947, consisting of all of Sakhalin and the Kuriles. With the end of the repatriation of Japanese civilians came the end of Karafuto and the definitive Sovietization of Sakhalin.[11]

MEMORIES AND PERCEPTIONS

How did this cohabitation work on a daily basis? Let us hear a voice from the Russian side first. Back to Colonel Kriukov's memoirs:

> We were facing a very urgent problem: to repair and re-establish the functioning of all industry with the hands of the Japanese themselves. . . . Even by January of 1946 only 25 per cent of the managing personnel were Soviet citizens. It was clear to us that for the time being we couldn't do much without the Japanese administration. In October we organized a meeting with all the owners, managers and chief engineers of the various enterprises and made arrangements concerning their relations

with our Trusts. . . . This was followed by a dinner party. We noticed, that the Japanese ate our white bread . . . and other Russian dishes with pleasure. After a traditional glass of saké and of our vodka they would easily get tipsy. We would then hear numerous frank expressions about our treatment of the Japanese; at the end they sang Russian songs together with us and were, all in all, very pleased with the reception.

This meeting was of great help in demobilizing most of the enterprises and workshops, and in raising the production for the needs of the Japanese population as well as for our country. . . . In fact, the civil administration and the trusts – with the help of the military – had the industry functioning in one-and-a-half or two months, got the workers back, and by the 28th anniversary of the Revolution [in November] the entire adult population was working. During these three months of 1945 . . . 400,000 tons of fish products, coal, paper, and other goods were shipped to the continent.

From October, all Japanese schools were already functioning, applying a new curriculum.

The Army political section was taking care of the cultural-propaganda activities. For this purpose they subordinated Japanese printing-houses and the local broadcasting centre with a staff of translators. From the first days of our presence shows and concerts were organized specially for the Japanese, and Soviet movies were often shown. At first the Japanese were either too shy or afraid to attend, but soon the hall would be entirely filled. Before the screening, a translator would explain the contents of the movie and use the occasion to address some pertinent issues of our everyday life. We showed both Japanese and Soviet movies, and there were lines for the Soviet ones – they got probably bored with their own. What's more, we sold the tickets about three times cheaper [than they used to be].

With the arrival of the army medical unit, a military hospital was immediately installed, as was a network of medical centres. 60,000 Japanese underwent medical check-ups: those who had spent a while in ports, forests and mountains. Thousands were hospitalized. Medical aid free of charge as well as the distribution of medicine was available at local points for the population.

So, what was the attitude of the Japanese towards all these measures and activities? One can say without doubt: the attitude of the majority was friendly. Did any acts of subversion or sabotage by the Japanese bourgeoisie and disguised army officers take place? The answer is clearly: yes. Several sabotage groups were unmasked and eliminated in the beginning of the cohabitation. During 1946, however, there were practically no such acts from the Japanese side, apart from some incidents of their careless attitude towards work.

Simple folk had lived nearly two years under the same roof with the Russian settlers, who kept arriving in droves. I remember calling on a Japanese, in whose house a family of one of our commanders had settled down. I asked them if they had any complaints about the 'new tenants'. The wife of the house owner told me: 'They have kids, so do we. The commander's wife brings us sugar and sweets, helps us, and invites us over to their room on holidays. We drink tea, and our children play together.' Such things were more than frequent.

Once we entered the main temple in Toyohara. Bits of paper and statuettes of Buddha were scattered about the floor. We found the priests and asked them why the temple wasn't visited by the people. They were surprised. Their chief said to us: 'We know that in the Soviet Union religion is forbidden and priests get jailed!' One of us answered indignantly: 'Yes, in our country the Church is separated from the State. Religious rituals are not compulsory, but those who wish to believe in God, may do so. And here, as you know, in towns and villages temples function, we don't forbid them.' The priest then said: 'We haven't been outside Toyohara, and thought that those were just false rumours.' We answered them: 'Don't be so naive. These rumours have one purpose – to set the Japanese against us. It's called provocation! Get this place in order and start your work.' One of the priests asked us: 'And how are we supposed to live? Before we were paid by the State and got extras for the rituals; nowadays nobody wants to pay us.' This talk made us think. As a matter of fact, there was a great number of priests here, and they were very much respected by the population. With no means of subsistence, they might start provocative actions against us. So, we fixed a salary and a food ration for them. This is how we dealt with the religious feelings of the Japanese: all temples and ash repositories were put under our protection; all Soviet citizens were warned against violating their religious habits. Letters of gratitude started coming to us from the priests. Later on, during the repatriation, we would allow the funeral urns to be taken to Japan (Kriukov, 1993 no. 1: 34-5, 40-1).

3. *'Friendship through black bread' – as remembered by Nakahara Shigeo, a witness.*

181

Colonel's Kriukov's testimony was largely confirmed by archival sources (*GASO*: f. 565, o. 1, d. 4, l. 9). For Soviet officials, this improvised 'cohabitation' was a success in all respects but for the eventual departure of its Japanese constituents. Nevertheless, who would have expected that their Sovietizing gauntlet would include the collectivization of Japanese priests.

How is this cohabitation remembered in Japan today, half a century after the events took place?

As mentioned earlier, the entire Karafuto population was repatriated to Japan, with the exception of the very few who could not or did not wish to leave. About 60,000 of them are presumed to be alive today, with 60 per cent of those, in turn, residing on Hokkaidō.

In the name of a place that ceased to exist fifty years ago, numerous associations of former Karafuto residents function are active today. The Union of Former Residents of Karafuto [*Karafuto remmei*], the main association, counts over 6000 members, with 36 branches all over Japan. The average members' age is 71. All members can be easily traced through a special members' guide that provides not only personal data, but also one's home town/village in Karafuto. *Karafuto remmei* publishes a monthly newsletter, re-prints old books on Karafuto, organizes trips to Sakhalin and holds an annual commemoration – *Karafuto day* – on 23 August, the official date of the Soviet occupation

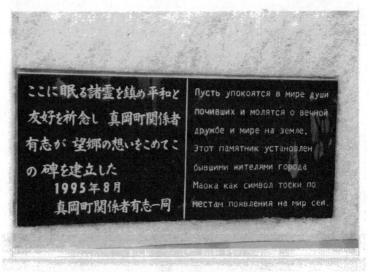

4. A memorial plaque erected by Maoka's former residents in present-day Kholmsk (August 1995).

of Karafuto, alternately in Tokyo and Sapporo. The commemoration includes a memorial ceremony and a luxurious luncheon, where people are seated according to their place of origin. Lunch is accompanied by nostalgic speeches, *Banzai* eruptions, and a warning – 'Never forget Karafuto!'. *Karafuto remmei*, with its salaried staff, subsists partly on rent, donations and membership fees, but mainly on a Health and Welfare Ministry [*Kōseishō*] allowance, which is the government's response to the compensations claimed by Karafuto evacuees for the loss of their hard-earned possessions or the property confiscated by the Russians (Kōseishō shakai, 1997: 449-50).

Apart from this main association, over a hundred others exist. Every (former) Karafuto town has an association, as does every school. The relatives of the victims who were on one of the three ships torpedoed by the Russians have an association, as do the POWs who were kept for several years in a camp in Okha (north Sakhalin). Yet another is busy arranging trips to Japan for those very few Japanese who continue living on Sakhalin today. All associations have annual meetings for its members. Moreover, for the past few years, there has been a literal *Karafuto boom* in Japan: memoirs are increasingly being published, inspired by the greater access to Sakhalin. During the past ten years various associations erected twelve memorial stones on the island.

The number of people who, once retired, devote their time to Karafuto-related research and consider it of prime importance is also remarkable. When asked why their past was of such importance to them, the most common answer was that they saw their lives as divided into two halves: before and after the repatriation, and that they have always considered themselves to be 'expellees'. One of my informants, a 67 year old gentleman, was planning to move back to his native Ōdomari (today's Korsakov) to rent an apartment in a building where his house used to stand and to start a Japanese language school for Russian children. When I asked why he would make such a momentous effort, he responded simply: 'Just as salmon go back to its original waters, I would like to die where I was born'.

Being a foreign historian collecting oral histories while working on a topic directly related to Japan's defeat in 1945, I encountered various reactions. But, above all, it was perhaps the eagerness of the informants to communicate their memories on what has been forgotten – the period of 'transition and cohabitation'. Most see themselves as double victims: not only of Russians, but also of the

Japanese government, whose renunciation of territorial claims over Karafuto they regard as betrayal.[12]

The fact that the Japanese stopped considering Karafuto as a *colony* may situate their presence there as more comparable to the settlement on Hokkaidō than in China or Korea. It explains as well the strong tendency to consider it as 'one's native land' [*kokyō*]. However, it also emerged from the interviews that there has been close to no transmission of this past to future generations. The main reason given was: 'It does not interest my children.' It was also evident from my survey that for the former residents of Karafuto, the Russian presence on the island before the Russo-Japanese War of 1904–05 was just as remote and insignificant as was the Japanese presence for the Russians born on Sakhalin after World War II. For both peoples, the history of the island had started with *them*.

The similarities between the eye-witness accounts and Soviet archival documents, autobiographies and newspapers are striking. Certainly, the interpretations may differ: the Soviets' euphoric descriptions of Japanese participation in building the future of the island, their eager parade on May Day 1946, or the unconcealed happiness on the face of Karafuto's ex-governor-turned prisoner, while listening to the official speech on Soviet victory, were less enthusiastic when related by the Japanese side. Nevertheless, the official interpretation of events by the conquerors remains surprisingly close to that of the conquered.

My Japanese informants hardly mentioned, if at all, the tales of violence, murder or rape. Archival sources tell us that they took place, but lasted a relatively short while, and had calmed down by October 1945. The military instructions concerning the treatment of the Japanese population were clear and strict – the army had no intention to repeat the 'vengeance campaign' that took place in Berlin the same year.[13] Colonel D. Kriukov clarifies in his memoirs:

> ... We passed a secret resolution to be obeyed by all the military formations: the Japanese administrative and economic body would be kept temporarily, but under the control of our department. It was said in the resolution that south Sakhalin and the Kuriles had been Russian lands from time immemorial, brought back to the Motherland. Everything found on them ... belonged to the State, and those who would steal or spoil any of it would be judged as criminals. It was suggested that no offence should be permitted [on the part of the Russians] towards the Japanese population, their being free citizens and

not war prisoners: one will not interfere with their national habits and traditions, one will respect all their rules while entering their houses, will not touch their possessions or provisions, will pay them according to the fixed prices when buying from them; no relations will be tolerated with their women, even with the consent of the latter; their shrines and temples will neither be visited [by Russians] nor destroyed. It was stated that those who violated the above order were to be punished most severely. ... At the beginning, it provoked hostile reactions from a number of commanders, who were still acting as they pleased and took what they liked in their zones (Kriukov, 1993 1: 23).

At times, the perception of the Red Army by the Japanese civilians borders on absurdity. What my informants all seem to remember was their amazement at how miserable the conquerors looked. Women would exclaim 'poor thing!' [*kawaisō datta*], referring to the Soviet soldiers, and shake their heads with a sigh. Indeed, the Soviet Army, after having triumphed on the European front, marched into Karafuto strangely dressed. Either the bottom or the top of their uniform was missing. As civilians watched them entering their towns and villages, they noticed, stupefied, that the Russian soldiers were wearing Japanese peasant clothes [*mompe*] obviously stolen along the way as the army was taking over the island. The soldiers were genuinely poor and stole all they could, which often left people, especially in the rural areas, without much to wear. Otherwise, wrist-watches, fountain-pens, knives, shoes and suitcases proved to be very popular. These incidents of robbery seem to rank among the most unpleasant memories of the Soviet army's presence in Karafuto. Just as the Russians were struck by the honesty of the Japanese, so were the Japanese appalled by Russian looting. A Korean informant who still lives on Sakhalin today shared his impressions:

We never thought that the Japanese could lose the war, never. At the very beginning of the Soviet occupation, some of us started to wonder what we should say to the Russians. Should we say that we were Japanese, in other words their enemy, or should we say that we were Korean? And would they understand the difference, and how do you say 'Korean' in Russian? There was no language to explain. It is hard to say if we were all happy to see the Russians. I would say that those who were particularly badly treated by the Japanese, welcomed them, but not all of us. Because at least we knew the Japanese but what could we expect from the Russians? Maybe they will turn out to be even worse, who knows! We knew very little about the Russians, although they were so close by. And although the Japanese frequently accused the

Koreans of spying for the Russians, this was untrue, of course. And this is why the Japanese were yelling that we should all be killed, as the Soviets were approaching. My first impression of the Soviet soldiers left me speechless, they looked so awful, real beggars and wild, I could not believe my eyes, were those the winners? They were stealing all the time, grabbing even kimonos from the women and wearing them! And they were so hungry! But later I learnt that this was the penal battalion – the released convicts. So that was only in the beginning, because the rules were very tough and the soldiers were punished constantly for misbehaving.[14]

Instead of the expected fear, one could clearly detect a feeling of contempt and superiority on the part of the Japanese. As another witness admitted:

How could you fear or respect such an enemy? They were poor, dirty, illiterate – beasts, in one word, but they weren't mean. . . Frankly, we expected it to be much worse! They were the winners, after all.

Indeed, if one goes through the Soviet press of August 1945, full of reminders of the brutal Japanese presence in the Russian Far East 20 years earlier, one cannot but wonder at this relatively quiet invasion.

From 1946, the Soviet settlers were arriving in Sakhalin in increasing number. They not only worked with the Japanese but also lived in their houses, sharing kitchens and bathrooms. Apart from party officials, these were often people who had lost everything during the war. They came to the island from all over the country, attracted by special resettlement benefits and new opportunities. It was not rare to see them arrive with no shoes on their feet, with just a sack containing all their belongings. One Japanese witness recalled:

How poor these people were! They would arrive just with a pillow or a small suitcase, that's all they had! There were no houses for them, so they would sleep on the floor at the train station. Then the Japanese were asked to share their houses with the newcomers, and of course they were afraid to. So they were told that those who would let the Russians in will be allowed to leave for Japan before the others.

Here, for the first time, the Japanese could witness communist society in practice, with rich and poor side by side. The class differences were striking. The low level of education among the newcomers had left a strong impression on the Japanese; many Russians were illiterate and even the new schoolteachers had trouble with arithmetic. However, the desire to build a better life than on the war-torn continent was strong, and the new colonizers worked hard. The rapid organization of free schools and medical services were welcomed by the Japanese – their own doctors were known to be excessively expensive.

Perhaps most shocking in the eyes of the Japanese was the loose way of living and lack of morals in this post-war Soviet society. They seemed to have no respect for family structure or chastity. As one informant pointed out:

> It's probably also something to do with Communism – nobody belongs to anybody, so you can have as many men or women as you like. But then they are so physically active, that by the age of thirty they look completely used up. Japanese could never be the same. You probably have to eat a lot of meat to be that lustful.

Another remembers:

> When leaving Sakhalin in 1947 and getting permission from the authorities, I was asked about my family ... 'This is my wife and my children', I said. 'Are they your and your wife's children?', asked a suspicious Russian. 'Well, yes, they are', I answered, surprised. The Soviet official explained: 'If they are your wife's children it doesn't necessarily mean that you are the father, you know.'

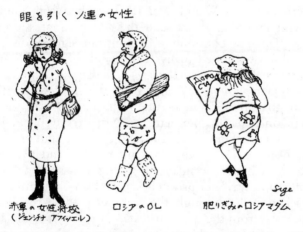

眼を引く ソ連の女性

赤軍の女性将校
（ジェンシナ アフィツェル）　　ロシアのOL　　肥りぎみのロシアマダム

5. *Three Soviet women: the officer, the secretary and the modern gal (by Nakahara Shigeo)*

Another phenomenon, incomprehensible to the Japanese, was the Soviets' attitude towards Karafuto's White Russians. This small Russian and Polish community, about 200 people, enjoyed a peaceful coexistence under Japanese rule since the Russo-Japanese War until 1943. These people were mainly farmers, who either preferred to stay on their land after the Japanese victory of 1905, or escaped to the south from the north with the beginning of the Soviet regime. Today, many Japanese still remember their 'foreign' classmates and the Russian bread that was sold at the train stations. For the last two years of the war, however, the life of this minority grew much harder in a ghetto-like area known as the 'Russian village'. Following the Soviet occupation, they were asked to work as translators and advisers for the new government, an offer they could hardly refuse. Being neither Soviet nor Japanese citizens, they feared the worst and it was not long in coming. Nearly all of them were judged by Article 58 of the Soviet penal code, accused of espionage against Russia, and sent to the labour camps by their fellow compatriots. A few of those who survived still live on Sakhalin today. All that is left to them from the Karafuto period are the rare photographs, Japanese school graduation certificates, and of course their memories.

★　★　★

Japan has been no exception to the thriving industry of retrospection that took new impetus in the 1990s from the 50th anniversary of World War II. Torn between 'coming to terms with its military past' and the active suppression of the same past, Japanese continue to demonstrate signs of discomfort.

1998 alone witnessed many such events. The publication of Iris Chang's book, *The Rape of Nanking* (Chang, 1998a), provoked such violent reactions from the right-wing academy in Japan that the Chinese-American author was forced to comment on it in an open letter to *Newsweek* (Chang, 1998b). The screening in Tokyo of a Taiwanese feature film on the same subject, *Don't Cry, Nanking*, was interrupted and permanently withdrawn, when a scandalized spectator slashed the screen. (The same film was later privately shown by a Communist group in a packed hall, although the only way to learn about the screening was from the daily *Akahata*.) For a short while another film, *Pride: The Fateful Moment* – a revisionist whitewash portrait of Tōjō Hideki whom the International Military Tribunal for the Far East sentenced to death – enjoyed a peaceful season throughout Japan despite protests and picketing by the left.

Each year in Japan, starting from the anniversary of the atomic bomb on Hiroshima and through to the date of surrender on 15 August, various television channels show documentaries on the

Pacific War. August 1998 was no different. Out of a dozen shows I was able to watch, only two dealt with issues other than the Japanese victims. One was on the Korean prisoners in Nagasaki and the other about a Japanese history professor on a visit to China where he discovered some unpleasant facts concerning the Japanese military presence in the 30s and later shared his impressions with unsuspecting students. At the same time, NHK commented on the results of a recent survey among junior high school students: the majority of them knew nothing of the link between Japan's war activities and the atomic bombings. All of this is happening in today's Japan which, after official apologies to South Korea and China, continues to debate on the 'right and wrong' of the annual visit to the Yasukuni Shrine made by Japan's political leaders.

It was in this atmosphere of partial war amnesia that the period of *cohabitation* on Sakhalin ceased to exist in Japan's contemporary history. Japan, badly hurt by its defeat, had more than 300,000 of its citizens indoctrinated by the Soviets and forced to participate in the destruction of their own land. It bears this humiliation still today.

The negative images of 'Russia-as-an-enemy', and the 'threat and temptation from the north' go a long way back. The Russo-Japanese War (1904-05), the Siberian intervention (1918-22), the Nomonhan Incident (1939), the 1945 abrogation of the neutrality pact by the Soviets and the general belief that this led to the August 1945 war, *despite* Japan's surrender,[15] are strongly implanted in the national consciousness. Moreover, this was greatly reinforced by public discourse during the cold war.

The oral histories I collected, however, remind us that these public images are often in contradiction with individual or private memories. Most interestingly, the apparent contempt and bitterness that the Japanese have towards the Russians is strongly interlaced with a feeling of sympathy for this 'white but poor enemy'. The Japanese considered this enemy, unlike the Americans, socially inferior and therefore pitiful, if not even likeable. Many of the interviewees regard this period as 'the most exciting experience of [their] lives', while others recalled their Russian neighbours, both civilians and military, with a clear fondness. 'They were good, simple people, we made friends and were sorry to part with them' – was a common comment on the end of this forced cohabitation.

BIBLIOGRAPHY

Chang, Iris. 1998a. *The Rape of Nanking: The Forgotten Holocaust of World War II.* New York: Penguin.

——. 1998b. 'It's History, Not a Lie.' *Newsweek*, 20 July: 19.

Choung, II Chee. 1987. 'Repatriation of Stateless Koreans from Sakhalin Island.' *Korea and World Affairs*, vol. 11(4): 708-744.

GASO [State Archive of the Sakhalin Region]: f. 171, o. 1, d. 4, l. 23; d. 5, l. 41; f. 4, o. 1, d. 306, l. 222, l. 162; f. 565, o. 1, d. 4, l. 9; f. 17, o. 36, d. 5, 8-10.

Karafuto shūsenshi kankōkai, ed. 1973. *Karafuto shūsenshi* [History of the end of the war on Karafuto]. Tokyo: Zenkoku Karafuto remmei.

Kōseishō shakai, ed. 1997. *Engo 50 nen shi* [50 years of protection: a history]. Tokyo: Gyōsei.

Kriukov, Dmitrii. 1993. 'Grazhdanskoe upravlenie na Iuzhnom Sakhaline i Kuril'skikh ostrovakh v 1945-1948 gg.Vospominania' [Civil administration on south Sakhalin and the Kurile islands, 1945-1948. Memoirs]. *Kraevedcheskii Biulleten'*, 1: 7-44, 2: 3-23, 3: 3-40.

MIS GHQ SCAP [Military Intelligence Section, General Headquarters, Supreme Commander for the Allied Powers]. 1947. *Daily Intelligence Summary*, 8 April.

Naimark, Norman M. 1997. *The Russians in Germany: A History of the Soviet Zone of Occupation, 1945-49.* Cambridge: Harvard University Press.

Nakayama, Takashi. 1995. *1945 nen natsu. Saigo no nissosen* [Summer 1945: The last Soviet-Japanese War]. Tokyo: Kokusho Kankōsha.

Nimmo, William F. 1988. *Behind a Curtain of Silence: Japanese in Soviet Custody, 1945-56.* New York: Greenwood Press.

SCAP [Supreme Commander for the Allied Powers]. 1946. *Directive to Japanese government.* 927, 7 May.

Sevela, Mariya. 1995. '*Nihon wa Soren ni natta toki*' [When Japan became the USSR]. *Rekishigakukenkū*, 676: 26-35, 63.

Stephan, John. 1971. *Sakhalin: A History.* Oxford: Clarendon Press.

Takagi Ken'ichi. 1990. *Saharin to Nihon no sensō sekinin* [Sakhalin and Japan's war responsibility]. Tokyo: Gaifūsha.

Verbitskaia, O. P. 1986. 'Planovoe sel'skokhoziaistvennoe pereselenie v RSFSR v 1946-58 godakh' [Planned rural resettlement within the Russian Federation, 1946-58]. *Voprosy istorii*, 12: 13-26.

Wakatsuki Yasuo. 1991. *Sengo hikiage no kiroku* [Post-war Repatriation Record]. Tokyo: Jiji Tsūshinsha.

FOOTNOTES:

1. Following the Allied victory, a total of seven million Japanese, both military personnel and civilians, were waiting to be repatriated at the end of 1945, of which 2,700,000 found themselves in Soviet-controlled areas (Manchuria, Dairen and Port Arthur, the northern part of Korea, the southern part of Sakhalin and the Kurile Islands) in August 1945. By March 1947, 97 per cent of the Japanese from all non-Soviet areas were repatriated. The figure for the Soviet-controlled areas was a mere 53 per cent (MIS GHQ SCAP, 1947: 1).

2. – Treaty of Shimoda (of peace and friendship), 7 February 1855: Sakhalin (Karafuto) Island remains non-divided, while the boundary between Russia and Japan passes between the islands Etorofu and Uruppu.

– Treaty of St Petersburg (Sakhalin-Kurile Islands exchange), 7 May 1875: grants Russia the possession of the entire island while Japan obtains the Kuriles.

– Treaty of Portsmouth (the transfer of South Sakhalin from Russia to Japan), 5 September 1905: the island is divided at the 50th parallel of latitude.

– Japanese occupation of North Sakhalin (1920-25).

– The Peking convention, 20 January 1925: Japan's recognition of the Soviet Union and withdrawal of its troops from North Sakhalin.

– Yalta agreement (entry of the Soviet Union into the war with Japan), 11 February 1945: by its military invasion the Soviet Union regains South Sakhalin and the Kurile Islands.

3.   These figures vary depending on sources. According to the archival records of the [Soviet] civil administration, on 1 July 1946 there were 305,800 'non-Soviet' residents on south Sakhalin and the Kurile Islands: 277,649 Japanese, 27,088 Koreans, 406 Ainu, 288 Ul'ta, 81 Evenk, 24 Nivkhi, 11 Nanai, 103 Chinese, 27 Poles, 97 Russians, 16 others (GASO: f. 17, o. 36, d. 5; 8-10). Japanese figures tend to be higher.

4.   The Soviet Union was not a signatory to the 1929 Geneva Convention which required a rapid repatriation of the enemy soldiers after the cessation of hostilities. It did adhere, however, to the Potsdam Declaration in 1945, which specified the same obligation concerning POWs. This obligation was not honoured by the Kremlin.

5.   And there was plenty of work indeed, some of it even creative. To give an example: one of my informant's occupations was to paint bed sheets in red and then make flags for the new government's offices.

6.   Anastas Mikoyan (1895-1978) was a member of the Central Committee of the Communist Party between 1923 and 1976. He was people's commissioner for foreign and domestic trade and distribution 1926-46 and minister of foreign trade 1946-49.

7.   Among numerous absurdities from the 'transition period' was a long telegram (12 pages) of 2 February 1946 with detailed instructions from Moscow, addressed to Colonel Kriukov. It concerned the general transformation of Japan into Russia, printed on the 'Imperial Japanese Telegraphs' forms, with a Japanese 'Toyohara city' stamp on each page.

8.   The Red Army's Newspaper for the Japanese Population was the official subtitle of this Japanese-language publication. It was published from 15 October 1945 until (at least) 2 September 1948. With a Russian editor-in-chief (Mishalov) and former journalists from Karafuto nichi nichi shimbun, it was published three times a week with a circulation of 30,000. Translations of Soviet articles, full of optimism and idyllic local news, made it very cheerful reading. Kriukov notes later on in his memoirs that: 'If one goes through the whole file of Shinseimei today, one can imagine how interesting the process was of re-educating the Japanese in the Soviet spirit' (Kriukov, 1993, 2: 6).

9.   In 1950 Soviet authorities made a false declaration that there were no more Japanese civilians on Russian soil.

10.   The 'question of Sakhalin Koreans' is one of the war crimes that Japan has been accused of recently. As Japanese nationals, Koreans were forced to serve in the Japanese military as soldiers or forced labourers attached to military units during World War II. Most of those Koreans were able to return to Korea when the war was over. Sakhalin was an exception, however. Although taken to the island mainly by force during different stages of the colony's development, they were denied repatriation either to Japan or Korea on the ground that they were no longer Japanese nationals, and thus were excluded from agreements concluded between the United States and the Soviet Union in 1946. Consequently, they were abandoned on Sakhalin as 'stateless', with no right to leave the island. Today they number about 40,000 (Choung, 1987).

11. By 1949 there were 450,000 Soviet settlers on Sakhalin, in other words exactly the same figure as for the Japanese population of Karafuto in 1945. It also proved to be the most successful region among those which were settled after the war in the USSR; officially, for the period between 1946-53 only 2.8 per cent of all new households had left the island (Verbitskaia, 1986: 23).

12. The San Francisco Peace Treaty (1951), intended to end the state of war between Japan and the former Allied powers, states in one of its 27 articles that Japan 'renounces all right, title and claim to the Kurile Islands, and to that portion of Sakhalin and the islands adjacent to it over which Japan acquired sovereignty as a consequence of the Treaty of Portsmouth of 5 September 1905.' The ambiguity of the document, however, and the absence of mention of the Soviet Union as the rightful proprietor led the Soviet delegation to walk out of the 'Japanese peace conference'. Consequently, the treaty was never signed by the Russians, creating what would later become known as the 'Japanese-Russian territorial dispute'. While Japan's territorial claims to the Kuriles have grown into serious political tension between the two countries, the loss of Karafuto has come to be a mere painful reminder of Japan's lost war, without possible reversion. Moreover, the recent opening of a Japanese consulate on Sakhalin acknowledges Russia's sovereignty over the island and puts an end to the remaining private hopes of recovering Karafuto.

13. On the occupation of Germany, see, for example, Naimark 1997.

14. This quotation and the following ones are drawn from my interviews and questionnaires conducted in Japan and Russia in 1992-98.

15. This is a perfect example of a popular national myth. In reality, the Soviet Union's entry into the war against Japan came seven days *before* Japan's surrender.

ACKNOWLEDGEMENTS:
I am grateful to the Canon Foundation for their support of the present research.

Japan, Europe and Cold War Issues

12

Japan and Europe in the Occupation Period, 1945-52

PETER LOWE

E urope and Japan had one fundamental feature in common in 1945 and this affected their attitude for most, if not all, of the occupation era – each was devastated by the enormous demands of war and physical destruction. Each faced famine, malnutrition and very low standards of living. There was one important difference, too: most of Europe had been fought over bitterly, resulting in the most savage treatment of civilians in any large-scale conflict in world history whereas Japan surrendered without a contested invasion of the home islands.

Four European countries were involved significantly in Asia after 1945 and a fifth was involved to a minor degree. Great Britain was heavily committed in the Indian sub-continent, Ceylon (Sri Lanka) and Burma until 1947-48; in Malaya the Communist insurrection occupied time and resources from 1948; and developments in China raised a question-mark over the future viability or survival of Hong Kong. France became locked in a brutal and ultimately disastrous conflict with a tenacious indigenous foe in Indo-China from 1945 to 1954. The Netherlands wrestled with the invidious challenges of assertive nationalism in Indonesia from 1945 to 1949. Portugal retained its interests in Macao and East Timor but little attention focused on Portuguese concerns. The Soviet Union was, of course, involved deeply as an Asian power in its own right; Russian territorial concerns were accentuated by Stalin's determination to foster Soviet interests in Korea and Manchuria. Colonial issues did not affect Japan particularly except for the desire a little later to develop an economic role in Asia in areas where Japan had

THE JAPANESE AND EUROPE

developed the Coprosperity Sphere in the first half of the 1940s. Eventually, Japan would require a working relationship with Russia but this would not become a priority until the occupation ended.

Europe and Asia were brought together by the growth of the cold war (Gaddis, 1982, 1987). In Europe, acrimonious disputes between the Soviet Union and the Western allies over Poland, the other countries of Central and Eastern Europe occupied by Soviet forces (plus, originally, Yugoslavia until Tito's break with Stalin), fuelled the take-off of the situation depicted sombrely by Winston Churchill in his 'Iron Curtain' address in Fulton, Missouri, in 1946. The proclamation of the Truman Doctrine and the offer of Marshall aid marked the real commitment of the United States to resist the perceived threat of Communist expansion. The majority of American politicians accepted that Europe must be the priority but some of the leading figures in the right wing of the Republican party deplored the emphasis on Europe and argued that Asia was neglected to a dangerous degree. In Asia the Truman administration and General Douglas MacArthur made it very clear that the Soviet Union's contribution to the allied occupation of Japan would be essentially nominal. Perhaps the only Soviet role of significance was to provide one of the judges for the International Military Tribunal for the Far East (IMTFE) (Minear, 1971).

The most dangerous confrontation between the United States and Russia in Asia developed in Korea, following the sharp deterioration in relations between the rival military administrations in South and North Korea in 1946-7 (Cumings, 1997). British politicians and civil servants regarded the fraught situation in the Korean peninsula in 1946-47 as the most dangerous in the world, apart from Berlin (Lowe, 1997a: 36). The decisive victory of the Chinese Communists in 1948-49 added a whole new dimension, if one that posed no shortage of problems for the Soviet Union. The Communist take-over of Czechoslovakia in 1948, soon followed by the tensions surrounding the Berlin blockade in 1948-49, produced a potentially combustible global struggle, rendered more dangerous by the successful testing of an atomic bomb by Russia in August 1949 (Lowe, 1997a: 150-63; Holloway, 1994).

NATURE OF THE OCCUPATION

The occupation of Japan proceeded with only a very limited

194

contribution from Europe. In 1945 Britain and the Soviet Union both hoped that they could participate positively in allied decision-making, although it is doubtful whether Stalin believed that Russia would achieve a great deal. British ministers and officials were more sanguine initially because of their somewhat complacent faith in Britain's historic role in eastern Asia receiving suitable acknowledgement. President Truman and General MacArthur did not share very much in common but both agreed that the allied occupation should be controlled by the United States with only minimal contributions from the other allied states. The principal British representative in Tokyo for most of the occupation was Alvary Gascoigne, a diplomat of military origins which rendered him better placed to exchange views with MacArthur and his staff (Lowe, 1994). Gascoigne was shrewd and showed considerable skill in his numerous meetings with MacArthur. He realized that he would have to listen patiently to the general's lengthy monologues but that he must then expound British policies as vigorously as he could (Lowe, 1994: 280). He gained MacArthur's trust and their meetings were mostly of a productive nature until the outbreak of the Korean War, in June 1950, when the general's preoccupation with Korean strategy, plus the voicing of a more critical British view of MacArthur, led to friction and to Gascoigne's service in Tokyo concluding on a sour note (Lowe, 1994: 293). However, MacArthur appreciated Gascoigne's ability and later described him as being 'sharper' than Esler Dening, Britain's first ambassador to Japan, following the end of the occupation (Lowe, 1997: 46, note 44).

British reactions to the policies of reform and rebuilding implemented by SCAP (the Supreme Commander for the Allied Powers) tended to be mildly critical and, in certain specific cases, more openly critical. The phase of hectic reform, political, constitutional, social and economic, was regarded as too radical, smacking of the more naïve aspects of the New Deal introduced by Franklin D. Roosevelt's administration in the 1930s. Basically, officials in the Foreign Office held that SCAP was trying to achieve too much too quickly and that a reaction would set in after the occupation, which would reverse the trend that the Americans were seeking to accomplish (FO 371/9254/5). Thus the constitution was regarded as too Westernized and idealistic, not least in article 9 where the possession of armed forces was forbidden.

The British then felt that the occupation lurched in the opposite direction quite suddenly with the adoption of the 'reverse course' in 1947–48. This contained implications that could be more immediately dangerous for British interests. A renewal of Japanese economic competition was viewed with deep anxiety. This was the result of vivid recollections of pre-war competition in cotton textiles where Japanese exports undermined Lancashire products. It was believed that Japanese competition was dangerous because of 'sweated labour' and devious commercial practices. The Lancashire textile industry was vociferous: employers and trade unions conveyed their fears to ministers, MPs, and the media (Lowe, 1997a: 85–6). The Labour government of Clement Attlee was committed firmly to implementing a full employment policy and to achieving an effective exports drive. While there was no profound faith in Lancashire's ability to restore its former glory in cotton textiles, ministers believed in emphasizing to SCAP and to Japanese representatives that Japanese labour should be treated fairly as regards acceptable wages and that undesirable commercial methods should be avoided (Lowe, 1997b: 72). Anxiety extended to shipbuilding and Japanese capacity in this sphere. Ministers revealed more concern over this than over textiles. It was recognized reluctantly that a peace treaty with Japan could not include restrictive clauses on these issues and that British representations should be pursued outside the framework of a treaty. Competition for the Staffordshire potteries was a less demanding matter for ministers and officials but the local Labour MPs pressed the industry's case vehemently.

THE 'REVERSE COURSE'

Hector McNeil, the minister of state in the Foreign Office, wrote to Foreign Secretary Ernest Bevin in June 1948 that the Americans were in danger of creating 'a most nasty political mess' because of their failure to understand Australian fears over the possible revival of Japanese militarism. The Attlee government could face criticism from MPs representing Lancashire constituencies (FO 371/69927/8332). Rearmament was an emotive issue in the light of memories – or nightmares – concerning the recent war in Asia and the Pacific. The Truman administration changed direction towards the occupation in 1947–48, influenced by a combination of complaints from Congress at the cost of the occupation, which was onerous in the eyes of American taxpayers; pressure from the Japan lobby for developing the Japanese economy and encouraging trade; and the growing impact of the cold war. George F. Kennan, head of the Policy Planning Staff within the State Department, was influential in pressing for the rebuilding of Japan. He went to Japan in February–March 1948 and held lengthy discussions with MacArthur. While respecting the general's positive record, Kennan held that the occupation was intoxicated with radical reform, which had gone too far. The economy should be restored, so that Japan could become a pillar of Western defences in Asia (FRUS, 1948, 6: 697). MacArthur reiterated his faith in Japan as a 'Switzerland of East Asia and the Pacific' but Kennan's thinking ran in a different direction. Covert Japanese rearmament was supported by some within SCAP, notably by MacArthur's intelligence chief, General Charles Willoughby. Brigadier A.K. Ferguson, military adviser to the British mission, reported in May 1948:

> There would, however, appear to be one question on which there is unanimity of opinion and that is that Japan must be protected as far as possible from Communistic influences and from infiltration from the USSR. The motive behind this unanimity is definitely American fear of Russian penetration and the desire to use Japan as a bulwark (FO 371/69887/7999).

Ferguson provided examples of creeping rearmament – air bases were being strengthened so as to include longer runways, possibly for the use of B-36 bombers; army and navy ammunition storage facilities were being improved, as were underground oil storage facilities. Ferguson was convinced that American motives were defensive but he conceded that, from a Russian perspective, they could appear threatening (FO 371/69887/7999).

The British Government was not kept fully informed of developments pointing to accelerating rearmament. However, pieces of the jigsaw puzzle accumulated so that a broad pattern could be discerned. Taiwan featured as a prominent element in 1949-50, following the defeat of the Kuomintang in the Chinese civil war and Chiang Kai-shek's retreat to the island. MacArthur placed great emphasis on the necessity to prevent Taiwan from falling into Communist hands. Gascoigne reported in September 1949:

> Some seven months ago MacArthur pointed out to me that Formosa was obviously a vital strategic point in the 'Island Line' and must be kept at all costs within the Allied sphere of influence. He certainly,

therefore, holds the view that its domination by the Communists would be a grave threat, not only to communications between Japan/ Philippines but also to the United States 'front line' in the Pacific/ Philippines/Okinawa/Japan (FO 371/75770/14000).

Willoughby told Malcolm MacDonald, the British high commissioner for South-East Asia, then visiting Tokyo, that he included Taiwan within the essential island defence chain (Philippines/ Okinawa/Japan) (FO 371/75770/14000). A number of Japanese army officers were sent secretly to Taiwan from the summer of 1949 to help the Kuomintang regime prepare for the defence of Taiwan against a Communist invasion. The most prominent of the military men was General Nemoto Hiroshi. The British consul in Tamsui confirmed the presence of Japanese military advisers (FO 371/75778/8488). Discussion of rearmament was extremely sensitive in the Commonwealth, particularly in Australia and New Zealand. The swift descent of Japanese forces into numerous Pacific islands in 1942-43 and Japanese naval and air operations in Australian waters, including the bombing of Darwin, caused immense anguish and exacerbated psychological reactions of insecurity in Australia and New Zealand. The only way to persuade the southern dominions to acquiesce in Japanese rearmament was to provide guarantees of their defence.

The triumph of Communism in China in 1949, together with various Communist risings in most of Southeast Asia, produced another source of apprehension. The United States was more perturbed over the latter but recognized that appropriate assurances must be forthcoming over the former. It was impossible for Britain to guarantee the defence of the Pacific dominions; only the United States could fulfil this task. John Foster Dulles appreciated this clearly when he assumed responsibility for negotiating a peace treaty with Japan in 1950-51. Dulles conceived of the ANZUS alliance as the solution to this problem (Lowe, 1997b: 36). The new alliance structure would complement his ideas for consolidating American defence strategy in East Asia and the Pacific through a security treaty with Japan. Dulles saw Britain as too heavily committed in Europe, the Middle East and Malaya to be able to contribute meaningfully in the Pacific. The British chiefs of staff initially deplored this approach but acquiesced, as did the Attlee government (Lowe, 1997b: 36-7). Naturally, British exclusion was damaging for British prestige but it was a realistic assessment of British capabilities.

ROLE OF YOSHIDA SHIGERU

The most important personality in Japanese politics during the occupation era – and probably in the whole of post-1945 history – was Yoshida Shigeru (Dower, 1996). A comparison could be drawn between the career of Winston Churchill in British politics from 1940 and the career of Yoshida from 1945-46. During the 1930s Churchill's career appeared to be in irreversible decline, as he moved erratically to the right and assailed the Indian policies of the MacDonald and Baldwin governments. In the late 1930s Churchill seemed destined for a final cantankerous phase before retirement. Instead, the gravity of the world crisis in 1940 led to Churchill at last becoming prime minister and fulfilling a further fifteen years of active leadership. Yoshida was a diplomat of seemingly average ability who held one important post as ambassador to Great Britain, in the late 1930s, but whose career also appeared to be drawing to a close amidst the rise of raucous militarism which he detested.

The comprehensive defeat of Japan in 1945 provided an opportunity for Yoshida's career to develop along wholly unexpected lines. The discrediting of much of the Japanese leadership and establishment meant that a political figure who combined conservatism with repudiation of old-style militarism could establish himself as a major player, given innate shrewdness and luck (Dower, 1996). Yoshida's approach was based on certain principles which he regarded as realistic and as connoting the only sensible way of restoring Japan's fortunes. He held office as prime minister briefly in 1946-47 and then from 1948 to 1954 (Kohno, 1997: 30-67). It was in his opinion imperative to cooperate closely with the United States so as to persuade the latter to terminate the occupation sooner rather than later; this cooperation must extend into the post-occupation period and would mean that Japan could rely on the United States for protection. However, Yoshida had no desire to be an US puppet. Rather he wished to use the opportunities created by the room for manoeuvre in the relationship between SCAP and the Japanese government to modify SCAP initiatives which he regarded as unwise. In addition, Yoshida tried to encourage European involvement as a counter-balance to excessive US power. Yoshida wanted to promote Japanese economic recovery but in a relatively modest way, attuned to the circumstances prevailing in Japan in the later 1940s.

Yoshida's diplomatic experience and lack of previous

participation in Japanese domestic politics was an asset in 1946-48. He had lived in Europe and was conversant with the state of Europe after the First World War, with the aspirations and failings of the League of Nations and with the endeavours of British and French leaders to handle the developing ascendancy of the dictators in the 1930s. Clearly, it was not feasible to expect France to play an active role in East Asian affairs after 1945, given the serious problems facing the Fourth Republic in Europe and in Indochina. The Netherlands was occupied similarly with Europe and Indonesia. The political evolution of West Germany was of considerable interest and afforded certain parallels with Japan. However, the existence of the various allied zones in Germany and Berlin also pointed to differences which remained highly significant for years ahead. Russia was excluded from effective involvement in the occupation and Yoshida felt – unlike the purged Hatoyama Ichirō – that little would be gained from pursuing relations with Moscow in the near future. Therefore, only Britain remained.

Yoshida regarded Britain with some warmth, which was not surprising for a former diplomat of his generation and moderation. He had grown up during a period when relations between Japan and Britain were cordial and Yoshida tended to speak of the Anglo-Japanese Alliance (1902-23) as part of a 'golden age' in Japan's development and in relations between the two countries. As is often the case, looking back enhanced the attractive features while blurring those that were less palatable. Yoshida genuinely liked Britain but there was political calculation in his attitude. He met the head or acting head of the British Liaison Mission (UKLIM) frequently and these encounters permitted Yoshida to float ideas so that he could ascertain British reactions. When he returned as prime minister in 1948, he emphasized to Alvary Gascoigne his desire for improved relations (FO 371/69819/3508). Since Yoshida and Gascoigne had known one another for twenty-five years as fellow diplomats, their approach was free of the constraints that would otherwise have prevailed.

Gascoigne liked Yoshida but it was, as yet, too early to assess whether Yoshida was well qualified for guiding Japan through the latter part of the occupation (FO 371/69819/3508). MacArthur was rather dismissive of Yoshida in 1948: he regarded him as indolent and not possessing the political skills for establishing lasting influence in Japanese politics. MacArthur lamented the mediocrity of Japanese politicians (FO 371/69819/ 3508). Officials in the Foreign Office also doubted whether Yoshida was the right man to lead Japan through a demanding period which would include preparing for a peace treaty establishing Japan's position while the cold war was extended to Asia, and handling economic issues. In February 1949 F.S. Tomlinson observed, 'The truth is that Mr Yoshida, although able in his own way, does not give the impression of being particularly well-qualified to cope with the intricate political and economic situation in which Japan now finds herself' (FO 371/ 76179/2420).

The Foreign Office was wary as regards Yoshida's oft repeated desire for warmer relations with Britain. Some friction had occurred already in Anglo-American relations because of the resentment of MacArthur or the Truman administration at attempted British interference. By 1948 British officials had adjusted to acceptance of American control, subject to pressing particular British interests vigorously when the occasion demanded. However, they wished to determine which issues should be emphasized to SCAP. Suspicion of Yoshida's motives existed and the Foreign Office did not wish to be drawn into Yoshida's manoeuvres to modify or divert American initiatives. To do this would be to risk American ire and this would be counter-productive to British aims to draw the United States more deeply into European commitments. Thus Gascoigne, although sympathetic to Yoshida, wrote in a private communication: 'Yoshida, who is likeable enough, is an intriguer and a trouble-maker. He would love to split us and the Americans and to complicate our inter-Commonwealth relations' (FO 371/ 69827/14706).

Yoshida urged the importance of an early peace treaty on the British: he shrewdly anticipated the character of the eventual San Francisco settlement in stating that, '. . . he thought it would be necessary for a number of allied troops to remain in Japan even after the peace Treaty, since the Japanese police were too few and their armament inadequate to maintain public order should the Communists attempt an offensive in Asia as they had already done in Europe' (FO 371/659825/14829). Implicitly this indicated Japanese cooperation in a measure of rearmament. Yoshida favoured ambiguity on this subject: it was highly contentious in Japan and Yoshida was opposed to rapid rearmament, since he was determined to prevent the old militarism reappearing (Lowe, 1997b: 101). John Dower has written, correctly, that Yoshida's principal achievement in Japanese-American relations lay in his successful resistance to John Foster Dulles's excessive enthusiasm for swift rearmament (Dower, 1996: 230). Here British politicians and officials agreed with Yoshida. The British were not properly informed of the limited and partially clandestine rearmament which occurred in the late 1940s under the encouragement of MacArthur's intelligence chief, Willoughby. MacArthur himself opposed rearmament and adhered to his preference for Japan as 'the Switzerland of the Pacific' (Welfield, 1988: 60-88). UKLIM and the Foreign Office interpreted the trend in the light of information gleaned. It was an extremely sensitive topic, given the recent proximity of war and the powerful feelings held among British POWs and civilian internees, not to mention the fervently-held opinions in Australia and New Zealand.

The British largely but not entirely concurred with Yoshida concerning the necessity for firm action to suppress Communist agitation in Japan. The Japan Communist Party (JCP) became more vocal and truculent in criticizing SCAP and the Truman administration in 1949-50. At the same time, trade unions should not be hindered unduly. Ernest Bevin, the foreign secretary, had been a great trade union leader and Bevin felt that democratization in Japan would not succeed unless the trade union movement was placed on an enduring foundation. Yoshida sought to assure the British that he was fully committed to democratization and was interested only in curbing the extremes of left and right (FO 371/76179/16818). Yoshida and the British united in applauding MacArthur's decision to purge the central committee of the JCP in mid-June 1950 (FO 371/ 83831/93).

NEGOTIATION OF A PEACE TREATY

On the eve of the outbreak of the Korean War, Robert Scott of the Foreign Office, reflected on British reactions to the unfolding of American policies towards Japan and China:

> Both in China and in Japan, after the war, we felt that American and British objectives were broadly the same. They were able and willing to assume the responsibility, we were not. Therefore, though we might have had private doubts about some aspects of their policy (and sometimes expressed them) on the whole we refrained from backseat

driving because we could not take over the wheel ourselves. That, as I see it, is a summary of the policy we followed and have been following in Japan. We had in fact no alternative.

The outcome in China was calamitous to Western interests, friction has been caused in Anglo-American relations arising out of our efforts to take over the helm of the Western ship after she had foundered and (most important of all) the Russian position has been greatly strengthened.

It may be that American policy in Japan will also fail. We may see the renaissance of a truculent and independent-minded Japan, ostensibly 'neutral', chafing at security controls and slowly gravitating to an East Asiatic orbit. In the short run Japan is dependent on the USA but in the long run her life hangs on ties with the mainland of East Asia. All of which will again work to the profit of Russia.

The time may thus be coming when we have to indulge in back-seat driving. The outlook is made more obscure by the lack of a clear American policy. The administration ... is trying to get a bi-partisan policy on Japanese and other issues but there is no knowing what it will be or when it will crystallize. Meanwhile the situation in Japan is drifting, in our view dangerously (FO 371/83831/93).

The biggest single issue facing the American, British and Japanese governments concerned the nature of a peace treaty. British leaders urged the conclusion of an early treaty, fearing that indefinite extension of the occupation would allow feelings of resentment and disgruntlement to fester in Japan. Divisions within the Truman administration over the wisdom of concluding an early treaty, given the deteriorating world situation, delayed progress until Truman decided that action was imperative and appointed John Foster Dulles to direct US negotiations. Yoshida desired an early peace treaty but viewed the subject with some trepidation. The signs pointed towards the United States supporting a relatively liberal, rather than harsh, treaty: this blended with the evolution of SCAP's policy since the early stages of the occupation, in addition to which the extension of the cold war to Asia increased the value of Japan to the United States. But aspects of the treaty were bound to be unpalatable to many Japanese and Yoshida had no wish to become a scapegoat; he told George Clutton, acting head of UKLIM, in March 1951 that he personally did not wish to sign a peace treaty (FO 371/92536/186). Yoshida was well aware that the British government leaned towards a less magnanimous approach than the US government, so that the scope for invoking British intervention was limited. However, it should be noted that the ministers in the Attlee cabinet were more critical of Japan than were the civil servants in the Foreign Office (Lowe, 1997b: 33-65). Yoshida intimated to Gascoigne in January 1951 that a more sympathetic British attitude would be appreciated: he deprecated the lack of enthusiasm in London for establishing a Japanese overseas agency in London and the critical line displayed by *The Times* correspondent in Japan, Frank Hawley, in his reports. According to Gascoigne, Yoshida felt hurt because '. . . we are not at present actively wooing Japan to the same extent as the United States' (FO 371/92521/4). Gascoigne clearly believed that Britain should adopt a more positive attitude towards Japan. Yoshida was vigorous and astute at the advanced age of 76 and 'had no particular axe to grind' (FO 371/9254/4).

Negotiations were handled very capably by Dulles who was confronted by daunting challenges. He had to secure agreement upon a liberal treaty which would ensure future stability in Japan, locked into a Western defence system guaranteed by the United States. The allies of the United States had to be persuaded to acquiesce in a treaty which made more concessions to Japan than they themselves would have initiated. At the same time, the peace treaty must be ratified by the US Senate. Differences between the US and British views were gradually reduced in April 1951 and Yoshida expressed satisfaction to Clutton at the progress made (FO 371/92547/383). John Dower has commented critically on Yoshida's attitude to the difficult issue of China and which Chinese government should be recognized eventually by Japan – 'Yoshida's policy was at best desultory and lackadaisical and his private actions belied his occasional public criticisms of the US containment policy' (Dower, 1996: 213). Dower continues that American and British diplomatic records lead historians to ponder why '. . . Yoshida never really seriously tried to exploit internal Anglo-American differences on the issue of dealing with communist China . . .' (Dower, 1996: 213).

ISSUE OF CHINA

The issue of China was peculiarly difficult and constituted the most contentious single aspect of Anglo-American exchanges over a peace treaty. The contention resulted from two developments: in January 1950 Britain recognized the People's Republic of China (PRC) and US ire at the emergence of the PRC, later compounded by Chinese military intervention in

Korea in October–November 1950. Critics of the Truman administration in the Republican party used the 'loss' of China as a weapon with which to weaken the Democrats before the presidential election in 1952. It was impossible for Dulles to permit a scenario in which the peace treaty he had negotiated led to the recognition of the PRC by Japan. To do so would be to risk refusal of the Senate to ratify the treaty by the requisite margin (and could doom Dulles's aspiration to become the next secretary of state in the new administration). Dulles and Herbert Morrison, the new British foreign secretary, agreed in June 1951 that neither the PRC nor the Kuomintang regime in Taiwan should attend the peace conference in San Francisco in September 1951 and that Japan should be free to decide which Chinese administration to recognize on regaining sovereignty.

Curiously, neither Morrison nor his Conservative successor, Anthony Eden, seems to have assessed carefully the political challenges facing Dulles or to have anticipated that Dulles would play matters as he did. When it became clear, in November–December 1951, that Dulles was pressurizing Yoshida to ensure that Japan would recognize Chiang Kai-shek's regime on Taiwan, Eden reacted angrily (Lowe, 1997b: 73-8). As with the distinction between the ministers in the Attlee government and the officials in the Foreign Office over the degree of generosity to be contained in the peace treaty earlier in 1951, so a similar difference in approach can be discerned between Eden and his officials. To the latter Dulles's strategy came as no surprise.

Yoshida was in an invidious dilemma regarding China and the peace treaty. Certain of his previous pronouncements indicated a pragmatic attitude along the lines that whatever the character of the Chinese government, geography and economics dictated that Japan should deal with it (Drifte, 1983: 128). In essence, this was only common sense. MacArthur condoned a significant quantity of trade between Japan and the PRC in 1950-51, despite his fulminations against the menace of 'Red China' (Lowe, 1997b: 131). But Yoshida's appreciation of political realities in Washington was greater than that revealed by Morrison and Eden. He discussed China with Morrison during the San Francisco conference, after Morrison underlined the vital importance of maintaining progress with democratization in Japan. Yoshida responded that democratization was required urgently in China, adding that future developments in Japan would be affected significantly by China. Morrison reiterated the essence of the understanding he had reached with Dulles in June, strictly applied:

> I mentioned recognition of China, emphasizing that we were not seeking to interfere. It was a decision to be taken by the Government and people of Japan for themselves. I thought, however, that he would be well advised to ponder very carefully and to take no precipitate action. Though the Treaty was signed, it was not yet in force; and it would be unwise of Japan by some hasty action on this important matter to stir up controversy in the various legislative bodies in the countries which had to ratify the Treaty. He took the point and was non-committal (FO 371/92616/5).

Once Dulles applied pressure, Yoshida complied and assented to the text of a letter Dulles drafted. Dower argues that Yoshida was too 'timid' in responding to the United States over China but it would surely have been dangerous for Yoshida to clash seriously with Dulles at a delicate stage in securing ratification of the peace treaty by the Senate (Dower, 1996: 213). It was more important for Yoshida to concentrate on restraining Dulles's enthusiasm for rapid rearmament.

CONCLUSION

British defence policy established the priorities as being the defence of Great Britain itself, the rebuilding and defence of Western Europe against external and internal threats, the defence of British interests in the Middle East and in East and Southeast Asia and the Pacific. As throughout the twentieth century, there was no doubt that Europe came first, although every reasonable effort should be made to ensure harmony within the Commonwealth (Lowe, 1997b: 5). Japan was viewed with considerable reservations. Limited rearmament came to be accepted grudgingly but British leaders and civil servants did not share the growing American enthusiasm for hastening Japan's economic recovery. Yoshida tried to nudge Britain towards a more assertive policy on occasion but the difficulty here was that if the British became too assertive, it was not likely to be in a direction helpful to Yoshida's ultimate objectives. Yoshida and the Attlee government agreed on the desirability of an early peace treaty in 1947-50 but the British favoured a tougher treaty than Yoshida contemplated. When the British did argue with the Americans over the peace treaty in 1951, what did the British want? They pondered a war-guilt clause, reparations, confiscation of Japanese gold deposits, removing Japanese rights under the Congo Basin treaties, other elements of constraint, and looked ahead to possibly sharp exchanges over cotton textiles, shipbuilding and the Staffordshire potteries. Yoshida and the British did concur over rearmament but Dulles excluded Britain from the ANZUS treaty structure, in which decision Australia and New Zealand acquiesced.

Yoshida was fond of referring to the 'good old days' of the Anglo-Japanese Alliance, days when the United States had not occupied centre-stage. However, British power had waned and would not be restored through nostalgic recollections of former Anglo-Japanese cooperation. Therefore, reduced to its essentials, Europe could not influence events in Japan during the occupation to a significant degree in the sense of European countries intervening in Washington or with SCAP. In a broader sense Europe did affect Japan because of the intensification of the cold war with the result that the United States changed policy, stimulated Japanese revival, and moved to consolidate Japan's role within the Western defence system. But the principal agent of change in Japan was the United States. Europe and Britain were on the sidelines.

BIBLIOGRAPHY

Cumings, Bruce. 1997. *Korea's Place in the Sun: A Modern History*. London: Norton.
Dower, John. 1996. *Japan In War and Peace: Essays on History, Culture and Race*. London: Penguin Books, 208-42.
Drifte, Reinhard. 1983. *The Security Factor in Japan's Foreign Policy, 1945-1952*. Ripe, East Sussex: Saltire Press.
FO, Foreign Office Files, Public Record office, Kew.
FRUS *Foreign Relations of the United States*.
Gaddis, John Lewis. 1982. *Strategies of Containment*. Oxford: Oxford University Press.
———. 1987. *The Long Peace: Enquiries into the History of the Cold War*. Oxford: Oxford University Press.
Holloway, David. 1994. *Stalin and the Bomb: The Soviet Union and Atomic Energy, 1939-1956*. London: Yale University Press.
Kohno, Masaru. 1997. *Japan's Postwar Party Politics*. Princeton, N.J.: Princeton University Press.
Lowe, Peter. 1994. 'Sir Alvary Gascoigne in Japan, 1946-1951'. In *Britain and Japan: Biographical Portraits*, edited by Ian Nish. Folkestone: Japan Library, 279-94.
———. 1997a. *The Origins of the Korean War*, Second edition. London: Longman.
———. 1997b. *Containing the Cold War in East Asia: British Policies Towards Japan, China and Korea, 1948-1953*. Manchester: Manchester University Press.
Minear, Richard H. 1971. *Victors' Justice*. Princeton, N.J.: Princeton University Press.
Welfield, John. 1988. *An Empire in Eclipse: Japan in the Postwar American Alliance System*. London: Athlone Press.

13

Europe in Japan's Foreign Policy

KAZUKI IWANAGA

A review of current writings on Japan's foreign policy reveals that its policy towards Europe has received little attention. During the postwar period, Japanese-European relations have been influenced overwhelmingly by the primacy of the critical relationship with the United States in Japan's foreign and security policies. In their world views, the Japanese have not placed Europe in the same category as the United States and Asia. From Tokyo's perspective, there are several factors as to why relations between Japan and Europe have been the weakest within the trilateral framework of Japan, Europe and the United States. For Tokyo's policy-makers Europe is remote, not only geographically but also psychologically. Moreover, Japan and the countries of Western Europe have had different regional interests, and Japan and Europe have paid little attention to their relations. Instead, they have concentrated on the maintenance and strengthening of their respective alliance relationships with the United States (Ministry of Foreign Affairs, 1991: 21).[1] Because of the centrality of the United States to Japan in the postwar period, Japanese policy-makers have tended to view specific foreign-policy issues through the prism of the dominant bilateral relationship with the United States (Iwanaga, 1996). With the end of the cold war, Japan came to recognize that it must pursue an assertive foreign policy commensurate with its economic clout, a process that requires it to move beyond its preoccupation with dominant bilateral relations with the United States and to develop closer and broader relationships with Europe.

In its relations with Europe, Japan has had considerable success during the past four-and-a-half decades. Its ties, especially economic ones, have expanded, and interest in Japan has grown. Yet there are limits to what Japan can hope to achieve in its relations with European nations due to a basic asymmetry in Japan's relationship with them. Clearly, they are potentially more important to Japan than Japan is to them. The crucial immediate interests of the member nations of the European Union lie in their relations with each other and with the United States. Geographical distances separate them from Japan. The overlap in interests is quite limited compared with Japanese-US or European-US relations. Although Japan sees a congruence of certain fundamental values with the countries of Western Europe such as a sharing of common beliefs in freedom and democracy as well as in the market economy, cultural differences create a deep gulf. Nevertheless, improved ties with these nations have served Japan's interests. Japan is a major industrial democracy, even though it is also an Asian nation, and on many international issues its leaders see a congruence of interests with other Western industrial democracies.

Until quite recently many Japanese had an outdated view of Europe and individual European states. Even at the governmental level, Japanese policy-makers looked on Europe with disdain. The official report of the Industrial Structure Council at the Ministry of International Trade and Industry in the early 1970s, for example, stated: 'As Western Europe is, generally speaking, a closed and tradition-filled society, it is necessary by all means to approach it fully respectful of its views of values and customs in expanding economic exchange' (Industrial Structure Council, MITI, 1972: 166). That view has changed at least at the policy-making level. The Japanese are developing new views of Europe and re-evaluating its ties with the nations therein. Euro-Japanese relations have taken on an increased importance. Europe has become the object of a different sort of interest to Japan than before. The interest is no longer exclusively economic. Japan has become more interested in political and security issues which has led it to view Europe in a new light.

The uniting of Europe, Japan's quest for a global role, and the decline of US hegemonic power are the most important background factors in this process of reassessing ties with Europe. Judging from their public statements, Japanese policy-makers tend to argue that, in order to play a global role, Japan needs to have a closer relationship with Europe (and, of course, the United States), within the trilateral framework of the global partnership. Western Europe, in turn, needs Japan for the management of the world economy, for many of the economic and financial problems could not be solved without the participation of the second largest economy of the world.

The catalytic shock of the end of the cold war and the inability of Japan to contribute manpower to the coalition efforts during the Gulf War have raised questions about how Japan can actively take part in global affairs. As in many other countries, the radical changes in world politics brought about by these events have greatly recast the foreign policy issues and challenges facing Japan. In Japan, changed circumstances have stimulated a lively debate over future foreign policy directions.

Japan's relationship with the United States, as well as Japanese participation in the peacekeeping operations of the United Nations and permanent seat on the UN Security Council attract a considerable amount of public attention. In contrast to such matters, the issue of Japanese-European relations is primarily confined to a small group of academics, intellectuals and policy-makers.

The main purpose of this paper is to analyze the evolving role of Europe in Japanese foreign policy. The main questions posed are:

- How and where has Europe fitted into Japanese foreign policy at different times in the postwar era?
- Has there been a restructuring of Japan's policy towards Europe?
- Has Japan given different weight to economic, political and security considerations in relation to Europe over the years?

It is useful and important, in dealing with these questions, to make a distinction between a government's policy as reflected in its foreign-policy pronouncements and actual behaviour. Governments' foreign-policy rhetoric may give strong evidence of intent to change policy, yet in actuality, changes that achieve this are rare. This study is concerned with the question of foreign-policy change. In recent years, the study of change in foreign policy has received increasing attention in the literature of international relations (Holsti, 1982; Hermann, 1990; Carlsnaes, 1993; Rosati, Hagan and Sampson, 1994; Iwanaga, 1996). It is assumed in this paper that Japanese policy-makers' attitude toward any specific foreign-policy issue (e.g., policy towards Europe) is constrained by more general foreign policy beliefs (e.g., postures and images of other nations) which, in turn, are constrained by even more general core values (e.g., ideology, belief in democracy, or belief in market economy) (Hurwitz and Peffley, 1987).

Before proceeding, several qualifications should be made. First, Europe, for the purposes of this paper, means Western Europe, excluding the former Soviet Union and the countries of Eastern Europe. The narrow definition of Europe includes essentially the member states of the European Union plus Norway and Switzerland. Of course, this is not to say that these countries are not important. Second, the analysis of Europe in Japanese foreign policy relies, to a great extent, on the statements of prime ministers and foreign ministers and the official reports of the foreign ministry as well as parliamentary proceedings. Where relevant, public statements and other hard data are not available, I have made use of the writings of policy-makers and other secondary sources.

EUROPE'S INCONSPICUOUS ROLE IN JAPAN'S FOREIGN POLICY

To fully understand the role of Europe in Japanese foreign policy over the years, especially how Europe fits into the Japanese world view, it is first necessary to consider the thinking of Prime Minister Yoshida Shigeru, for he laid the basis for Japan's postwar foreign and security policies or what has come to be known as the Yoshida doctrine. Yoshida accepted the international environment as a given and Japan's national interest, being a defeated minor power, best served by adapting to the existing international order maintained by the United States, the *Pax Americana*.

According to his line of reasoning, nation states in the international order were confronted with constraints and opportunities, the effects of which tended to vary with their positions within the international power structure. Yoshida acknowledged the inherent disparity in the distribution of power between the major powers and the minor states and that there were severe limitations in the extent to which a defeated minor power like Japan could alter the international system (Iwanaga, 1993: 83). Therefore, under Yoshida's leadership, the foreign policy of Japan took a passive stance towards the existing international environment. He recognized that whatever actions Japan took had only a marginal impact on world politics.

Nevertheless, Yoshida took full advantage of the international order supported by the United States in order to insure Japan's goals of security and prosperity.

The primacy of the Japan–US relationship firmly anchored in the 1951 and 1960 security treaties allowed Japan to define its foreign policy primarily in economic terms and adopt a low external political posture. Under Yoshida's leadership, Japanese foreign policy came to be coloured by a strong element of dominant bilateralism. Japan has for four-and-a-half decades pursued one of the most successful and consistent foreign policies of any industrialized democratic country. As former US Secretary of State Henry Kissinger put it, 'Japanese decisions have been the most farsighted and intelligent of any major nation of the postwar era' (Kissinger, 1979: 324).

Because Japan's foreign-policy framework was very US-centric, Europe occupied an inconspicuous role in it. This is not to say that Europe was totally unimportant to Yoshida. That Yoshida was the first prime minister to visit Europe after the war and to have talks with national leaders was proof of his interest in Western Europe (albeit a limited one). He made a trip to Europe (the United Kingdom, France, West Germany, and Italy) and the United States in 1954, the final year of his administration. Europe was important to him in two respects. First, Yoshida was interested in developing relations with Europe, for he, a strong anti-Communist, believed that the solidarity of the Western alliance was essential in countering the Soviet Union's policy towards the West and fighting Communism in East and Southeast Asia. Considering Yoshida's greater esteem for the British foreign policy, it was not surprising that he emphasized especially the strengthening of Japan's friendly relations with Great Britain to meet the threat of Communism (Yoshida, 1957: 224-7).

Second, Yoshida worked hard to attract European leaders to his Asian policy when he visited Western Europe in 1954. His tour there should be regarded as a strategic step towards his forthcoming talks with the US leaders: he needed the support of European leaders for his Asian policy, especially the policy towards China, before he went on to the United States. By getting support from European leaders, Yoshida hoped that he could nudge the United States towards softening its position on China. He found the China policy of the US rigid in comparison to the British policy which to him seemed more pragmatic and wise. Prime Minister Yoshida's attempts to secure British support in persuading Washington to change its China policy did not succeed. The British were simply noncommittal. For the British and other European political leaders, Japan was of little political importance, viewed as being closely allied with, and subordinate to, the United States.

EUROPE IN PRIME MINISTER IKEDA'S THREE-PILLAR SCHEME

Japan's relations with Europe were of little concern and importance to the Japanese until the early 1960s. When Ikeda Hayato replaced Kishi Nobusuke as prime minister in July 1960, Japan's relations with Europe entered a new phase. Ikeda created the foreign policy of 'cooperation with the free world community'. During Kishi's administration (1957-60), Japan's collaboration with the other free countries was almost entirely confined to the United States.

During the Ikeda administration, ties with Western European countries were forged. He described Japan as one of the three pillars supporting the free world, the other two being the United States and Western Europe. Referring to the East–West conflict, he stated that the 'free world' was supported by three pillars: Western Europe, the United States and Canada, and Japan. Ikeda's three-pillar scheme stressing the importance of the links with the United States and Western Europe revealed important facets of Japanese foreign policy. For the first time since the war, Europe had become an important component in Japan's foreign policy. Japan had now begun to show an increased interest in strengthening its contacts with European countries.

In their policy speeches to the Diet, Ikeda and his foreign ministers frequently mentioned Western Europe and the European Community. Ikeda argued that it was necessary to place more emphasis on Japan's relations with Europe than had been the case in the past. Their frequent reference to Europe indicates a perception of Europe as important to Japan's economic growth and the enhancement of its international status and prestige. However, he was not oblivious to its political implications. Ikeda was deeply concerned about the danger of Japan being left out of the new economic order that would result from the economic integration of Europe and her need to participate in the mainstream of the world economy, together with a 'United Europe' and the United States. In the Diet debate, Ikeda pointed out that Japanese-European relationship,

213

compared with US–European and US–Japanese relations, was inadequate and that the trilateral relationship between Japan, Western Europe, and the US should be taken into consideration (Shūgiin, 1964b: 3).

Ikeda approached Western Europe primarily from an economic perspective. He stressed the importance of the European Economic Community (EEC) for Japan in the following way: 'The fact that it has now become a "New Europe" matching in power the Soviet Union and the United States, and that Washington is trying to strengthen America's economic ties with the EEC is a matter of grave concern to us' (Ministry of Foreign Affairs, 1962: 13). As Japan's need for an export market had grown, it had turned to Europe as a source of demand. Conscious that Japan needed access to the European market, Ikeda emphasized closer ties between the business community in Japan and that in Europe:

> I wish to mention the importance of mutual understanding between the business community in Japan and that in Europe through closer contacts between them. The deep-rooted mistrust and suspicion of Japan by the European business community which arises from their unfamiliarity with actual conditions in Japan seem to be the cause of the continued discrimination against Japanese goods. In order to eliminate them, it is desirable that our business community cooperate with the Government and on their part improve their export systems and at the same time make a more positive approach to their counterparts in Europe (Ministry of Foreign Affairs, 1962: 7f).

In 1962 top political leaders of Japan and several major European countries visited each others' capitals to promote friendly relations. Between September and October 1962, Foreign Minister Ōhira Masayoshi made a European tour, followed by Prime Minister Ikeda in November. Ikeda visited the United Kingdom, West Germany, France, Italy, Holland, and Belgium and stressed 'the need of setting up a strong international cooperation structure with North America, West Europe and Japan as the three pillars of the free world' and pointed out 'the importance of establishing intimate relations between our country and West Europe such as exist between Japan and the United States' (Ministry of Foreign Affairs, 1962: 50). In return, the foreign ministers of Great Britain, France and West Germany visited Japan in 1963. Thus, Japan widened her diplomatic contacts, which included periodic routine meetings not only with the United States but also with Canada, Britain, France,

West Germany, and Australia. In his speech to the Diet soon after visiting West European countries, Ikeda stated that these countries were 'eager to expand their relations with Japan, the leading advanced nation of Asia, by eliminating the existing trade barriers' (Ministry of Foreign Affairs, 1962: 51). A Treaty of Commerce and Navigation between Japan and Great Britain was concluded in November 1962 when Ikeda visited London. Similar agreements were reached with other West European countries concerning the relaxation or removal of import restrictions against Japanese goods.

Overall, European countries looked on Japan with a complicated mixture of apprehension, envy, and admiration. Watching its rapid economic development, with US assistance, European leaders almost certainly resented the fact that Japan was surging ahead of their countries. And they looked with some apprehension at Japan's growing economic strength. However, they had become increasingly interested in expanding economic ties with Japan. They recognized Japan as an advanced industrial nation and thus were ready to accept Japan as a member of the 'club' of first-class economic powers.

The Japanese government under Prime Minister Ikeda saw Japan's membership in the Organization for Economic Co-operation and Development (OECD) as a way of establishing ties with Western Europe because 18 of the 20 member states were European (Itō, 1966: 153, 167). Ikeda's European tour increased West European support for Japanese entry into the OECD. Ikeda found that the countries of Western Europe placed 'an increased confidence in Japan' and desired to have 'closer cooperative ties with Japan as they have with North America' (Ministry of Foreign Affairs, 1963: 12). Foreign Minister Ōhira, in his foreign-policy speech to the Diet in 1963, emphasized that 'Japan's diplomatic intercourse with West Europe has undergone a significant development following the European tour of Prime Minister Ikeda.' 'It means', Ōhira continued, 'that the way has been paved for cultivating with West European countries intimate relationships such as exists now between Japan and the United States' (Ministry of Foreign Affairs, 1963: 16).

Prime Minister Ikeda raised the question of Japanese membership in the OECD with President Kennedy as early as June 1961 when he visited the United States. Ikeda did not succeed in convincing the US President to support the membership. Kennedy told his guest that the time was not ripe

215

for Japan's entry into the organization. Soon, however, an awareness emerged in Europe and the United States that, recognizing the growing strength of Japan's economy, Japanese participation was essential if the problems of world economy were to be solved. This was articulated by Foreign Minister Ōhira in his reply to an interpellation in February 1964 as to why the OECD accepted Japan's membership: 'I believe they correctly evaluated that the world economy cannot be smoothly managed by disregarding Japan's economic power'. This also meant that Japan's participation was deemed crucial in solving economic problems in Asia where Japan is the only developed country in the region (Shūgiin, 1964a: 8).

For Ikeda, policy towards Europe became in a sense a way of asserting independence from the United States. Six months after he became prime minister, he stated before the Budget Committee of the Lower House: 'Japan has taken many foreign policy actions similar to those of the United States, but hereafter we shall pursue an independent course of action' (*Asahi shimbun*, 16 December 1960, evening ed.). The policy of external diversification was pursued through trade relations, as well as political and cultural relations. This meant departing from Japan's excessive emphasis upon the United States, something which was carried out through improved commercial agreements with the European countries.

Compared with other major foreign-policy issues, Japan's quest for membership in the OECD did not arouse sustained and strong criticism from Japan's opposition parties. This is evident from the infrequent reference to OECD during Diet foreign-policy debates during 1961-63. The only time there was a debate on it was in January-April 1964, when the Ikeda government attempted to obtain the Diet's approval. Circumstances surrounding the membership were technical in nature. Moreover, because of the political turmoil Japan had just experienced, the Ikeda government adopted, from the outset, its well-known 'low political posture' towards the opposition parties and played down the political aspects of the country's membership in the OECD. Ikeda's most urgent task was to restore domestic peace, so badly damaged by the struggle against the revision of the security treaty with the United States. Japan's economic development interests and the pursuit of a more independent foreign policy required domestic political stability, for Ikeda was deeply conscious of the inseparability of domestic politics and foreign policy. Ikeda was convinced that the achievement of his goals required him to assume a conciliatory attitude towards opposition parties, rather than to continue the confrontation politics of his predecessor.

The most vocal critics on the question of Japan's membership in the OECD were the Socialists. The major differences between the ruling Liberal Democratic and the Socialist parties on the policy towards Japanese membership had deep roots. They arose, in part, because of differing ideological perspectives and priorities regarding Europe and Asia. It is questionable whether the Socialists (or at least some leading Socialist Diet members) had any deep understanding of the nature and functions of the OECD. The Socialists opposed Japan's membership in the OECD, claiming that it was an anti-Communist organization led by the United States. One Socialist Diet member even portrayed the organization as an 'economic version' of the NATO (Shūgiin, 1964b: 5). In a reply to the question on the nature of the OECD and its relationship with NATO, Foreign Minister Ōhira had to emphasize the fact that there was absolutely no association between the two organizations (Shūgiin, 1964b: 4). To support this, the government stressed that Sweden, Austria and Switzerland were also members of the OECD.

Japanese opinion was in favour of developing relations with European countries after the extended political turmoil in the country in connection with the revision of the security treaty with the United States. Therefore, public opinion was in favour of Japanese membership in the OECD. Many Japanese viewed the establishment of ties with Western Europe as a test of Japan's ability to pursue a foreign policy independent of Washington. Ikeda reasoned that his role in this would not only enhance the country's status and prestige, but would also strengthen the LDP's public support. Ikeda was one of the postwar prime ministers who probably paid the most attention to public opinion. Itō Masaya, his secretary and biographer, for example, wrote that, for Ikeda, the interests of the people counted 60 per cent and those of the LDP counted 40 per cent on his political scale (Itō, 1965).

Japan's relations with Western European nations were consolidated when Japan was admitted to the OECD in April 1964. The Japanese membership was a boost for Japanese international recognition as one of the leading industrial economies of the world and its only Asian member.

Ikeda's successor, Satō Eisaku, had not been able to follow up on this motif. For Satō, Europe was peripheral to an America-centred world view. Indeed, except for rhetorical references to Western Europe, the words and deeds of the Japanese governments from 1964 to the early 1970s were dominated by relations with the United States. The concern about 'the American factor' was natural. Japan-Europe relations remained predominantly economic until the late 1970s and the early 1980s.

EUROPE IN JAPAN'S RESOURCE DIPLOMACY

Under the government headed by Prime Minister Tanaka Kakuei (1972-74), Japan tried to establish closer ties with the European Common Market countries to offset those with the United States. Tanaka expressed concern about the lack of close ties between Japan and Western Europe and her need to establish a trilateral relationship (Saito, 1990: 39). More importantly, Japan took an interest in Europe hoping to gain access to oil and markets. In 1973 Tanaka's top priority was to secure oil for Japan. The Tanaka government was thus concerned with Japan's energy situation and his advocacy of closer ties with Western Europe should be seen in the context of that concern (Hayasaka, 1987: 327-31). Tanaka declared:

> In light of the Japanese situation, with its heavy dependence upon overseas sources of energy and raw materials, I have long been acutely aware of the need to ensure stable supplies and to diversify our sources, and we have made repeated efforts to secure supplies from the resource-possessing nations. Since forming my first Cabinet, I have met with leaders in the United States, Europe, and the Soviet Union and have actively utilized these meetings to discuss with them the joint development and stable supply of natural resources. The issue of natural resources is an important element in Japanese foreign policy (Ministry of Foreign Affairs, 1973: 83f).

That Tanaka was the first Japanese prime minister since Ikeda to make an official European tour illustrates his interest in the region. He visited three West European states and the Soviet Union in the wake of the oil crisis. Although Tanaka's policy of developing a balanced triangular relationship between Japan, Europe, and the United States was similar to Ikeda's so-called 'three pillars of the free world', the circumstances for and basic objective of Tanaka's European tour were different from Ikeda's trip. Tanaka was an advocate of close cooperation on energy issues among Japan, Western Europe, and the United States. He was the first of the leaders of the industrial democracies of the West to support Kissinger's concept of a new Atlantic Charter regarding trilateral cooperation between Japan, North America, and Western Europe (Wakaizumi, 1974: 45f).

The Tanaka administration had moved towards the adoption of the so-called resource diplomacy for securing stable oil supplies. When Tanaka visited Britain, France and West Germany, he stressed close cooperation and interdependence among advanced industrial democracies of the world regarding energy questions. He proposed to Prime Minister Edward Heath Japanese participation in the development of North Sea oil resources and to President Georges Pompidou he proposed a joint venture in developing oil and other natural resources in Africa. In Bonn, he reached an agreement with Chancellor Willy Brandt that a joint committee would be established to study the possibility of cooperation between the two countries in the field of natural resources and energy supply. Tanaka continued his resources diplomacy in a quest for diversified sources of energy supply in Moscow and met Leonid Brezhnev to discuss, among other things, Japanese participation in the Tyumen oil develop-ment project in Western Siberia.

Despite the Tanaka government's interest in establishing close ties with Western Europe, there was something of a gap between the rhetoric of cooperating with Europe and the actual policy pursued by the government. Europe was still of little political and strategic importance to Japanese foreign policy-makers until the late 1970s. Even economic relations between Japan and the European Community as a whole were very weak and highly asymmetrical. In the early 1970s, Japan's share in the export of West European countries accounted for only 1.1 per cent and import 1.7 per cent (Industrial Structure Council, MITI, 1972: 166).

Japan began to involve itself in world affairs through its participation in the Group of Seven (G-7) summits. Japanese participation in trilateral cooperation on economic issues between Japan, Western Europe and North America began in November 1975 when Prime Minister Miki Takeo participated in the summit meeting of Western industrial democracies at Rambouillet. It was the first time since World War II that Japan was able to exchange views within the trilateral framework and even discuss policy coordination on the management of the world economy. After their inception in 1975, particularly from the turn of the decade onwards, the meetings of the annual Western summits came to serve as a forum for Japan to discuss cooperation and policy coordination between Japan, Europe and North America on global and regional issues.

THE INDIVISIBILITY OF THE WESTERN ALLIANCE

After years of avoiding getting itself actively involved in global politics, Japan was moving slowly and cautiously towards playing an important political and security role in the world. Towards the end of the 1970s and the beginning of the 1980s, Japan's foreign policy was for the first time in the postwar period expanded on a global scale, while elsewhere East–West relations were deteriorating. Under these new circumstances, Tokyo began to show a keen interest in policy coordination with Western Europe. Tokyo's increased interest in the countries in Europe were primarily based on political and strategic considerations, rather than on economic factors. As the cold war resumed, the problem of global security was perceived in terms of Japan's position as a member of the Western alliance: to act in concert with Western Europe and the United States would conform with and strengthen Japan's view that Western security was indivisible. The *Diplomatic Bluebook* of the foreign ministry stated:

> While Japan's relations with the countries of Western Europe were friendly enough, they were not, at least until the late 1970s, such as to facilitate cooperation on international political issues of importance. However, as Japan became an increasingly important member of the international community, it became crucial that Japan and Western Europe cooperate in dealing with international political issues of mutual concern, including such issues as the Afghan problem in 1979, the Polish problem in 1980 and beyond, and the stepped-up Soviet deployment of SS-20s in the late 1970s and early 1980s, and efforts were made on both sides to strengthen the political dialogue between Japan and Western Europe (Ministry of Foreign Affairs, 1985: 95).

Subsequent Japanese responses to these events brought about the common concerns and intensification of political consultations with the Western European nations and the United States. The Japanese government recognized the insufficiency of focusing merely on the dominant-bilateral relations and the importance of the coordination and adjustment of policies on many political and strategic issues between the United States, Western Europe and Japan.

In response to the collapse of the US–Soviet détente, Japan emphasized the shared values of democracy and freedom with regard to the West European link and stressed common interests and called for cooperation between Japan and Western Europe. Former Vice-foreign Minister Murata noted that Japan's participation in the boycott of the 1980 Moscow Olympic and the economic sanctions taken by the Western bloc after the Soviet invasion of Afghanistan was the first time since the end of World War II that Japan had acted in close cooperation with the countries of Western Europe and North America on an important political and strategic issue that had global ramifications (Murata, 1987: 4).

It is interesting to note that the Japanese became increasingly aware of the fact that the peace and security of Europe was closely linked to that of East Asia. What made the Japanese realize this was the Soviet military build-up in the Far East. including the question of transferring Soviet intermediate range nuclear force (INF) from Europe to the Far East. Referring to the Soviet arms build-up, Foreign Minister Abe Shintarō, in his speech to the Diet in January 1983, expressed profound concern, stating that it was threatening peace and stability in the Far East (Gaimushō, 1983: 372). Tokyo realized that the US–Soviet arms control talks on the INF, especially the Soviet deployment of the SS-20 missile, 'are of crucial importance to this country' (Gaimushō, 1983: 15). Accordingly, the Japanese government advocated a global solution to the INF incorporating Tokyo's viewpoint.

In the postwar era it was Prime Minister Nakasone Yasuhiro who spoke out more forcibly on a forthright alignment of Japan with its European and US allies than any of his predecessors since Yoshida Shigeru. In the political statement at the Williamsburg summit in June 1983, the Japanese prime minister, well-known for his high-posture political style, took the initiative in its formulation and agreed with the leaders of the other participating countries that 'Western security is indivisible and must be approached on a global basis' (Ministry of Foreign Affairs, 1985: 97). Prime Minister Nakasone recalled more than ten years later:

> If the Soviets were to be persuaded, or pressured into withdrawing their SS-22 missiles from Europe, the SS-20s deployed in Asia would also

have to be similarly dealt with. And, to force the Soviets to agree with such a demand, Japan, Western Europe and the United States would need to form a united front. With this goal in mind, I persuaded President Francois Mitterand of France to make a public statement at the time of the 1983 Williamsburg Summit to the effect that national security was a globally indivisible issue, and that the West would stand firmly together against the Soviet threat (Nakasone, 1995: 26f).

The West European countries responded positively to the Williamsburg statement and the consequence of this statement was to make 'the European factor' more important in Japan's foreign policy. The Japanese foreign ministry claimed that '. . . it became an important factor in promoting subsequent cooperative relations between Japan and Western Europe' (Ministry of Foreign Affairs, 1985: 97). This declaration, according to one top official of the foreign ministry, '. . . was an epoch-making event for Japan giving notice as it did of new Japanese interest in political and security cooperation between the Western nations' (Murata, 1987: 4). Moreover, Japan's active participation in the formulation of the political declaration should be seen as Nakasone's effort to 'break free of the Yoshida doctrine' (Nakasone, 1995: 24). Nakasone was the first postwar Japanese prime minister who forthrightly challenged the Yoshida doctrine that lay behind Japan's passive and withdrawn foreign policy.

The Nakasone administration stated that relations with the West European countries were an important pillar of Japanese foreign policy (Ministry of Foreign Affairs, 1986: 136). The Japanese government continued to maintain that Japan and Western Europe shared common interests concerning the East-West relations and security issues as is evident not only from political declarations at the 1983 Williamsburg summit, but also from the London summit in 1984 and the Bonn summit in 1985. Japan expanded its dialogue with Western Europe through consultation. In addition to the existing high-level administrative meetings between Japan and the EC (from 1973) and annual exchange meetings between Diet members in Japan and parliament representatives from the EC (from 1978), twice-yearly consultations between the foreign ministers of Japan and the EC and the member of the EC Commission responsible for external relations were initiated from 1983.

It was hoped that regular official consultations would strengthen a cooperative relationship with Europe and concrete efforts would be made to give substance to the relations.

However, the tangible results in establishing Euro-Japanese communications in terms of both quantity and quality were far from satisfactory. Murata wrote:

> Regular foreign ministers' meetings are held between Japan and Britain, France, West Germany, and Italy, as well as political consultations with the European Community under its troika set-up. However, many of these consultations tend to be nothing more than *tours d'horizon* of the political situation in the Soviet Union and the Third World, if we exclude discussions on bilateral problems. Nor do they lead to concrete policy coordination (Murata, 1987: 9).

Murata called for more meaningful dialogue between Japan and Western Europe.

TRILATERAL COOPERATION

In the late 1980s, Japan began to flex its economic muscles in pursuit of a trilateral relationship that would provide greater recognition of Japanese perspectives. Tokyo's policy-makers became increasingly aware of their country's growing international presence as Japan had emerged as an economic superpower with global interests. This realization was accompanied by increasing recognition of Japan's capability to influence world events. Many of the long-standing features of Japanese foreign policy were changing and a subtle but important transformation was taking place in the way Japanese saw their role in the world. The 1988 *Diplomatic Bluebook*, for example, declared:

> Occupying a relatively inconspicuous place in the international community for many years following World War II, Japan considered the international environment as a given. It was inconceivable then that Japan would have any major impact on the international situation... Japanese actions today have a major impact, which they have never had, not only economically but across the entire spectrum of international relations (Ministry of Foreign Affairs, 1988: 1-3).

In seeking to contribute to international peace and prosperity, the government headed by Prime Minister Takeshita Noboru took steps to become a more active player in international politics and announced the International Cooperation Initiative in 1988 built around the three pillars of 'cooperation for peace', 'expansion of official development assistance (ODA) to the developing countries', and 'promotion of international cultural exchange'. The initiative was a blueprint for global and regional action and was designed to provide concrete policies through which Japan showed how it intended to bear a greater responsibility and play a more active role as a major power for promoting the international order.

Takeshita recognized the importance of Western Europe, along with the United States, for international peace and prosperity and made it clear that he would like to see a further strengthening of trilateral cooperation among Japan, Europe and the United States as Japan strove for a larger role in world affairs: 'Close and cooperative relations with the United States and Europe are indispensable if Japan is to play a significant role for world peace and prosperity' (Ministry of Foreign Affairs, 1988: 291). Takeshita's remark implied that Japan needed Europe if Japan was to play a global role. He acknowledged that '... the relations between Japan and Europe, which form one side of the triangle, have perhaps not been close enough, compared with the other two sides, that is, the relations between Japan and the United States on the one hand, and Europe and the United States on the other' (Ministry of Foreign Affairs, 1988: 296). Takeshita stressed the need to strengthen the relationship between Japan and Europe in order to '... create a better balance in the trilateral relations among Japan, the United States, and Europe' (Ministry of Foreign Affairs, 1988: 291). In his speech to the Diet after assuming office as Prime Minister he declared that cooperation with the West European countries was 'an important pillar of Japanese foreign policy' (Ministry of Foreign Affairs, 1988: 265). He visited Western European countries twice in 1988 in order to strengthen Japan-Europe relations and was one of the postwar prime ministers who attached most importance to Japan's ties with Western Europe.

As a part of the first pillar of the International Cooperation Initiative, 'cooperation for peace', Japan collaborated with Western Europe in providing assistance to Eastern Europe. Regarding the issue of support to Eastern Europe, the congruence of Japanese-European concerns were affirmed during the G-24 meetings.[2] During his visit to Europe in January 1990, Prime Minister Kaifu Toshiki announced Japan's assistance measures amounting to a total of almost two billion dollars to Poland and Hungary and expressed readiness to extend Japan's assistance to other East European countries if there was progress in their democratic reforms. Japan had also actively participated in the European Bank for Reconstruction and Development (EBRD), established in 1990, and was its second largest contributor after the United States.

What motivated Japan's participation in the reconstruction of East Europe? Japan joined the Bank not primarily for the purpose of reconstructing eastern and central Europe as such but in the broader implications for its global role. Tokyo's strong support for the EBRD is a sign of her determination to play a global role beyond Asia's borders (Yasutomo, 1993: 326). As former Vice-Foreign Minister Kuriyama explained, Japan's extensive involvement in Eastern Europe was launched, partly, on the basis of the realization that '... not only is the achievement of political and economic reforms in the Eastern European countries of vital importance for the building of a new international order in Europe, but such reforms will significantly contribute to the restructuring of global East-West relations' (Kuriyama, 1990: 19). Japan's involvement in the development and democratization of Eastern Europe can also be seen as its way of showing the solidarity with Western Europe (and the United States) (Bridges, 1992: 237). By joining what might be considered a European scheme for the part of the world in which Japan had no immediate political or strategic interests, the Japanese government sought to deepen relations with West Europe. Its involvement in the Bank was the first occasion on which Japan deliberately attempted to play a political role in Eastern European affairs using economic aid as a political lever to move the region toward democracy. Naturally, this would most likely serve as a point of reference for future activities in the region.

EUROPE IN JAPAN'S FOREIGN POLICY IN THE 1990S

Japan's increasing interest and involvement in political and security issues of the world can be ascribed primarily to three factors:

1) its growing economic strength;
2) the decline of US hegemonic power; and
3) recognition of the importance of Western Europe in world politics as the European Community's integration process accelerated

Basic issues for Japan include how to adjust to changed circumstances. The United States alone cannot establish a new international system. Without key participation by Western Europe and Japan, such a system cannot be created. Former

Vice-Foreign Minister Kuriyama described the distribution of the three world economic powers of the late 1980s – the US, the European Community and Japan – as the '5-5-3' structure. As a member of such a structure, he declared, Japan is in a position to share responsibility for the creation and maintenance of the international order together with the United States and Western Europe (Kuriyama, 1990: 13).[3]

Kuriyama argues that, having become one of the major powers based on economic strength, Japan can no longer take a passive posture by regarding the international order as given. In his view, it has to redefine the country's basic foreign-policy posture. For Kuriyama and the Japanese foreign ministry, Japan's foreign policy must outgrow from that of an inconspicuous minor power to the foreign policy of a major global power. It is only through consultation and coordination with the United States and Europe that Japan can make effective use of its strength to contribute to the peace and prosperity of the world: 'The era in which the United States could by itself support the international political and economic orders is long past, and the key to world peace and prosperity today rests in the cooperative structure of Japan, the United States, and Western Europe' (Kuriyama, 1990: 12f).

The end of the cold war and the Gulf War accelerated the pace of change in Japan's approach to its role in the arena of international politics and security. As the bipolar order collapsed, the dominant bilateral framework that had guided foreign and security policy thinking and planning for four decades appeared increasingly irrelevant. An awareness that the era of US hegemonic power was over and that the peace and stability of the world requires the trilateral cooperation of Japan, Europe, and the United States has been growing since the latter half of the 1980s. This awareness, strengthened by the Gulf crisis, was articulated by the foreign ministry. As the 1991 *Diplomatic Bluebook* stated, the Japanese government, while recognizing the military strength and political leadership of the United States, stressed the limitations in its power: 'The posture of the United States Government in strongly seeking a burden sharing among the allied countries in coping with the Gulf crisis reflects the awareness on the part of the United States of its limitations. Particularly in the economic aspect, the relative erosion of American strength is notable' (Ministry of Foreign Affairs, 1991: 18).

The European Community's move towards an integrated single market, coupled with this relative decline of the United States, has led to increased awareness of Europe among Japanese policy-makers. As Europe has moved closer towards the single market (the so-called 1992 process), the Japanese have increasingly attached more weight to the role of the EC in world affairs. Tokyo has repeatedly stressed that Japan, the US, and the EC, sharing a belief in democracy and the market economy, have important roles to play in assuring the peace and stability of the world. Japanese policy-makers believe that there is now a pressing need to bring Japan and Europe closer together and to strengthen a trilateral cooperation between Japan, Europe, and the United States to address not only such global issues as nuclear non-proliferation, disarmament and UN reform but also such regional issues with global implications as the Middle East peace process, the conflict among the former Yugoslav states, and development of North Korea's nuclear capability. The emphasis hitherto in Euro-Japanese relations has been on economic issues, but for the sake of forming a new international order in the post-cold war era and establishing comprehensive cooperation between the developed countries, a new political relationship between Japan and Europe is necessary.

The view that Japan needs a 'special relationship' with Europe, especially the European Community, in order to play a global role (not to mention a 'special relationship' with the United States) has become slowly but steadily anchored in the minds of Tokyo's foreign-policy decision-makers after the end of the cold war and the Gulf crisis. They reasoned that it was the forging of closer political coordination with Europe that would provide the necessary base for Japan to play this new role as a global power in the post-hegemonic era that made up the essence of such a relationship.

The role of Europe in enhancing Japan's role has become an integral part of Japanese foreign policy at the declaratory level. In order to forge a 'special relationship' with Europe, Japan took the initiative to propose a strengthening of political dialogue through an agreement with Japan similar to that concluded by the EC and the United States. The European Community was responsive, since strengthened ties with Japan was clearly of political benefit. At the Japanese initiative, the Japan-EC joint declaration was issued in July 1991 at the Hague to establish a cooperative relationship between the two parties as global partners and it symbolized a new chapter in Euro-Japanese relations. Japan's relationship with Western Europe has differed from its relations with the United States in that the former has hitherto been based on a two-tier structure, with political and diplomatic questions handled on a bilateral basis with the individual members of the European Community and economic and trade issues handled directly between Japan and the EC.

The declaration could be read as a road map for more multilayered Japanese-European relationships. It emphasized joint efforts in support of democracy, freedom, market principles, the promotion of free trade, human rights, and the formation of a new international order. Furthermore, the declaration strengthened the dialogue framework through holding more regular consultations between Japan and the EC on political and foreign affairs.

The attempt to strengthen and broaden ties with Europe is not an entirely new policy for Japan, as we have seen. The joint declaration outlined above, does, however, represent a new departure in its comprehensiveness and degree of intent. Since the 1991 joint declaration, there has been a widening and deepening of political dialogue between Japan and the EU through more direct and regular channels for communications and policy coordination. One of the most important forums for political dialogue is the annual summit between the Japanese prime minister, the president of the EU Commission and the president of the European Council. Other important fora for political dialogue include annual meetings between Japan and the EU Commission at ministerial level, and twice-yearly political consultations between the foreign ministers of Japan and the EU and the member of the EU Commission responsible for external relations (troika).

The Japanese government perceived that it was important for Japan, in the post-cold war era, to strengthen its relations with international organizations other than the EU based in Europe. Japan, for example, viewed the role of the Conference on Security and Cooperation in Europe, CSCE (later the Organization for Security and Cooperation in Europe, OSCE), important for the security of Europe and regional stability and the construction of a new international order in the post-Cold War period. 'Given this, it is beneficial both for Japan and the CSCE to build closer relations' (Ministry of Foreign Affairs, 1992: 251).

Furthermore, the Russian membership in the CSCE in 1992 has added global dimensions to the role and functions of the organization with significant implications for the security of Japan. This meant that '... the jurisdiction of the CSCE extends all the way to the western shores of the Sea of Japan and that the decisions of the CSCE, therefore, have a decisive impact on the security of Japan, at least theoretically' (Japan Forum on International Relations, 1993: 19). Tokyo felt that it was important to establish closer relations with CSCE and Foreign Minister Watanabe Michio disclosed in the foreign policy debate in the Diet on 26 February 1992 that the discussion was already under way for special membership in the CSCE (Shūgiin, 1992: 12). In fact, Japan obtained a special status as a 'Partner for Cooperation' at the Helsinki Summit meeting in 1992, enabling her to participate in various meetings but not in adoption of its decisions. In fact, since 1992, representatives from Japan have participated in the Foreign Ministers Council and the High Level Administrative Committee, and activities in the former Yugoslavia.

As Japan seeks to respond to the changing demands and challenges placed upon it by the post-Cold War security agenda, many Japanese have become interested in transplanting CSCE institutions from Europe to Asia. The end of the Cold War has given rise to opportunities for new ideas to be articulated about specific problems in the new security environment in the region. There has been an intensive debate in the Diet on the question of whether the creation of an equivalent of the CSCE for Asia is possible. There has been little support for such an idea within the foreign-policy establishment. Foreign Minister Kōno Yōhei has stated in the Diet, on several occasions, that in contrast to Europe where the peace and security is conducted within an interlocking network of multilateral institutions such as the CSCE, NATO, and the EU/WEU, a NATO-type multilateral security organization and an Asian version of the CSCE would be inappropriate. There are, however, some influential politicians who have openly supported the establishment of a CSCE clone in Asia-Pacific. Nakasone Yasuhiro, a former prime minister, for example, calls for what he terms the 'Asia-Pacific Common House', the idea of a CSCE arrangement for Asia-Pacific: 'The time is ripe to build an international framework in the region comparable to the CSCE...' (Nakasone, 1995: 34).

Japan has also sought greater dialogue with the North Atlantic

Treaty Organization (NATO). 'As NATO strengthens its political role and plays a broader part in constructing a new order in Europe, the strengthening of the dialogue between NATO and Japan will contribute to the reinforcement of Japan-European relations and Japan-US-European relations as a whole' (Ministry of Foreign Affairs, 1992: 249). Japanese Diet members have been attending North Atlantic Assembly meetings since 1980 and there have been visits by Japanese foreign ministers to NATO Headquarters since 1986. In 1990 Japanese senior foreign-ministry officials attended a NATO seminar for the first time. Since the joint declaration, personal exchange has increased as evident from the visits by NATO secretaries-general to Japan and the hosting of a high-level Japan-NATO seminar, but regular, official relations have never been established. As previously mentioned, one of the main reasons for Japanese interest in European security issues was the growing awareness that the questions of European regional security have the significant implications for Asian security in the post-Cold War era.

Japan considers such global multilateral fora as the annual Group of Seven summit meetings, the United Nations, and the OECD to be of great importance in promoting and strengthening policy coordination among Japan, Europe and the United States (Ministry of Foreign Affairs, 1995: 22). Created to deal with economic issues, the G-7 has, nonetheless, also addressed political and strategic issues and played an important role as a forum for policy coordination among the major industrial democracies of the world during the cold war. Japanese policy-makers believe that, with the end of the cold war, the uncertainty of the complex international situation will increasingly require close cooperation between Japan, Europe and the United States. Moreover, they believe that the importance of the G-7, which accounts for about 70 per cent of the world's GNP, as a forum for trilateral cooperation will be even greater than before and Japan should actively contribute to strengthen the G-7 framework. Among the seven, Japan is the only country that is not involved in any institutional policy-coordinating mechanism on political issues. Japan is not a member of the permanent five on the UN Security Council, the NATO, nor the CSCE. Thus, the Group of Seven seems to be the only possible framework for effective policy consultation and coorrdination.

One recent addition to multilateral fora for cooperation

between Europe and Japan is the Asia-Europe Meeting (ASEM) at which leaders from Europe and Asia gather and discuss various global and interregional issues. The first ASEM meeting was held in March 1996. Prime Minister Hashimoto Ryūtarō and Foreign Minister Ikeda Yukihiko articulated the government's expectations for the ASEM as a forum for the promotion of closer bonds between Europe and Asia in a debate in the Diet on 27 February 1996. Compared to the Asian-North American relations and European-North American relations, they said, ties between Asia and Europe are weak and the relationship should be strengthened. They further argued that the ASEM will give Japan the chance to assume a constructive role in bringing Asia and Europe closer together, drawing on its position as an Asian nation with global economic clout, as well as a member of the G-7 and on its experience in dealing with Europe (Shūgiin, 1996: 3-5).

Japan's relations with Europe have grown closer since the 1991 Japan-EC Joint Declaration. In the field of politics and economics, Japan has moved toward greater policy coordination with Europe (and the United States). The Japanese foreign ministry in its annual report in 1995, for example, stated:

> Looking back on the main events of 1994, multilateral cooperation centering on Japan, the United States, and Europe played an important role. In the political arena, this trilateral cooperation was essential in dealing with such regional issues as the problems in the former Yugoslavia and North Korea's suspected development of nuclear weapons, as well as in such areas as arms control and disarmament. In the economic arena, the roles of Japan, the United States, and Europe were, respectively and collectively, determining factors in ensuring continued growth of the world economy, maintaining momentum towards the establishment of the WTO, tackling various post-Uruguay Round issues, extending economic aid to developing countries, and providing support for efforts by market economy (Ministry of Foreign Affairs, 1995: 21f).

The Japanese would like to see their bands with Europe, specifically the European Union, deepened and expanded. Tokyo's policy-makers argue that Europe's influence in global politics would greatly increase as the EU proceeds with an eastern enlargement. The EU has increasingly come to believe that it would need Japan not only for the management of the world economy but also for global and regional politics. On the whole, however, Euro-Japanese relations have not been transformed into ties as broad or as deep as Japan's ties with the United States. Former Vice-Foreign Minister Kuriyama argues that it would require greater efforts to strengthen these relations than the task of improving the Japanese-US partnership (Kuriyama, 1991: 122).

SUMMARY AND CONCLUSION

The key feature of postwar Japan's foreign policy has been that it was made within the framework of a dominant bilateral relationship with the United States. Relations with the United States have for the four-and-a-half decades, since the recovery of national independence in 1952, been the principal consideration of Japan's foreign and security policy calculations. The 1951 and 1960 security treaties have been the core of this relationship. The US-Japan Security Treaty firmly anchored Japan to the United States and successive Japanese governments were resolved to act in concert with the United States.

The postwar phase of Japanese policies toward Europe has been far from static. Over the past 50 years, they have been repeatedly modified or adjusted. Many of the changes have paralleled broad shifts in Tokyo's world view and foreign policy. At different times, in defining their immediate goals and current policies in relation to Europe, the Japanese have given quite different weight to economic, political and security considerations. The evolution of Japan's Europe policy can be conveyed by phases of development. In the initial phase, from 1952 to 1960, Europe occupied an inconspicuous place in Japanese foreign policy reflecting the tremendous weight of Japanese-US relations. Almost any foreign policy issue seemed to be linked in some way with the US relationship.

During the second phase, from the early 1960s to 1964, Japan's initial attitude of indifference to Europe turned into a positive posture. The era of the Ikeda government was, economically, an important milestone for Japanese policy towards Europe because it shifted government policy for the Japanese-European relationship and led to Japan's membership in the OECD. Ikeda's three-pillar scheme incorporated Western Europe as one of the three pillars supporting the free world. The importance of Europe in the thinking of foreign-policy decision-makers eroded during the third stage, from 1964 to the late 1970s with a few exceptions, however. Although prime ministers and foreign ministers continued to refer to the strengthening of relations with Europe at the declaratory level, the rhetorical references to Europe were not as frequent as they used to be.

Until the late 1970s Japanese-European relations were mainly limited to the realm of economy. As the East-West relations worsened in the late 1970s and early 1980s, Japan's policy towards Europe began to take a new course to reflect new realities and, for the first time, the efforts were made to effect policy coordination between Japan, Europe, and the United States on military and strategic issues. During the Nakasone administration, the Japanese emphasized that the three global economic powers had a common interest in the security of the Western world. Japan's efforts at broadening relations with Europe met with only limited success.

It was during the fourth phase, from the late 1980s, especially after the end of the cold war order, that the field was cleared for a more assertive Japan in global politics. The 1990s represent an era of transition for Japan-Europe relations. The Cold War having ended, both sides were challenged to reorder their foreign-policy priorities. New and complex global and regional issues present Japan with foreign-policy challenges that cannot be met merely with the Cold War *modus operandi*. Japanese relations with the outside world can no longer be viewed through the dominant-bilateral lens of the Cold-War era, instead the Japanese have to peer through their own global trilateral lens in line with Japan's national interests. What will be Japan's international role in the post-hegemonic era? This question has been repeatedly raised since the end of the Cold War. It appears that Japan is slowly moving from a foreign policy posture based on a global partnership with the United States to one that is based on a Japan-US-EU tripartite global partnership.

Despite Japan's rhetorical commitment to forge a global tripartite partnership following the momentum created by the end of the Cold War and the Gulf crisis, it has failed to achieve significant change, making only limited progress in its attempt to redefine its role in world politics. In surveying Japanese relations with Europe, one is made aware of a gap between rhetoric and practice. Changing Japan's relations with Europe is much easier said than done.

BIBLIOGRAPHY

Asahi shimbun, 16 December 1960, evening ed.

Bridges, Brian. 1992. 'Japan and Europe: Rebalancing a Relationship'. *Asian Survey*, 32(3): 230-45.

Carlsnaes, Walter. 1993. 'On Analysing the Dynamics of Foreign Policy Change: A Critique and Reconceptualization'. *Cooperation and Conflict*, 28(l): 5-30.

Gaimushō [Ministry of Foreign Affairs]. 1983. *Waga gaikō no kinkyō* [Diplomatic bluebook]. Tokyo: Ōkurashō insatsukyoku.

Hayasaka Shigezō. 1987. *Seijika Tanaka Kakuei* [Tanaka Kakuei, the politician]. Tokyo: Chūō kōronsha 1987.

Hermann, Charles F. 1990. 'Changing Course: When Governments Choose to Redirect Foreign Policy'. *International Studies Quarterly*, 34(1): 3-21.

Holsti, K. J. 1982. *Why Nations Realign: Foreign Policy Restructuring in the Postwar World*. London: Allen and Unwin.

Hurwitz, John and Mark Peffley. 1987. 'How are Foreign Policy Attitudes Structured? A Hierarchical Model'. *American Political Science Review* 81(4): 1099-119.

Industrial Structure Council, MITI. 1972. *Japan in World Economy*. Tokyo: The Ministry of International Trade and Industry and Press International.

Itō Masaya. 1965. 'Hishokan no mita ningen Ikeda Hayato'. *Chūō koron*, October, 208-21.

——. 1966. *Ikeda Hayato: sono sei to shi* [Ikeda Hayato: His life and death]. Tokyo: Shiseidō.

Iwanaga, Kazuki. 1993. *Images, Decisions and Consequences in Japan's Foreign Policy*. Lund: Lund University Press.

——.1996. 'From Passive to Active Foreign Policy'. In Bert Edström, ed., *Japan's Foreign and Security Policies in Transition*. Stockholm: The Swedish Institute of International Affairs, 15-40.

Japan Forum on International Relations. 1993. *The Policy Recommendation on Political Cooperation with Europe: Japan's Agenda for 21st Century*. Tokyo, November.

Kissinger, Henry A. 1979. *The White House Years*. London: Weidenfeld and Nicolson.

Kuriyama, Takakazu. 1990. *New Directions for Japanese Foreign Policy in the Changing World of the 1990s: Making Active Contributions to the Creation of a New International Order*. Tokyo: Foreign Press Center.

——. 1991. 'Japan's Foreign Policy: My Two-Year Experience at a Crossroads'. *Japan Review of International Affairs*, 5(2): 109-33.

Ministry of Foreign Affairs. 1962-63, 1973. *Gaimusho Press Releases*. Tokyo: Ministry of Foreign Affairs.

——. 1985-86, 1988, 1991, 1992, 1995. *Diplomatic Bluebook*. Tokyo: Ministry of Foreign Affairs.

Murata, Ryohei. 1987. 'Political Relations between the United States and Western Europe: Their Implications for Japan'. *International Affairs*, 64(1): 1-10.

Nakasone, Yasuhiro. 1995. *Reflections on Japan's Past and the Need for a Third Opening: Looking Towards the Future*. Tokyo: IIPS.

Rosati, Jerel A., Joe D. Hagan and Martin W. Sampson III, eds. 1994. *Foreign Policy Restructuring: How Governments Respond to Global Change*. Columbia, SC: University of South Carolina Press.

Saito, Shiro. 1990. *Japan at the Summit: Japan's Role in the Western Alliance and Asian Pacific Co-operation*. London: Routledge for the Royal Institute of International Affairs.

Shūgiin [Lower House]. 1964a. *Dai 46 kai kokkai shūgiin gaimu iinkai giroku*

[Proceedings of the Lower House Foreign Policy Committee of the 46th session of the Diet], 5, 21 February.

——. 1964b. *Dai 46 kai kokkai shūgiin gaimu iinkai giroku* [Proceedings of the Lower House Foreign Policy Committee of the 46th session of the Diet], 17, 7-8 April.

——. 1992. *Dai 123 kai kokkai shūgiin gaimu iinkai giroku* [Proceedings of the Lower House Foreign Policy Committee of the 123rd session of the Diet], 2, 26 February.

——. 1996. *Dai 136 kai kokkai shūgiin yosan iinkai giroku* [Proceedings of the Lower House Budget Committee of the 136th session of the Diet], 19, 27 February.

Wakaizumi, Kei. 1974. 'Japan's Dilemma: To Act Or Not To Act'. *Foreign Policy*, 16, Fall, 30-47.

Yasutomo, Dennis. 1993. 'Japan and the New Multilateralism'. In Gerald L. Curtis, ed., *Japan's Foreign Policy After the Cold War: Coping with Change*. London and New York: M. E. Sharpe, 323-46.

Yoshida Shigeru. 1957. *Kaiso jūnen* [Memoirs of a decade], 1. Tokyo: Shinchōsha.

FOOTNOTES

1. In this paper, dominant bilateral relationship or dominant bilateralism refers to Japan's relations with the United States.

2. The G-24 group consists of 24 member countries of the OECD concerned with support to the democratization in Eastern Europe. The first G-24 high working-level meeting was held in August 1989.

3. The '5-5-3' structure of global economic strength is similar to the one that existed in the pre-war period as a result of the naval agreements at the Washington Conference of 1921-22 limiting the tonnage of capital naval vessels of the United States, Britain, and Japan to a ratio of 5:5:3. As one of the major world powers, Japan was in a position to fulfil its international responsibilities in cooperation with the United States and Britain.

14

Opportunities and Constraints in Euro-Japanese Relations: A Multidimensional Approach

GLENN D. HOOK

During the Cold War era the ideological poles of capitalism and Communism structured global and regional orders around modes of order-building based especially on the military might of nations. Military alliances were constructed largely around ideology, irrespective of the spatial separation of the member states, with the nuclear superpowers, the United States and the Soviet Union, binding their respective allies to a non-spatial understanding of the Cold-War identities, 'East' and 'West'. Now, with the ending of the Cold War, the tripolarization of the global economy is structuring global and regional orders around modes of order-building based especially on the economic might of nations. Economic alliances are being built on different spatial scales (see Gamble and Payne, 1996; Hook and Kearns, 1999), with the three core regions of the United States and the North American Free Trade Agreement (NAFTA), Germany and the European Union (EU), and Japan and a more inchoate East Asian region emerging as the new economic cores of global and regional orders. In the Cold War, bipolar, military confrontation led observers to focus overwhelmingly on the military aspect of power; in the post-Cold War, tripolar economic competition if not confrontation has led observers to focus overwhelmingly on the economic aspects of power. Consequently, in the same way that an analysis of military might was at the heart of studies of order in the Cold War era, so economics are now being placed at the centre of studies of order in the post-Cold War era.

Nevertheless, global and regional orders emerge out of a complex process of order-building involving not only the military and economic dimensions of power, but also the political and cultural. For order is based on consensual as well as coercive elements of power (Cox, 1987: 7). What is more, as in the Cold-War era the non-aligned movement sought to puncture the bipolarism and bilateralism at the heart of the global and regional orders, so in the post-Cold War era processes and actions which link parts of different regions together are puncturing order-building based on discrete, tripolar economic alliances and regional identities. In this sense, the restructuring of global and regional orders involving the military, economic, political and cultural dimensions of power, on the one hand, and multidimensional interregional linkages, not just tripolar economic regionalization, on the other, need to be taken into account in seeking to provide a fuller understanding of Euro-Japanese relations in the emerging post-Cold War orders.

The main purpose of this chapter is to analyze some of the key multidimensional interlinkages forged between Japan and Europe, and to do so in the four dimensions of economy, politics, security, and culture. Beyond this, we also seek in the Conclusion to broaden our perspective by addressing the issue of how, in the process of the interlinkages between Japan and Europe being built and reinforced, late-comer, East Asian economies are catching up with early-starter, European economies and forcing them to respond. The main objectives of this chapter are thus to: (1) address the restructuring of the global and regional orders taking a multidimensional approach; (2) challenge the image of the new world order as being rooted in three emerging economic blocs by producing a more complex picture, where interregional linkages, especially Euro-Japanese linkages, are as much a part of the emerging post-Cold War order as is regionalization; and (3) reflect on the broader question of how the early-starters of Europe have responded to the challenge of the East Asian late-starters and the transformation of their relationship.

EURO-JAPANESE INTERLINKAGES

The globalization and regionalization of economy, politics, security and culture have gone hand in hand with interregional

237

developments. As in the case of globalization and regionalization, interregionalization is uneven, creating constraints on, yet opportunities for, change in relations in and between different regional and global orders (on opportunities and constraints, see Cox, 1996). Here interregionalization refers to the process of expanding economic, political, security and cultural links between the emerging tripolar regions of the world. Narrowly, the interlinkages among the three core regional economies of Japan, the United States and Germany are being strengthened, maintained or weakened in the context of unfolding regionalist projects, promoted by purposive actors, such as states, and ongoing regionalization processes, as spurred by market and other social forces. More broadly, restructuring on regional and subregional scales is occurring within the context of unfolding globalist projects and ongoing globalization processes (on these concepts, see Hook and Kearns, 1999). Given the Allied occupation of Japan between 1945-52 and the economic, political, security and cultural integration of Japan into the capitalist world order under the asymmetric structure of power topped by the United States, on the one wing, and the European's general commitment to post-war US order-building, on the other, interregionalization processes linking Japan to Western Europe, the European Economic Community (EEC), the European Community (EC) and now the European Union (EU) have been constrained severely by omnipresent, US-Japan bilateralism.

With the restructuring of global power in the 1970s, strategic attempts to nurture élite links among the three cores emerged, as seen in the setting up of the Trilateral Commission (Gill, 1990). While attempts to understand the EC (hereafter, EU)-Japanese relationship within this tripartite view of the world abound (e.g. Mendl, 1984), the Euro-Japanese leg of the triad always has been weaker. Again, while this is the leitmotif of a trilateral understanding of the relative weight of these three cores, the ascendance of Japan globally, the restructuring of the global economy following the 1985 Plaza Accord currency realignments, the recent end of the global Cold War, and the increased international demands on both Europe and Japan to play a greater global role have bolstered substantially the Euro-Japanese leg of the tripod. Indeed, over time, the constrained interregional linkages symbolic of the Euro-Japanese leg have moved beyond a mainly economic focus: now, stronger political

and security links, as well as cultural exchange, are quintessentially part of the wider EU-Japanese relationship. As recognized
at a recent summit, in moving forward towards a new
relationship, the two sides are seeking to promote 'dialogue
and cooperation on, *inter alia*, political and security, economic as
well as cultural matters' (Joint Press Statement, the Japan-EU
summit 1995, 1995: 1). Crucial to this transition has been the
ending of the Cold War and the emerging opportunities to play
a bigger role in interregional political and security affairs.

ECONOMY

Still, over the longer term, economic links have been central.
The strengthening of Japan's economic relationship with Europe
followed the asymmetric penetration of key sectors of European
economies by Japanese manufacturers, who flooded their
markets with internationally competitive goods. As in the case
of the United States, the surge of manufacturing exports in
automobiles, colour televisions, video-cassette recorders and
other key products, especially in the 1980s, engendered trade
conflicts. The result was a cacophony of European voices calling
for the implementation of Voluntary Export Restraints (VERs)
in these and other sectors of the economy. Such measures were
implemented bilaterally within the EU as part of the overall
measures taken to try to reduce the huge trade surplus enjoyed
by Japan as a major exporter, with exports to the EU rising from
13.6-20.2 per cent between 1984-93. Another EU tactic was the
implementation of anti-dumping duties, although in 1990 Japan
successfully fought the EU under the General Agreement on
Trade and Tariffs (GATT) over the issue of local content.
Similarly, the Europeans joined the American chorus in
demanding the 'opening' of the Japanese market. Their demands
have ranged from sectoral issues, such as pharmaceuticals and
cosmetics, through services, such as access for lawyers and
openness and transparency in financial markets, to the revamping
of economic structures, as in the distribution system and *keiretsu*
relationships. Some success in boosting EU exports clearly was
achieved as a result of these pressures, with EU exports to Japan
rising from 7.2-12.5 per cent between 1984-93, and in loosening
restrictive practices, as in the liberalization of financial markets
symbolized by the 1998 Japanese 'big bang'. In this sense, both
the United States and the EU share an interest in stimulating
changes in the Japanese political economy, both externally and

internally, in order to address trade conflicts, reduce trade surpluses, and open up the Japanese economy to the outside.

Nevertheless, in pursuing this two-pronged approach of restricting Japanese imports and expanding European exports, the EU is in a weak position in comparison with the United States. For unlike in the US case, pressure from the Europeans, whether exerted bilaterally or through EU institutions, can not be reinforced by a 'security lever', which continues to offer the United States an additional means to exert pressure on Japan, even after the Cold War's ending. The Commission recognizes as much: 'it can be argued that Japan has done much to accommodate US economic demands in order not to damage their overall relationship, including the security alliance (Commission of the European Communities, 1995a:5).

Nor is the EU able to manipulate the levers of global finance like the United States, as even with the launch of the euro the EU still falls under the dollar's shadow. The American's dashing of the Japanese initiative to set up an Asian Monetary Fund in response to the recent financial crisis in East Asia demonstrates the US ability to use financial instruments to reshape the regional economic order. By acting strategically to maintain a strong or weak dollar, moreover, the US is able to exert global as well as regional influence, far beyond the reach of the EU, unless the euro gains significantly in international importance. In this situation, the Europeans remain less effective than the Americans in influencing Japanese trade and investment practices, with the additional potential for differences emerging between EU member states enabling the Japanese to exploit intra-EU policy gaps. Similarly, the United States has been able to exert greater leverage to open the Japanese market, as seen in the case of the signing of the semi-conductor agreement (Tsuchiya, 1995).

Finally, the EU's commitment to 'open regionalism' as an integral part of the European élite's regionalist project, has been cast into some doubt by the implementation of VERs against exports from Japan, on the one hand, and restrictions on Japanese transplants in exporting to other parts of the Community, on the other. The erection of barriers to external and internal trade reflects the intra-European dilemma over exposure to the sharp breeze of East Asian competition. During the 1980s, the laissez-faire United Kingdom (UK) was at odds with the French strategic traders, as seen in the 1988 cross-Channel stand-off, when the French sought, albeit unsuccessfully, to prevent intra-EU exports of automobiles from Japanese transplants in the UK (Julius and Thomsen, 1988).

Thus, despite a commitment to 'open regionalism' on the part of Europe's economic and political élites, their call to 'open Japan' has on occasion gone hand-in-hand with concrete measures to constrain the activities of Japanese enterprises. The 1993 implementation of EU-wide VERs on automobiles, whether exported from Japan or from Japanese transplants located within the EU, illustrates how Europeans have resisted the opening of certain sectors of their economy to the full power of Japanese competition. It must also be noted that, under the Maastricht Treaty, anti-dumping measures and countervailing duties no longer require a qualified majority, but only a simply majority, with Article 130 of the Treaty also seeking to ensure 'the conditions necessary for the competitiveness of the Community's industries' (Sideri, 1995: 238).

Still, the general direction of European attitudes regarding Japan's presence has been towards convergence with the British in supporting the benefits of Japanese and other Foreign Direct Investment (FDI), especially in the 1990s, so that the 'threat' perception has been complemented if not totally replaced by a perception of the Japanese presence as a benefit. The amount of Japanese investment in Europe, especially the UK, increased significantly in the wake of the Plaza Accord, although between 1990-5 East Asia has grown in significance, as evidenced by the decrease from 25.1 per cent to 16.7 per cent investment in Europe, and an increase from 12.4 per cent to 24.0 per cent in East Asia (for details, see Hook, 1998a). In this sense, a consensus seems to be emerging among the European élite that the benefits of Japanese FDI outweigh the costs: the Japanese, and other East Asian presence, can serve to make EU businesses competitive, create employment opportunities, and introduce cutting-edge technology and efficient management practices. As noted by the Commission's Sir Leon Brittan, the Japanese should '... ensure that their massive investment in Europe – -which I whole-heartedly welcome ... is seen and felt to be mutually beneficial' (Brittan, 1991: 6).

At the same time, the EU has expressed strong support for multilateral, rather than bilateral, solutions to trade conflicts through the World Trade Organization (WTO), as evidenced by the Commission's negative attitude towards the US-Japan autovehicle-sector dispute (Commission of the European

Communities, 1995b: 73). In this, Japan and the EU have found common ground for cooperation in support of 'globalism' and 'open regionalism', in contrast to the Clinton Administration's approach, which at least started out as being more confrontational, and has relied more on bilateral negotiations to resolve trade disputes. The tone was set for the Euro-Japanese approach at the 1995 Japan-EU summit, where the two sides agreed:

> It is vital for the operation of the WTO, that all its Members, without exception, respect fully the obligations as set out in the WTO Agreement. Disputes between Members of the WTO which cannot be resolved through bilateral consultations should be referred to the new, strengthened dispute settlement procedures, on which all have agreed' (Joint Press Statement, the Japan-EU summit 1995, 1995).

In this situation, the Japanese élite has sought to gain support for the beneficial effects of Japanese competition, technology and investment within the EU. The Japanese tactic of exploiting differences among members, playing off one country, national region or even city against another in the battle to attract Japanese investments and manufacturers, has turned the political and certain of the economic élite of Japan and those of especially Britain into close collaborators. By setting ceilings on the incentives member states are supposed to offer to Japanese investors, the EU is able to ameliorate, at least to some extent, the competition and conflict among the membership in struggling to attract Japanese investments, but the discretion on incentives allowed under EU rulings, which make the UK especially attractive; the added advantage of the City, which even after the launch of the euro remains Europe's main financial centre; low corporation taxes; English as the medium of communication; and Labour's policy of continuing in the Conservative's footsteps as far as welcoming FDI is concerned, means that Britain emerged in the late 1980s and has remained in the 1990s as a key destination for Japanese investors. This followed the radical shift in British policy in 1988 (Nuttall, 1995: 7), with the clarion call of the then Conservative government changing from 'bash the Japanese' to 'boost the Japanese investment' in the UK economy.

Looking back on the pre-Blairite days, the Conservative's pro-Japanese policy appears clearly set on establishing Britain as a key, low-cost production platform, with no minimum wage, no Protocol on Social Policy (as annexed to the Maastricht Treaty), and no 'Japan bashing' to court the possibility of a popular anti-

Japanese backlash. The contrast with Edith Cresson's France is telling, as her outbursts about the Japanese as 'ants' went far beyond the 1960s French image of the country's prime minister as a travelling transistor radio salesman. Whatever cultural differences might remain as a source of conflict between Britain and Japan, the 'transistor salesmen' from Japan were clearly seen to serve centrally the Conservative's statist project of making British workers and businesses alike swallow the bitter pill of East Asian competition. Smashing worker solidarity, on the one hand, and introducing efficient management practices and production techniques, on the other, was part of a strategy to ensure the UK's survival in a globalized economy. In weeding out the weak in the face of East Asian competition, therefore, the Conservatives sought to make British manufacturers and other industries globally competitive. For the globalization of the economy has meant that, by supporting 'open regionalism', Britain and other European economies must face the competitive pressures from Japan and the other economies of East Asia, even if arising from within the EU. In this sense, Thatcherite conservatism embraced two 'special relationships': with the US, in the areas of security and foreign policy; and with Japan, in the areas of investment and industrial policy.

Despite differences brought about by the downturn in the Japanese economy and the fallout from the Asian financial crisis, the Blair government has followed basically the Conservative's 'special relationship' with Japan by maintaining an economy open towards Japanese FDI. The Labour government's passage of legislation introducing a minimum wage does not seem to have affected the continuing attractiveness of Britain as a destination for foreign investment. If anything, the legacy of the Conservative's anti-European policy, as rumoured in the case of the decision of Toyota to build a plant in Valencia, Northern France, rather than Britain, appears of greater significance than any increase in the cost of labour associated with the minimum wage. For Toyota went ahead with the French investment '. . . despite high labour costs and the Jospin government's plan to introduce a 35-hour week' (Graham and Simonion, 1997: 7). As is illustrated by Britain's cooperation with the United States in the 1998 bombing of Iraq, the special relationship with the United States in the areas of security and foreign policy remains intact, too, under the new Labour government.

The dynamic overseas march of Japanese capital and business

into Europe in the wake of global restructuring in the mid-1980s thus was a reaction to global, regional and interregional pressures. The rise in the value of the yen after the Plaza Accord made Europe an attractive outlet for surplus capital, with a surge in Japanese investments occurring in the late 1980s, but the Japanese advance also was spurred regionally by the signing of the Single European Act in 1986 and the fear that the completion of the Single Market in 1992 would restrict, if not totally exclude, service sector, manufacturing and other investors from European market opportunities. Investments focused on real estate, finance and insurance as well as on electronics, chemicals and automobile manufacturing, with the bulk of Japanese FDI concentrated in the non-manufacturing sector. Reflecting Britain's regional and global role, by far the largest proportion of investments have been located in the United Kingdom, with around 40-45 per cent of the cumulative total by the early 1990s. In 1996 the annual investment in the UK was triple that of the Netherlands, the second most popular destination that year (JETRO, 1998: 528). The City's continuing power in global finance as well as the attractiveness of the investment climate for regional manufacturers, as seen in the location of over one-quarter of the total number of Euro-Japanese manufacturers in the UK, suggests the important position Britain continues to occupy in the Euro-Japanese relationship will be hard to displace.

POLITICS

It is in the context of the strengthening of links between Japan and Europe in the economic dimension that interlinkages have gone forward in the political field. Thus, up until the end of the Cold War, political dialogue between Japan and the EU was quintessentially economic dialogue, with the sole purpose of meetings between the political and bureaucratic élites of Japan and the EU being to address outstanding economic issues. In this most fundamental sense, the emergence of trade disputes and other economic problems created the need for some form of political dialogue, as resolving economic issues is a political as well as an economic process. The main issues have continued to be trade and the 'opening' of the Japanese market, but political cooperation between the two in the 1990s has moved far beyond these narrow areas. The EU's competencies on trade were set out in the Treaty of Rome, and were strengthened immeasurably in 1970, when the Commission formally gained the power to negotiate a common commercial policy, with Japan as the first nation with which it carried out trade negotiations. At the same time, however, bilateral negotiations were set to continue, as seen in the bilateral agreements between member states and Japan on VERs.

The demands to open the Japanese market similarly went forward along the dual track of EU and bilateral pressure on Japan. This created a 'unity of purpose' between the Europeans and the Americans (Commission of the European Communities, 1995a: 6). Nonetheless, the omnipresent bilateralism at the heart of Japan-US relations, on the one hand, and the bilateralism embedded in the multilateralism of EU-US relations, on the other, stumped the growth of Euro-Japanese political relations during the Cold War, with even trilateralism largely centring on the 'thick but inflexible leg' of Japanese-American relations and the multilateral relations between the United States and the EU member states (Nakanishi, 1995). In the nascent global order of the post-Cold War era, the new political relationship between Japan and the EU is being pushed forward not simply in terms of a new interregional relations, 'but as a counterweight to the US' (Commission of the European Communities, 1995a: 19).

At the same time, however, creeping institutionalization of élite political dialogue between Japan and the EU, and recognition of the EU as a separate political entity, was moving forward slowly along with the continuing predominance of the member states in the political relationship (Gilson, forthcoming). True, the limited nature of the EU's political competency has constrained the development of the political side of the relationship. The start of European Political Cooperation (EPC) in 1970 occurred outside the formal treaty framework of the EU, and foreign and security policy remains beyond the competency of the Commission under the terms of the 1985 Single European Act and the 1991 Maastricht Treaty – a far different situation than in trade, with the move to a common foreign and security policy having failed to make much headway. That been said, the institutionalization of political links has been central to the development of stronger ties between Japan and Europe, with a number of frameworks and fora being set up over the past twenty-five years as the Japanese government gradually has come to recognize the EU as an actor separate from the EU member states. At the outset, semi-annual consultations were held between Japan and the Commission from 1973, with the Commission opening a delegation in Tokyo in the following year, and regular meetings involving Diet members being held from 1978 onwards. Then, in the 1980s, an institutional framework for political dialogue was established: meetings between the Japanese Foreign Minister and the Foreign Ministers of the Community (the troika) began in 1983 on a biannual basis; and ministerial-level meetings between the Japanese government and the Commission began in 1984, albeit with a gap between the 1986 and 1990 meetings. Both sides also have carried out briefings on foreign policy, with the EU briefing Japanese representatives on the EPC. Finally, in 1993 the Japanese side set up a Consulate-General in Strasbourg in order to monitor developments in the European Parliament (For details, see Tanaka, 1995).

These and other activities laid a somewhat shaky but nevertheless a foundation for the development of the political relationship in the post-Cold War era, as expressed by the signing of the Hague Declaration in 1991. The EU and Japan decided at that time '... to intensify their dialogue and to strengthen their cooperation and partnership in order that the challenges of the future may be met' (Joint Declaration, 1991). Thereafter, a Euro-Japanese summit was set to take place annually following the first meeting in the Hague, although the continuing weakness of the political relationship is evident from the failure to hold a summit in 1994, partly due to the political turmoil in Japan. Still, a new importance has been given to firmly institutionalizing the political dialogue in the emerging post-Cold War global order, as seen in the Commission's call for the EU to '... actively support and participate in Japan's greater political involvement in global foreign and security policy' (Commission of the European Communities, 1995a: 3). Similarly, the Japanese government has expressed support for the increased political role of the EU. This strategy of the two sides mutually reinforcing each other's aspirations to carry out global and regional political roles was confirmed at the Fourth Japan-EU summit in June 1995 (Joint Press Statement, the Japan-EU summit 1995, 1995).

The concrete areas of political cooperation are still limited, but have expanded significantly in the 1990s and can be expected to move forward even further in the context of the strengthening of the two poles of the tripolar global structure.

The Euro-Japanese attempt to give shape to the newly emerging global order can be seen from a number of areas of cooperation. In the first place, the two sides cooperated by submitting a joint proposal for the establishment of a United Nations (UN) Arms Register, which was successfully instituted in 1992, with the first report issued in 1993 (For details, see Chalmers et al., 1995). This serves to enhance a Euro-Japanese profile in the UN, apart from the security aspects of the initiative.

Second, Japan and the EU have implemented cooperation in the use of Overseas Development Assistance (ODA), in line with the duo's declaratory commitment to free-market ideology and interregional support in the use of aid for the development of the East Asian wing and East European wing of the newly emerging global order. In the case of the European wing, the Japanese have joined in developing the emerging market economies of the former Soviet Union, and also are assisting Central and East European economies, as seen in Japan's founding membership in the European Bank for Reconstruction and Development from 1990. The efforts to contribute to the economic reconstruction of the region in the post-Cold War era are illustrated by such contrasts as the economic assistance offered to Poland and Hungary as well as business training of students carried out in a Russian business school by Niigata prefecture. In the case of the Asian wing, the EU follows Japan as the second most important aid donor (Commission of the European Communities, 1994: 5), with a focus on South Asia, and also has been involved in discussions to offer aid to Mongolia and Cambodia. The two have complementary aid strategies in terms of overall geographic focus and amounts, with the Asian share of EU aid having declined from 33.7 per cent to 18.5 per cent between 1981-2 and 1991-2 (Sideri, 1995: 228), whereas Japan still remains as Asia's number one donor. As the Commission recognizes: 'The Community has a strong and well-established presence in Africa, Middle East and Central and South America whereas Japan has tended to concentrate on Asia' (Commission of the European Communities, 1992: 13).

Third, EU-Japan cooperation has moved forward in the area of the environment, with the institutionalization of the Japan-EU High Level Meeting on the Environment taking place in 1992. In particular, the two sides now seek to work together in carrying out research in areas of global concern, global warming and acid rain, and to prevent the destruction of tropical forests.

This form of cooperation can be expected to develop further in the future, as environmental issues gain in importance in the restructuring of the global order.

Fourth, the emergence of a Euro-Japanese role in global politics is symbolized by the EU's endorsement of Japan's bid for a permanent seat on the United Nation's Security Council (Commission for the European Communities, 1995a: 8), a central plank in the statist Japanese project of carving out a more powerful role for the nation in the newly emerging global order. In this, Japan and the EU share ambitions to play a greater political role in world affairs.

Fifth, with the end of the Cold War the interregionalization of politics is taking place regionally as well as in the cores. Indeed, the EU has set the evolving political relationship with Japan within the context of the Commission's new Asia strategy (Commission of the European Communities, 1994; Commission of the European Communities, 1995a: 3). A number of regional fora facilitate the broadening of interregional political links. At a general level, the EU signed a formal agreement with the Association of Southeast Asian Nations (ASEAN) in 1980 (On this relationship, see Robles, 1998). Within this ASEAN-EU context, Euro-Japanese political dialogue takes place at the annual ASEAN Postministerial Conference, where Japan and the EU are both dialogue partners, consolidating the position of the EU as an independent actor in Japanese eyes. The same can be said for meetings of the ASEAN Regional Forum, which also involves Japan and the EU, and acts as a forum for political as well as security dialogue (on Japan's role, see Hook, 1998b). In light of the EU's lack of bilateral dialogue with individual members of ASEAN, these regional fora can be expected to take on increasing importance in the development of a wider strategy of cooperation between Europe and Asia, as with the Asia-Europe meetings (ASEM). In these meetings, too, Japan and the EU are able to hold political dialogue (for details on ASEM, see Segal, 1997; 1998). Finally, Japan and the EU both play a role in the Korean Peninsula Energy Development Organization (KEDO), with Japan and the EU serving to supplement the role of the United States, at least financially (on KEDO, see Hughes, 1998: 390-4). The financial contribution to KEDO the EU made in 1996 is symbolic of the interregionalization of security issues.

Beyond this, in a broader understanding of politics, which

includes social forces outside of the governing élite, we find interregionalization went forward during the Cold War era based on the asymmetrical penetration of Japan by European political ideals. In this sense, Marxist philosophy, ideas of the welfare state, Eurosocialism, social democracy, and so on, exerted a profound influence on the political make-up of Japan. It still remains that, even in the post-Cold War era, the Communists continue to play a role as part of the political opposition in Japan. Now, with the socialist party spent as a force likely to provide any hope of a political alternative, the Euro-Japanese relationship is firmly embedded in the ideology of the capitalist, free-market economy and democracy, as confirmed in the Hague Declaration.

At the other end of the political spectrum, the continuation of the Japanese imperial system ensures that strong political links are maintained with European monarchies, especially the royal household in Britain. Of course, the links between the Japanese and British imperial institutions are bilateral, but the meeting of President Jacques Delors with the emperor of Japan in 1991 suggests how, in institutionalizing political relations between Japan and the EU, the traditional trappings of sovereignty can be used as a force for political legitimization.

SECURITY

The interlinkages between Japan and the EU in the security dimension remain the most constrained by the legacy of the Cold War security structures set in place by the United States as well as by the domestic constraints on the use of the military as a legitimate instrument of state policy in Japan (Hook, 1996). On the EU side, the lack of competency in security affairs, which remain the preserve of the member states, has limited the development of cooperation in this field. In such a situation, Euro-Japanese initiatives have gone forward outside of the traditional paradigm of 'security through strength', as illustrated by the Euro-Japanese attempts to promote confidence-building measures in the newly emerging post-Cold War order and to tackle the problem of the former Yugoslavia. This can be seen in the case of the UN Arms Register mentioned above, in the commitment to act jointly to prevent 'the dissemination of antipersonnel mines' (Joint Press Statement, the Japan-EU summit 1995, 1995), and in the EU proposal to launch a satellite with Japan in order to monitor maritime activities in the region. In the case of the former Yugoslavia, the appointment of a Japanese national, Akashi Yasushi, as the UN's special envoy helped those in favour of Japan taking a more active international role. For not only did the government send a fact-finding mission in 1994, but thereafter attempts were made to push forward with the despatch of the Self-Defence Forces (SDF) on a peace-keeping mission to Macedonia, although domestic resistance to their overseas despatch meant that, in the end, the Japanese contribution was limited to financial and humanitarian aid in Bosnia and in wider support for UN efforts (on popular resistance to SDF despatch, see Hook, 1996: 114-8). In this way, cooperation on security is contributing to the establishment of a framework of restraint on the proliferation of weapons, with Japan and the EU carving out a fledgling role as 'civilian powers' (on 'civilian powers', see Maull, 1991). As seen in the case of the EU's involvement in KEDO and Japan's involvement in the former Yugoslavia, such a role is emerging in the post-Cold War era as interregional, not just regional, in nature.

In the broader context, external and internal constraints on a military role for the SDF have limited Japanese links with the North Atlantic Treaty Organization (NATO) during the Cold War era, and even in the post-Cold War period, these links have proven less important than those outside of the traditional paradigm of 'security through strength'. It is true that, at the time of the controversy over the SS-20 deployments in Europe in the early 1980s, Prime Minister Nakasone Yasuhiro made an open connection between European and Japanese security interests as part of his attempt to strengthen the Cold War identity of Japan as a member of the 'West', but this connection was made within the context of trilateral cooperation within the West and competition with the East, symbolized by his concern over the US-Japan security treaty and the Soviet's intentions in Asia-Pacific, rather than in the narrow context of interregional cooperation between Japan and Europe. Although no formal links exist with NATO, informal contacts gradually have been developed following the 1985 visit of the Japanese Foreign Minister to NATO Headquarters, with the Director General of the Defence Agency following up by making several visits to NATO, and a reciprocal visit to Japan being made in 1991 by the NATO Secretary-General. On another level, Japanese and European bureaucratic and academic élites have participated in the NATO High Level Seminar on Global Security, first held in 1990, thereby starting to nurture élite networks among those involved in military affairs. More formally, Japanese links have been gradually forged with the Conference on Security and Cooperation in Europe (CSCE), with Japan gaining observer status in 1992, although this precludes participation in CSCE decision-making. In this way, the ending of the Cold War has created opportunities for the development of new security links between Japan and Europe through both formal and informal mechanisms.

Finally, Euro-Japanese dialogue, linkages and exchanges in the field of security at the same time represent a process of interregionalizing ideas about security. During the Cold War, this ideological dimension was manifest in the swing from Europe to Asia, where the threat of Communist expansion in the Euro wing of the global confrontation between capitalism and Communism was transferred to the Asian wing, where nationalist aspirations, North-South disparities, and post colonial tensions were inserted into the European and more broadly Western framework of understanding Cold War security. In the post-Cold War era, the most significant aspect of such an ideological linkage is the attempt to institutionalize European ideas of regional security in East Asia, as seen in the proposal to establish an Asia version of the CSCE, and the attempt to introduce confidence-building measures through the ASEAN Regional Forum. In the field of security, therefore, linkages with Japan and East Asia more generally still remain dominated by the European wing of the newly emerging regional and global orders.

CULTURE

Interlinkages in the field of culture have been forged mostly within the structural constraint of the bilateral relationships between Japan and the member states of the EU, but the 'hard' and 'soft' aspects of culture also have influenced the evolution of the EU-Japan relationship. The legacy of European cultural influence in Japan means that, in tandem with the globalization of the Japanese economy, cultural exchange has proceeded on the basis of Japanese 'soft culture' starting to 'catch up' with the penetration of Japanese 'hard culture' in the EU (on the case of *manga*, see Bouissou, 1998). Japanese language and culture more generally have been important parts of this process. In this the

Japan Foundation and other bodies have played an important role, seeking in their broad-set mandate to increase foreign understanding of Japan and thereby eradicate the sort of cultural misunderstandings, perception gaps, and prejudices which can blight diplomatic and other relations.

The Japan Foundation, which is budgeted through the Ministry of Foreign Affairs (MOFA), and is under the super-vision of the Minister's Secretariat in the MOFA, seeks as one of its tasks to develop Japanese studies in Europe, with programmes to stimulate the learning of Japanese and support for advanced study of Japan. Similarly, a number of Japanese transplants, such as Nissan, have helped to fund Japanese studies in Britain and elsewhere. In line with the burgeoning attempt to strengthen the Euro-Japanese leg of the tripod, the Japan Foundation in the mid-1990s also instituted a programme to promote academic cooperation between the EU and Japan in areas of global concern to both partners, as in the case of disarmament and the environment. In this sense, the promotion of an understanding of Japanese language and Japan more generally appears as part of a broader political and economic strategy to increase the acceptability of Japan as an international player, on the one hand, and in pushing forward with the new Euro-Japanese relationship based on greater global cooperation, on the other. Such efforts serve to erase the negative image of Japan left over from World War II, ameliorate the impact of any remaining European 'Japan bashers', and build up a sense that, far from being 'different', Japan is rather a 'normal' player in the restructuring of the global and regional orders. Indeed, the end of the Cold War has highlighted how, increasingly, the Japanese are being regarded more 'like us', as both Europe and Japan start to face similar issues, such as defining a new role in the world, dealing with an aging population pyramid, and restructuring the economy in the face of globalization processes.

On the European side, the flood of made-in-Japans and FDI has promoted a genuine interest in Japanese language and culture, on the one hand, at the same time as it has prompted the development of a strategy to study Japan in order to penetrate the Japanese market, on the other. There has been an increase in the provision of Japanese language programmes in schools and universities, especially from the 1980s onwards, as illustrated by the case of the United Kingdom (The Japan Foundation and the Daiwa Anglo-Japanese Foundation, 1996-7). Indeed, Britain is both a linchpin for Japanese cultural diplomacy as well as the country where the government has actively promoted the study of Japan. The 'Parker initiatives' of the late 1980s, for instance, increased the provision of Japanese language and Japanese studies at universities by boosting the number of posts in the field for lecturers and professors. The understanding of Japan also is seen as a way to penetrate the Japanese market, as in the Department of Trade and Industry's 'Opportunity Japan Campaign'. Similarly, the EU has taken the initiative in promoting the study of Japanese language and culture as a way to penetrate the Japanese market, as in initiatives like the 'Gateway to Japan' and the 'Executive Training Programme'. The strategy of pushing forward with this use of culture to promote Euro-Japanese relations was highlighted in early 1995, when the Commission suggested the possibility of '... promoting a network of universities in Europe which offer joint diplomas combining business or economics with a first-hand knowledge of Japan', and '... encouraging teaching of modern Japanese in higher education throughout the EU...' (*European Report*, 1995: 6).

In terms of ideology, the EU and Japan have both clearly espoused a shared commitment to 'democracy' and the 'free-market economy', as part of the Hague Declaration. In pushing forward with Euro-Japanese interlinkages, therefore, these principles can be employed as political tools by both sides. In the case of the former, for instance, the Commission has noted how the transformation of the party political system in Japan shows '... a desire to change the bureaucratic system so that it becomes more responsive to the democratic will' (Commission of the European Communities, 1995a: 3). In this, the EU is seeking to employ 'democracy' as a lever to bring about changes in the economic structures blocked by the bureaucracy, as in the EU's continuing desire for further deregulation of the Japanese market. Similarly, in pressing for the 'opening' of this market, the EU has used free-market ideology, calling on Japan to remove obstacles to market access, as EU exports '... can benefit the consumer and lower the costs of intermediate manufactured products and services to industrial buyers' (Commission of the European Communities, 1995a: 9). In this way, the EU seeks to make allies of Japanese consumers in their struggle to break the stranglehold of the distribution system and the *keiretsu*. In the case of Japan, appeals to 'free-market' principles have served in its attempt to block or remove VERs and 'anti-dumping'

253

measures proposed by the EU. In the context of the historical legacy of democratic developments in Europe, however, failings in 'European democracy' have not played a role in Japan's attempt to legitimize attacks on European practices. At the same time, their joint declaratory commitment to these two principles can be used in their efforts to spread the post-Cold War ideology to other parts of the globe, enforcing discipline on the newly emerging market economies, if not necessarily putting a high priority on democratization in either wing of the emerging order. The recent Japanese response to the Asian financial crisis also leaves in doubt the degree of Japanese commitment to free-market principles, too.

In the broadest sense, therefore, cultural interlinkages have set in motion the 'Japanization' of Europe, but within the constraints of the emerging post-Cold War order. It is 'Japanization' as a process of increased understanding of Japan, on the one hand, and 'Japanization' as a process of Europe meeting the Japanese challenge, on the other. In this we are witnessing how, in a late-comer's attempt to catch up with the front-runners, a degree of 'cultural convergence' is underway between Japan and the EU in the context of the deeper and wider dynamics of globalization processes. The expansion of the EU's interest from Japan to other East Asian economies, as witnessed by the promulgation of the Community's new 'Asia policy', suggests the dialectic relationship between the front-runners and late-comers will over the longer term lead to a boost in interest in 'Asian culture' and language in an attempt to remain competitive in the face of globalization processes.

CONCLUSION

These interlinkages in economy, politics, security and culture have forged a multifaceted, complex set of symmetric and asymmetric relations between Japan and Europe. The scale of international trade, the significant penetration of Japanese FDI in Europe, and the emergence of spatially disparate production processes in industries such as automobiles and electronics has served to structure interregional economic interdependence between East Asia and Europe. The need to respond to economic and security issues on interregional levels has pushed forward political cooperation, as seen in the European support for a Japanese seat in the United Nations Security Council. The breakdown of the Cold War structures has provided increased opportunity for interregional cooperation, as evidenced by the implementation of the Euro-Japanese proposal for a UN Arms Register. The expansion in the reach of culture, both 'hard' and 'soft', has brought about the rise of Japan as a cultural presence in Europe, although this has been largely within the overall embrace of 'consumer culture' and the ideology of the 'free-market' and 'democracy'. In these ways, the transformation in regional and global orders is taking place in the context of Euro-Japanese interlinkages and the interregionalization of economy, politics, security and culture.

In the development of these relations with the EU, the Japanese economic penetration of Europe, first in trade and then in investment, has brought to the forefront of European concern the question of how to respond to the Japanese, and more broadly East Asian, challenge. In the post-Cold War era, interregionalization is moving beyond economics, to embrace political, security and cultural dimensions. New forms of cooperation between Japan and the EU have partly emerged as a balance to the predominance of the United States, partly as a response to the reconfiguration of the global order, with the two wings of the US-centred world order increasingly taking on a political role, and partly as a reaction to the fear of 'closed regionalism'. Overwhelmingly, however, Euro-Japanese coop-eration has emerged in response to the structural transformations brought about in regional and global orders as a result of the economic ascendance of Japan as a late-comer in the global political economy.

The shape of the emerging world order remains indetermi-nate, with forces for integration and disintegration, fragmenta-tion and unity, interacting in a complex process of constraint and opportunity. Within this context, what is the power of the Japan and the other East Asian newcomers to transform the global and regional orders? More specifically, how can the rise of Japan be understood in the context of Euro-Asian interregionalization? We have seen how the Japanese penetration of Europe set in motion internal dynamics of change. In the battle between the 'Japan bashing' school of thought and the 'Japan benefits' school of thought, European political forces now have come to coalesce most significantly around the 'benefits' school, as seen in the EU's new Asia strategy. In the face of competition from the newcomers, internal structural changes are being forced on European nations, with the introduction of highly competitive

East Asian transplants and the continuing flow of competitive goods into the markets of the EU transforming industrial and social relations. The fears on the part of especially the weak and downtrodden that, in the face of globalizing economic and other forces, the victories won by labour in the struggle with capital, as seen in the creation of the welfare state and other institutional structures, are being abandoned or trimmed in the face of the latecomers' challenge, which in the past had led to continental charges of this off-shore island's 'social dumping', are in themselves part of the impact of globalization in Britain and continental Europe.

In identifying Japan as a 'benefit', the political and economic élites of Britain and the EU have recognized the permeability of the state and the Union in the present world order. In building the institutions to protect workers at home, the early-starter, European powers penetrated and exploited the late-comers of Asia. These latecomers now have mounted a challenge to the early-starters, with East Asians seeking to legitimize this challenge by introducing a new ideology, giving central place to 'Asian values' and the caring services of the family, rather than the state, an ideology not unfamiliar to Thatcherite Britons (see, for instance, Ishihara and Mahathir, 1994; Zakaria, 1994). Strength in economic competitiveness can erode the safety nets for protecting the weak in Europe as well as sharpen the competitive edge of European business. To what extent the downturn in the Japanese economy and the Asian financial crisis will dampen the challenge for Europe remains to be seen. What is clear, however, is that, under ongoing globalization processes, competitive challenges will continue to arise for Europe as latecomers seek to catch up with the early-starters.

Thus, the question of how Europe should respond to the Japanese and more broadly Asian challenge cannot be answered by reference solely to different forms of capitalism (Albert, 1993). Rather, the more fundamental question is how, in the process of latecomer modernization and the erosion in the power of military might as an effective and cost-efficient instrument in the protection and pursuit of state interests, the advanced states can work to sustain the quality of life already achieved, on the one hand, and enable the poor and deprived, both within the advanced economies and in the developing regions of the world, to enjoy at least the basic minimum, on the other. In the struggle to establish a new, post–Cold War order, the states of Europe are grappling with how to achieve a balance between the demands for competitiveness and the demands for health, welfare and the good life. In striving towards a global transformation bringing about a more equitable distribution of life chances and resources, not only relations between the political, bureaucratic and economic élites of Europe and Japan, but also between transnational social movements, need to be strengthened. In this way, the Euro-Japanese élites' emphasis on the 'free market' can be complemented by a popular emphasis on transnational 'democracy'. From this a new 'double movement' (Polanyi, 1944 [1957]) may arise which will enable both latecomers and early-starters to respond to the opportunities of the new era.

ACKNOWLEDGEMENT

The author wishes to express his gratitude to the Leverhulme Trust for the award of a Leverhulme Research Fellowship during the period this chapter was prepared.

BIBLIOGRAPHY

Albert, Michel. 1993. *Capitalism against Capitalism*. London: Whurr.

Bouissou, Jean-Marie. 1998. 'Toppling Disney's World: Why Japanese Manga Succeeded in France'. Paper presented at a conference on The Global Meaning of Japan, organized by the Centre for Japanese Studies, University of Sheffield, 20-22 March.

Brittan, Leon. 1991. 'Europe and Japan: the Evidence of Change'. Extract from a speech by Sir Leon Brittan, *Foreign Correspondents' Club of Japan*, Tokyo, 28 February.

Chalmers, Malcolm, Greene, Owen and Xie, Zhiqiong. 1995. *Asia Pacific Security and the United Nations*. Bradford: University of Bradford.

Commission of the European Communities. 1992. 'A Consistent and Global Approach'. *Com* (92) 219 final.

——. 1994. 'Towards a New Asia Strategy'. *Com* 94: 314 final.

——. 1995a. 'Europe and Japan: the Next Steps'. *Com* 95: 73 final.

——. 1995b. *Bull.* EU 5.

European Report. 1995. 11 March.

Cox, Robert W. 1987. *Production, Power and World Order: Social Forces in the Making of History*. New York: Columbia University Press.

Cox, Robert W. with Sinclair, Timothy. 1996. *Approaches to World Order*. Cambridge: Cambridge University Press.

Gamble, Andrew and Payne, Anthony, eds. 1996. *Regionalism and World Order*. Basingstoke: Macmillan.

Gill, Stephen. 1990. *American Hegemony and the Trilateral Commission*. Cambridge: Cambridge University Press.

Gilson, Julie. 1999. *Japan and the European Union*. Basingstoke: Macmillan.

Graham, Robert and Simonian, Hague. 1997. 'Toyota Picks France for New Plant.' *Financial Times*, 10 December.

Hook, Glenn D. 1996. *Militarization and Demilitarization in Contemporary Japan*. London: Routledge.

——. 1998a. 'Japanese Business in Triadic Regionalization'. In *Japanese Business Management. Restructuring for Low Growth and Globalization*, edited by Hasegawa Harukiyo and Glenn D. Hook. London: Routledge: 19-37.

——. 1998b. 'Japan and the ASEAN Regional Forum: Bilateralism, Multilateralism or Supplementalism?'. *Japanstudien*, 10:159-88.

Hook, Glenn D. and Kearns, Ian. 1999. 'Introduction'. In *Subregionalism and World Order*, edited by Glenn D. Hook and Ian Kearns. Basingstoke: Macmillan.

Hughes, Christopher W. 1998. 'Japanese Policy and the North Korean "Soft Landing"'. *The Pacific Review*, 11(3) 389-415.

Ishihara Shintarō and Mahathir, Mohammed. 1994. *'No' to ieru Ajia* [The Asia that can say 'no']. Tokyo: Kōbunsha.

Japan Foundation and the Daiwa Anglo-Japanese Foundation. 1996-7. *Japanese Degree Courses in Universities and other Tertiary Education Institutions in the United Kingdom*. London: Daiwa Anglo-Japanese Foundation.

JETRO [Japan External Trade Organization]. 1998. *Sekai to Nihon no kaigai chokusetsu tōshi* [World and Japanese foreign direct investment]. Tokyo: JETRO.

Joint Declaration. 1991. *Joint Declaration on Relations between the European Community and its Member States and Japan in the Hague*, 18 July.

Joint Press Statement, the Japan-EU Summit 1995. 1995. *Fourth Japan/EU Summit*, Paris, 19 June.

Julius, D. and Thomsen, S. 1988. 'Foreign-owned Firms, Trade and Economic Integration'. In *Tokyo Club Papers*, 2, Tokyo: Tokyo Club Foundation for Global Studies: 191-226.

Maull, Hans. W. 1991. 'Germany and Japan: the New Civilian Powers'. *Foreign Affairs*, 69(5) 91-106.

Mendl, Wolf. 1984. *Western Europe and Japan Between the Superpowers*. London: Croom Helm.

Nakanishi, Hiroshi. 1995. 'A Thick but Inflexible Leg: Japanese-American Relationship in the Trilateral Context'. Paper presented at the Hakone Conference (mimeo).

Nuttall, Simon. 1995. 'The Reluctant Partnership'. Paper presented at the Hakone Conference (mimeo).

Polanyi, Karl. 1944 (1957). *The Great Transformation*. Boston: Beacon.

Robles Jr, Alfredo C. 1998. 'ASEAN and the European Union: Conceptions of Interregional Relations and Regionalization in Southeast Asia'. Paper presented at the Joint Conference of the International Studies Association and the Standing Group on International Relations of the European Consortium for Political Research, Vienna, 16-19 September.

Segal, Gerald. 1997. 'Thinking Strategically about ASEM: The Subsidiarity Question'. *The Pacific Review*, 10(1): 124-34.

——. 1998. 'A New ASEM Agenda: A Report on the British Council's Meeting "Asia and Europe: Societies in Transition, 19-22 March 1998"'. *The Pacific Review*, 11(4) 561-72.

Sideri, Sandro. 1995. 'The Economic Relations of China and Asia-Pacific with Europe'. *Development Policy Review*, 13(3): 219-46.

Tanaka, Toshiro. 1995. 'EPC in World Society: the Picture from Japan'. *Hōgaku kenkyū* [Keio University], 66(2): 428-48.

Tsuchiya Motohiro. 1995. 'Nichibei handōtai māsatsu no bunseki' [An analysis of the friction between the Japanese and American semiconductor industries]. *Hōgaku seijigaku ronkyū* [Keiō University], 25: 343-73.

Zakaria, Fareed. 1994. 'A Conversation with Lee Kuan Yew'. *Foreign Affairs*, 73(2): 109-27.

15

The Structure of Soviet-Japanese Relations in the Cold War: Normalization in the Mid-1950s

TANAKA TAKAHIKO

On 19 October 1956, Japan and the Soviet Union restored their diplomatic relations by issuing a joint declaration in Moscow after a year-and-a-half of tough negotiations. Soviet-Japanese normalization in 1956 has multiple historical meanings. It marked a starting point of a more stable relationship between the two neighbouring countries than during the previous eleven years. It also made it clear, however, that they could not remove an intractable 'thorn' stuck in their relationship, that is, the northern territorial questions. Looking through the Cold War period, it should be pointed out that the process and results of normalization in the mid-1950s has influenced enormously later Soviet-Japanese relations. In this sense, in order to understand the transformation and stagnation of the relations during the Cold War period it is helpful and useful to clarify the structure of Soviet-Japanese relations at the time of normalization. At the same time, it would help us understand what the end of the Cold War in the Far East meant, because it will facilitate our grasping which factors of the Soviet-Japanese Relations really ended and what did not at the end of the Cold War.

Now that the Cold War has ended, international historians are faced with an urgent need to re-examine the history of the Cold War from new perspectives. One of them is to focus our attention upon the terminating process of the Cold War order or structure, even while we are looking at the origins of the Cold War or the process by which it intensified. Another is to treat international history as a structure composed of multiple dimensions and factors. The Cold War was a dynamic and complicated historical structure composed of various interconnecting dimensions. The Cold War structure has been transforming itself historically in accordance with the changing combination and constellation of those dimensions and factors. Perhaps the origins of the Cold War could be understood as an emerging particular set of those factors, and its end as erosion of another particular set (for a tentative attempt, see Tanaka, 1998). It seems rather fantastic to analyse the Cold War only as a stable bi-hegemonic structure, and it sounds rather silly to reach the peculiar conclusion that the Cold War was a long peace (Gaddis, 1987).

Soviet-Japanese relations after the Asia-Pacific War were no exception. They were multidimensional and deeply incorporated into the Cold War structure. The structure of Soviet-Japanese relations was closely connected with the overall and regional structure of the Cold War. In order to understand how Soviet-Japanese friction and conflicts started and developed – and how they will be dissolved – it is necessary to analyse the dynamic historical transformation of these relations. It seems a dominant trend among scholars, however, to concentrate on bilateral aspects of Soviet-Japanese relations. It is true that many of them tried to inject some American factors into their Soviet-Japanese diplomatic history, but treated them as a peripheral topic. Some scholars put too much emphasis on the domestic political struggles of the infamous factional politics [*habatsu seiji*] as the main factor shaping Japan's foreign policies (Hellmann, 1969). But it is now more necessary than ever to make more efforts to write a structural or multidimensional history of Soviet-Japanese relations during the Cold War period.

The main purpose of this essay is to present a tentative description of Soviet-Japanese relations in the mid-1950s from a multidimensional and structural perspective. In doing so, I shall focus on the following dimensions:

1) The global political dimension of the Cold War, which was in a transitional period from the serious East-West confrontation to the stabilization of the security dilemma;
2) the regional political dimension of the Cold War in the Far East, including Soviet-Japanese relations, US-Japanese relations, Sino-Soviet relations, Sino-US relations, US-Soviet relations and interconnection of them. In

addition, Anglo-Japanese and Anglo-American relations cannot be ignored; and

3) the domestic political dimension, such as politico-social changes in Japan (e.g., nationalism) and political changes in the Soviet Union.

THE TRANSFORMATION OF THE COLD WAR IN THE MID-1950S

The Cold War demonstrated undeniable changes in the mid-1950s. First of all, the trend of détente, the so-called 'thaw', emerged saliently around the time of the death of Soviet premier Joseph Stalin in March 1953, though signs of flexibility in Soviet Cold War policy could be seen much earlier with regional diversity (Shulman, 1963; Stephen, 1984). The Korean War reached a truce in July through Soviet initiatives. The five-power foreign ministers' conference in Geneva, with Britain and Russia as co-chairmen, succeeded in terminating the Indochina war in July 1954, despite of US objection. The Soviet flexibility also lead to significant change in Europe. From summer to autumn in 1955, the four-power summit and the four-power foreign ministers' conference in Geneva raised a mood of détente though they could not solve German problems. The Austria State Treaty was signed in May whereby the country regained her independent status, after the Soviets had altered their rigid stance over the re-independence of Austria. In September, West Germany restored her diplomatic relations with the Soviet Union.

Although the above-mentioned events were welcomed as a token of slackening East-West tensions, their significance should not be overestimated. The significance of the 'thaw' was rather amplified because there were more dangerous trends going on in parallel. In fact, the Cold War tensions intensified in various ways. First, the world entered the thermonuclear era as the two superpowers succeeded in developing the hydrogen bombs from 1952 to 1953. The advent of the H-bomb had more serious repercussions than the A-bombs dropped on Hiroshima and Nagasaki. Humankind was for the first time faced with the possibility of human annihilation. The Soviet-US nuclear arms race intensified. Secondly, both blocs almost accomplished construction of military alliances on a global scale. The Western European Union (WEU) was established in 1954 and West Germany was rearmed and joined the WEU and NATO.

Eastern Europe also set up the Warsaw Pact Organization (WPO) in May 1955. In Asia, the Southeast Asia Treaty Organization (SEATO) was formed in September 1954 and the Baghdad Treaty was concluded in the next year. The security dilemma between the two blocs reached a critical point, in other words, a dangerous stalemate.

Thus, the two opposite trends, 'thaw' and 'stalemate' emerged in the global dimension of the Cold War in the mid-1950s. But they were not contradictory but rather complementary. The dangerous development of the security dilemma made some communication channel between the two blocs a necessary measure for crisis management in order to avoid the possibility of an escalation to the third world war. The thaw was, in this sense, to be designed to stabilize the Cold War confrontation and reduce its risks without dissolving the hostile inter-bloc relationship.

Partly related to the slackening trends of East-West tensions, nationalism in various parts of the world became assertive in the mid-1950s. The 'blocism' as the superpower's disciplinary tool for maintaining the Cold War order of domination, as Mary Kaldor suggests, became less effective as the Cold War tensions were slackened (Kaldor, 1990). The retreat of blocism lead to the self-assertion of nationalism in the allies to the superpowers. In other words, the emerging mood of détente tempted the allies to conduct relatively independent diplomatic movement to escape from the straitjacket of the 'imaginary war'. In the third world, newly independent countries also attempted to have more say by taking advantage of the desires of superpowers for more influence. The Asian-African Conference in Bandung in 1955 and the result of the Suez crisis are good examples. The Cold War now started to enter into a different phase (LaFeber, 1991). The superpowers could not employ as violent methods as in the first ten years of the Cold War for fear of escalation. They had to rely on more psychological strategy *vis-à-vis* their allies and the countries of the third world, such as taming and inducing the emerging nationalism. In fact, the Truman administration started searching for a psychological strategy in 1952 and the Eisenhower administration employed psychological operations through the CIA (Cook, 1981). The peace offensive of the Soviet Union can also be interpreted as a psychological tactics to erode the solidarity of the Western bloc.

To summarize, the Cold War in the mid-1950s demonstrated

the following three interrelated streams: the deepened security dilemma, the mood of détente, and the emerging nationalism. By and large, those macro trends of the Cold War influenced every aspect of world politics in the period, in particular, relations between an ally of a bloc and the leader of the opposite bloc, such as Soviet-Japanese relations.

SOVIET-JAPANESE NORMALIZATION AND INTERNATIONAL POLITICS IN THE FAR EAST

It is helpful to describe here briefly the development of the Soviet-Japanese normalization talks in 1955-56. I shall then discuss impacts of regional political developments.

Normalization Talks

After the collapse of the scandal-ridden Yoshida government, Hatoyama Ichirō became prime minister in December 1954. His foreign minister Shigemitsu Mamoru announced that the new administration would make the normalization of Japan's relations with Communist countries one of its most significant foreign-policy goals. The Russians responded favourably and realistically. Official negotiations started in London in June 1955. The first round of the negotiations stuck on the territorial issue. The Japanese at first demanded the return of the Kuriles. In response, the Soviet plenipotentiary Yakob Malik suggested the possibility of returning the Habomais and Shikotan on the condition that Japan recognize Soviet sovereignty over the rest of the Kuriles. But a settlement could not be reached because the Japanese in return extended their demand to Kunashiri and Etorofu, which were essential to the Soviet Cold War strategy in the Pacific. The Russians rejected the Japanese request and the negotiations reached a deadlock.

The second round of the London talks was held in spring 1956. Both sides repeated rigidly their previous positions. The Hatoyama government started to reshape its policy and inclined to adapt a new policy line, the so-called 'Adenauer formula': that is, to restore diplomatic relations by postponing solution of the territorial problems.

The third round of the normalization talks were resumed in summer 1956. Foreign Minister Shigemitsu went to Moscow and played the major role in the negotiations. Faced with the rigid Soviet stance and Russian threat not to return even the

Habomais and Shikotan, Shigemitsu, who was against the 'Adenauer formula' and determined to conclude a peace treaty, reached the decision to accept the Soviet condition, Japanese recognition of Russian sovereignty over the Kuriles other than the Habomais and Shikotan. But Tokyo stopped him and the last opportunity for a peace treaty during the Cold War era disappeared.

The final round was held in October 1956. At this time, Hatoyama himself flew to Moscow. At last, Hatoyama and Khrushchev reached a settlement based on the 'Adenauer formula' and issued the joint declaration on 19 October. The territorial questions remained to be solved in the future, though the declaration provided that the Habomais and Shikotan would be restored when a peace treaty was concluded (for more detailed accounts, see Tanaka, 1990a).

Regional Environments around Japan

The softening of Soviet attitudes towards Japan seems to have begun in 1952 and the first initiative for normalization came from the Russians in summer 1953. It seems that the Korean War and the end of the occupation of Japan affected the Soviet leaders to a great degree. The war demonstrated the US determination to defend her sphere of influence in the Far East. The independence of Japan provided the Russians with a great opportunity to regain some influence on Japan and push back US dominance over Japan. In Japan the end of the occupation aroused nationalist sentiments whose proponents sought more autonomous or independent foreign relations of their country. It seems that the Soviet leaders took advantage of these sentiments in order to make the Japanese leave the American orbit. In proposals for normalization made in 1953, the Soviet government made an alteration of Japan's relationship with the US an essential condition for normalization.

In October 1954, the Russians issued a more realistic proposal for normalization in a Sino-Soviet joint statement. They removed the above-mentioned condition from their proposal. This suggests that the Soviet leaders had to reach some agreement with the Chinese before the Russian could present a substantial initiative to the Japanese and that Soviet-Japanese normalization was also regarded as beneficial by the Chinese (Stephen, 1984). Perhaps the resumption of Soviet-Japanese diplomatic relations was regarded by both of the Chinese and the

Russian leaders as a test case for the subsequent attempt at Sino-Japanese normalization. In fact, the Chinese government also started its own wooing to Japan in the mid-1950s.

At the end of Yoshida's long-lived administration, the Japanese people became fed up with his pro-American foreign policy. Restored independence led to an upsurge of nationalist sentiments in Japan and anti-Americanism which were intensified by some events such as the fifth Lucky Dragon incident. The new prime minister, Hatoyama Ichirō, was famous for being a nationalist and not so pro-American as Yoshida. This fact must have provided a great opportunity and political resources for the Russians, though Hatoyama's preference to large-scale rearmament alarmed them. Normalization with Japan emerged as a realistic and effective policy instrument for inducing the Japanese nationalism into stronger anti-Americanism. In this sense, the Soviet government exercised a psychological operation against Japan and the United States (Tanaka, 1993).

The Soviet gesture in the first London talks of offering a return of the Habomais and Shikotan can be understood in this context. Territorial questions can easily mobilize nationalist sentiments. The Soviet leaders must have intended to soften anti-Soviet sentiments in Japan and to let the Japanese become suspicious about the intention of the US occupying Okinawa. But the Soviet Union could not make more territorial concessions because of her anti-American military strategy in the Pacific. The Habomais and Shikotan were not at all significant in that sense, but she had to retain Kunashiri and Etorofu to keep the exit to the Pacific for its navy and the bases for its air forces. The Soviet policy towards Japan was restrained by the confrontational aspect of the Cold War.

The Eisenhower administration was carefully and unpleasantly watching the development. It is doubtless that the US leaders disliked the idea of improvement of relations between their allies and their arch-enemy. But they had to restrain themselves for various reasons. Because the US had diplomatic relations with the Soviet Union, she could not find a persuasive rationale to stop the Japanese from restoring their diplomatic relations with the Russians. Eisenhower and his staffs also had to take into full account the rising nationalism and anti-American sentiments in Japan after the effectuation of the San Francisco Peace Treaty. Although they considered that Japan should have sound nationalism, it should not be anti-Americanism. If they interfered with the normalization process, it was inevitable that the emerging anti-American sentiments in Japan would flare up. Secretary of State John Foster Dulles pressed the Japanese not to make too many concessions on the territorial issue, but it was because he considered that the Soviet Union would not return any territories she had once obtained. The Americans knew that the Soviet rigidity over the territorial issue would lead the Japanese nationalism in direction of anti-Sovietism. Their nightmare was that Japan became neutral and that it would make it difficult for them to keep their bases faced with strong anti-American sentiments.

They also manipulated Japanese nationalism by offering to return the Amami islands in August 1953 immediately after the first Soviet overture of normalization. It could be easily assumed that normalizing relations with the Soviet Union would become a symbol of Japan's autonomy and independence after the long occupation period. The US officials tried to neutralize the effect of the Soviet overture by appealling to the Japanese more by suggesting the returning of the islands occupied by the US (Tanaka, 1993).

Apart from that, Soviet-Japanese normalization itself was not very harmful to the Cold War strategy of the United States. But an expected effect of normalization was the increasing possibility for Japan to move to normalization with China which was vital to the Americans. The US administration considered any improvement of Sino-Japanese relations might stimulate the Japanese drive for trade with China. The increase of Japan's economic dependence on the Chinese market would enhance China's political leverage against Japan. In fact, the general Cold War strategy of the United States had been in transition in the mid-1950s. For the US officials, China became a more immediate menace than the Soviet Union. The Sino-US tensions had never been resolved since the Korean War but rather grown over the Taiwan Strait crisis. Moreover, China began to be more influential through playing a major role among Asian countries as was fully demonstrated by the Bandung conference. The possible Sino-Japanese rapprochement meant the possibility of a neutral Japan. NSC 5516 clearly proves that the United States regarded the possibility of Sino-Japanese rapprochement as something that the US should prevent (Tanaka, 1993).

The Eisenhower administration, which had kept its self-restrained and cautious attitude towards intervention in the normalization process since the start of the Soviet-Japanese talks, suddenly altered its policy line and issued the *aide-mémoire* in September 1956 saying that Kunashiri and Etorofu were historically Japanese territories. This was aimed at obstructing any Soviet-Japanese normalization achieved on the basis of Japanese acceptance of Soviet sovereignty over the two islands or even following the 'Adenauer formula'. This alteration of the US attitude seems to have been caused by a strong warning from Taiwan's president Chiang Kai-shek against the possibility of Sino-Japanese rapprochement fol Soviet-Japanese normalization (Tanaka, 1993). Although the previously cautious US attitude had widened the freedom of Japanese actions in the normalization talks, the US policy change narrowed Japan's option. Hatoyama in Moscow could not at all accept the Soviet territorial conditions, and had to demand strongly the return of the Habomais and Shikotan. The joint declaration was the best thing that Japan could achieve in those circumstances.

Thus, the process of Soviet-Japanese normalization was an international political process involving not only Soviet-Japanese relations but also Sino-Soviet and Sino-US relations as very significant and influential circumstantial factors. It is needless to repeat the effect of global transformation of the Cold War on the process.

Finally, it should be pointed out that there was a country which was not directly involved in Far Eastern political development but played a significant position: Britain. The British government could not keep completely aloof from the Soviet-Japanese negotiations, partly because the first and second rounds of negotiations took place in London, but more importantly because Britain was a co-author of the territorial clause of the San Francisco Peace Treaty. British attitudes over the northern territorial questions were remarkably different from the American ones. The British foreign office of the Eden administration took the stance that Kunashiri and Etorofu were Soviet territories not only *de facto* but also *de jure*. It even suspected that Japan could not claim their sovereignty over Shikotan.[3] The core principle of British Far Eastern policy was to stabilize tensions even by taking an unfavourable stance to her allies. It did not desire to stimulate Japanese irredentism that could cause Far Eastern instability. The Japanese hoped for establishing a common front with the co-authors of the San

Francisco Peace Treaty in order to strengthen their position on the territorial issue. But the severe stance of the British prevented it. It may have imposed significant constraints on the US and the Japanese attitudes towards the Russians and may have indirectly helped the Soviet-Japanese normalization.

SOVIET-JAPANESE NORMALIZATION AS AN INTERSECTION OF INTERNATIONAL POLITICS AND DOMESTIC POLITICS

It is well-known that the process and the results of Soviet-Japanese normalization were very much affected by domestic political struggles among Japanese conservatives. Researchers of Soviet-Japanese relations have usually, however, ignored the inter-relationship between domestic aspects and the on-going international transformation of the Cold War. In fact, the complex transformation of the Cold War made it quite difficult for policy-makers to establish firm consensus about the nature of international politics in the mid-1950s. This difficulty caused critical divergence among Japanese leaders over the policy of Soviet-Japanese normalization. The policy divergence complicated and confused Japanese diplomacy on this issue, being called 'dual diplomacy', and, then, affected the negotiating process of normalization in ways harmful to their own country.

Those who put more emphasis on the continuous trends of confrontation or dangerous stalemate in the Cold War tended to insist on a hard-line policy towards the Soviet Union and to be anxious about possible negative impacts on US-Japanese relations. They were, therefore, strongly against normalization and adamant on the territorial issue. This faction was represented by Yoshida. Yoshida even tried to obstruct normalization by utilizing his personal connection with the hard-liners in the United States such as Senator Alexander Smith.[4]

On the other hand, Hatoyama and his advisers, Matsumoto Shun'ichi and Sugihara Arata, emphasized that the aspect of détente was more important. They argued that the 'thaw' demonstrated the future tendencies of world politics and that Japan should adapt to them or take the initiative to promote these trends. The Socialists, who appreciated the flexible attitudes of the Soviet Union and called her a 'stabilizing force', were also pro-détente and pro-normalization. Although the Hatoyama group and the Socialists were different in their ideologies and in the extent to which Japan should become neutral in the Cold War *'feind und freund'* division, both shared the view that it was necessary to keep more distance from the US (Tanaka, 1990b).

It should be acknowledged that both pro-normalization and anti-normalization groups shared the growing nationalist feelings. The Yoshida group intended to improve Japan's international status by showing loyalty to her bloc leader and availing US military and economic power to reconstruct the economic power of their country. Yoshida is famous for being against the rearmament of Japan, but recent researches point out that his long-term goal was to strengthen Japan, first in economic terms and then in military terms (Uemura, 1995). In other words, these groups tried take full advantage of the beneficial elements of the Cold War in order to meet their nationalist desires. In this sense, therefore, they can be called 'Cold War nationalists'.

On the contrary, the Hatoyama group and the Socialists regarded slackening of US control over Japan as the core of their nationalist aims. By playing a positive role in promoting détente, they thought, Japan would be able to gain a firmer international position in world politics. In other words, they tried to gain political force within the context of the existing political contests between nationalism and 'blocism'. In this sense, the Hatoyama group and the Socialists can be characterized as 'détente nationalists'. It should not be overlooked, however, that the Socialists were strongly opposed to Hatoyama's positive attitude towards the rearmament. Hatoyama agreed with Yoshida in his desire to reconstruct Japan in the form of a traditional nation-state or 'normal state'. The Socialists insisted on keeping the Article 9 of the new constitution. This being so, there was a complicated divergence in Japan's nationalism both in terms of Japan's external roles and in terms of the desirable forms of future Japan.

The normalization talks became an arena of political struggles among those groups for inducing the growing Japanese nationalism to their own merits after the end of allied occupation. It certainly complicated the normalization talks, in particular, on the territorial issue. In order to absorb the nationalist sentiments broadly held by the Japanese public opinion, even the Hatoyama group could never make further territorial concessions.

Of interest is Shigemitsu's position. As a realistic and pragmatic diplomat, Shigemitsu realized the significance of both trends of the Cold War. The 'thaw' and the flexibility of Soviet policy struck him but also he knew the unstable nature of détente. As a proud professional diplomat, Shigemitsu was very contemptuous about Hatoyama's excessive emphasis on 'peaceful nature of the Soviet Union'. At the same time, he was unwilling to accept the rigid attitude held by the Yoshida group. From Shigemitsu's viewpoint, world politics was in transition, showing two ambivalent trends and it was his task to draw a more balanced picture of world politics and to base his Soviet policy on it. In other words, Shigemitsu was ready to take advantage of the trend of détente for Japan's sake, but he knew that everything should be cautiously done because of the existing East-West confrontation. He realized the necessity and feasibility of Soviet-Japanese normalization. He was also well aware of unpleasant feelings held by the Americans. He rightly expected that the 'Adenauer formula' would leave a 'thorn' which would cause a serious problem between the Soviets and the Japanese (Tanaka, 1990c).

Before and during his mission in Moscow in 1956, Shigemitsu seemed to make tireless efforts to solve every sort of problem caused by the complex nature of Soviet-Japanese normalization. Shigemitsu had been playing the role of hard-liner in the Hatoyama government, in order to diminish the anxiety held within the US government and also to mobilize support among the public sensitive to the territorial questions. He had constantly insisted that, in order to remove the 'thorn', normalization should take an officially legitimate form, that is, a peace treaty containing a provision of territorial solution, ambiguous as it may be. His decision in Moscow to accept the Soviet territorial claims was in the same line of thought. The tragedy for Shigemitsu was that the domestic political struggles among the main factions were evolving over the question: how to absorb the nationalism in Japanese public opinion. Shigemitsu himself had tried to make use of nationalistic public sentiments to support the strong territorial demands against the Russians. But the growing nationalist public opinion made even Hatoyama hesitate to support Shigemitsu's decision in Moscow. It cannot be denied also that the US psychological manoeuvring of Japanese nationalist sentiments as mentioned above had a certain effect of strengthening the irredentism of the Japanese public.

It is also necessary to pay full attention to the Soviet domestic situation. It seems that the Soviet leaders were faced with a dilemma. The political instability after the death of Stalin

271

remained until 1957 when Nikita Khrushchev finally established a firm political authority after a long political struggle. The Soviet leaders needed to make their external policy flexible and to liberate their nation from Stalin's oppressive rule. At the same time, they had to strengthen national unity that could be slackened by their external overtures of peaceful coexistence and by their domestic attempts to deny Stalinism. Under these circumstances, Khrushchev needed to improve the relations with Japan but could not make any territorial concessions that would make him being accused of losing parts of national territories. In other words, to remove the thorn from the postwar Soviet-Japanese relations was made difficult by Russian domestic politics and Russian nationalism that had to be cautiously treated in the transitional period of the Cold War. Now that the Russian historical archives are opening, historians should cast more analytical light on the impact of Russian domestic factors on Soviet-Japanese relations.

Here, I must admit that my analysis on domestic factors is far from being sufficient. It should be extended into the field of economic and social structures affecting Soviet-Japanese normalization. It would be of a great importance and interest to analyse more profoundly effects of nationalism or national sentiments both in Japan and the Soviet Union. For instance, as Glenn Hook has suggested, it is necessary to research the history of how education in both countries has treated national territory and its history. Mutual perceptions held by the two nations towards each other must be studied as well. So many factors to be reckoned with can be pointed out.

CONCLUSIONS

Postwar Soviet-Japanese relations can be characterized as an output of a Cold War process where the global, regional and domestic dimensions were interrelated. This does not mean that the bilateral aspects of Soviet-Japanese relations are not important. What should be realized is that the bilateral process of these relations was deeply affected by multidimensional factors and was dependent to a great degree on broader international circumstances and the domestic politico-social structure.

Until the end of the Cold War, we have seen a complicated transformation of the Far Eastern international political structure and the domestic politico-social structure of the Soviet Union and Japan. US policies towards the Soviet Union, China and

Japan have changed considerably. The Soviet Union has disappeared, and China is faced with the tasks of uneasy adjustment. In spite of these transformations, the territorial issue is still an obstructive thorn in Russian-Japanese relations, which are now in a transition from relations of the Cold War to the post-Cold War period. In order to understand this transitional process, it is essential to analyse which factors of the dynamic structure of Soviet-Japanese relations remain or disappeared. It is required that historians conduct more structural research on these relations, based on the significant works presented in the past and employing more interdisciplinary methodology. For this purpose, it would be necessary to initiate some projects of co-operative research composed by many historians from various fields. The European Association for Japanese Studies can provide, I believe, a suitable basis for such a cooperation.

BIBLIOGRAPHY

Cook, Blanche Wiesen. 1981. *Declassified Eisenhower: A Divided Legacy*. Garden City, NY: Doubleday.

FRUS. 1985. *Foreign Relations of the United States, 1952-54*, 14, 2. Washington, DC: Government Printing Office.

Gaddis, John Lewis. 1987. *The Long Peace: Inquiries into the History of the Cold War*. New York: Oxford University Press.

Hellmann, Donald C. 1969. *Japanese Foreign Policy and Domestic Politics: The Peace Agreement with the Soviet Union*. Berkeley and Los Angeles: University of California Press.

Kaldor, Mary. 1990. *The Imaginary War: Understanding the East-West Conflict*. Oxford: Blackwell.

LaFeber, Walter. 1991. *America, Russia, and the Cold War, 1945-90*. New York: McGraw-Hill Inc.

Shulmann, Marshall. 1963. *Stalin's Foreign Policy Reappraised*. Cambridge, Mass.: Harvard University Press.

Stephen, John J. 1984. 'Soviet Policy in Asia, 1945-1951: An Overview'. In Hosoya Chihiro, ed., *Japan and Postwar Diplomacy in the Asian-Pacific Region*. International University of Japan, Occasional Papers 1, 59-99.

Tanaka, Takahiko. 1990a. *Soviet-Japanese Normalization Talks in 1955-1956: with Special Reference to the Attitude of Britain*. Ph.D. diss. University of London.

——. 1990b. 'Soviet-Japanese Normalisation and the Foreign Policy Ideas of the Hatoyama Group'. In Peter Lowe and Herman Moeshart, eds. *Western Interactions With Japan: Expansion, the Armed Forces, and Readjustment, 1859-1956*. Sandgate, Folkstone, Kent: Japan Library, 105-14.

——. 1990c. 'Shigemitsu Mamoru Revisited: Shigemitsu as Foreign Minister and the Soviet-Japanese Normalization Talks'. *International Studies, Discussion Paper Series*, IS/90/219, 45-77.

——. 1993. 'The Soviet-Japanese Normalization Talks and US-Japanese Relations, 1955-1956'. *Hitotsubashi Journal of Law and Politics*, 21, 65-93.

———. 1998. 'International Relations in the Formation of the Cold War Structure, 1945-1955: Western Europe and the United States'. *Hitotsubashi Journal of Law and Politics*, 26, 63-78.

Uemura Hideki. 1995. *Saigumbi to 55 nen taisei* [Rearmament and the 1955 system]. Tokyo: Bokutakusha.

FOOTNOTES

1.   The arguments in this essay are largely based upon my research done for a Ph.D. dissertation submitted to the University of London in 1990, *Soviet-Japanese Normalization Talks in 1955-1956: with Special Reference to the Attitude of Britain.*

2.   *FRUS*, 1985: 1381.

3.   Minutes by Giles Bullard, 5 June 1956, F0371 121039, FJ10338/24, Foreign Office Files, Public Record Office, Kew.

4.   Alexander Smith to Robertson, 1 June 1956, 661.946/6-156, National Archives, Washington, D.C.

Index